Passive-Aggression

Passive-Aggression

Understanding the Sufferer, Helping the Victim

Second Edition

Martin Kantor, MD

PRAEGER™

An Imprint of ABC-CLIO, LLC

Santa Barbara, California • Denver, Colorado

Library of Congress Cataloging-in-Publication Data

Names: Kantor, Martin, author.
Title: Passive-aggression : understanding the sufferer, helping the victim / Martin Kantor.
Description: Second edition. | Santa Barbara, California : Praeger, [2017] |
    Includes bibliographical references and index.
Identifiers: LCCN 2017020996 (print) | LCCN 2017022157 (ebook) |
    ISBN 9781440837913 (ebook) | ISBN 9781440837906 (hardcopy : alk. paper)
Subjects: | MESH: Passive-Aggressive Personality Disorder | Passive-Aggressive
    Personality Disorder—therapy
Classification: LCC RC569.5.P37 (ebook) | LCC RC569.5.P37 (print) |
    NLM WM 190 | DDC 616.85/8—dc23
LC record available at https://lccn.loc.gov/2017020996

ISBN: 978-1-4408-3790-6 (print)
        978-1-4408-3791-3 (ebook)

21 20 19 18 17   1 2 3 4 5

This book is also available as an eBook.

Praeger
An Imprint of ABC-CLIO, LLC

ABC-CLIO, LLC
130 Cremona Drive, P.O. Box 1911
Santa Barbara, California 93116-1911
www.abc-clio.com

This book is printed on acid-free paper (∞)

Manufactured in the United States of America

This book discusses treatments (including types of medication and mental health therapies), diagnostic tests for various symptoms and mental health disorders, and organizations. The authors have made every effort to present accurate and up-to-date information. However, the information in this book is not intended to recommend or endorse particular treatments or organizations, or substitute for the care or medical advice of a qualified health professional, or used to alter any medical therapy without a medical doctor's advice. Specific situations may require specific therapeutic approaches not included in this book. For those reasons, we recommend that readers follow the advice of qualified health care professionals directly involved in their care. Readers who suspect they may have specific medical problems should consult a physician about any suggestions made in this book.

Dedicated to Michael

Contents

Part 3   Treatment

Acknowledgments

Many thanks to Bryn Devon for her highly skilled work in handling the mechanical aspects of this manuscript.

Introduction: An Overview

Around the turn of this century, "passive-aggressive personality disorder," or "PAPD," was fully accepted as being one among the true personality disorders. It was considered to be a valid, recognizable, reliably identifiable conglomerate of traits readily and accurately spotted by diverse clinicians each independently pinpointing its unique qualities while ignoring supposed artifacts that contaminated and confused some of the definitive, "official" models popular at the time. A specific identifiable syndrome, one that was essentially different from all the others, was believed to exist.

Then, in the past few years, the *DSM-5* removed PAPD from its list of valid diagnostic entities,[1] as Wetzler put it in a personal communication, relegating it to "the rubbish bin."[2]

Currently, passive-aggressive personality disorder is not even referenced in the index of the *DSM-5*.[3] (As many observers fail to note, it is still mentioned, albeit just once, and in passing, in the body of the *DSM-5* text, where it appears under the rubric of two categories: "other specified personality disorder" and "unspecified personality disorder.")

As the *DSM-5* notes, these two categories are provided for two situations:

"The individual's personality pattern meets the general criteria for a personality disorder, and traits of several different personality disorders are present, but the criteria for any specific personality disorder are not met;

The individual's personality pattern meets the general criteria for a personality disorder, but the individual is considered to have a personality disorder that is not included in the *DSM-5* classification (e.g., passive-aggressive personality disorder)."[4]

Currently, and as if in reply to the *DSM-5*, at least three groups of observers, Murphy and Oberlin, Wetzler and Jose, and Hopwood et al., seem to be leading a potent counterrevolution. Each strongly objects to the elimination of PAPD as a valid diagnostic entity. And each in his or her own way pushes for the reinstatement of PAPD as an official diagnosis:

One: Murphy and Oberlin. They note that "PAPD exists as an entity. This entity is characterized by anger and notable for the anger being expressed secretly—in an outwardly docile way."[5]

Two: Wetzler and Jose. They assert that PAPD is "reliably diagnosed . . . fairly prevalent, and ha[s] good internal consistency . . . best identified by [the victim's] own mounting frustration and anger."[6]

Wetzler and Jose also describe and define PAPD as what they call a "crime of hostility, often through omission"[7] and one accurately "reflect[ing in their anger styles] the specific form of hostility that passive-aggressive individuals manifest."[8]

Their definition reflects the close "association between passive-aggression and antagonism [and between] passive-aggression [and] hostility"[9] as manifest by "irritability, surliness, and angry reactions to minor slights [with] hostility . . . the only trait in the entire nomenclature at all related to passive-aggression."[10] "That PAPD [is] defined by a single underlying construct may well [be] an asset [for], in fact, defining a disorder as an extreme manifestation of a single trait [is] more in keeping with the general definition of PD [personality disorder] than most other definitions of personality pathology. Based on our review, we found that if the indirect expression of self-assertion or hostility [specifically the form of that hostility that passive-aggressive individuals manifest] was clearly defined [that led] to internal consistency values comparable if not superior to most PD diagnoses."[11]

Three: Hopwood et al. These authors note that: "The [passive] aggressive construct is unidimensional, internally consistent, and reasonably stable [so that] overall, results support the construct validity of PAPD. Both genetic and environmental factors are present in the genesis of PAPD [with a] heritability of the disorder . . . estimated at .50 in school-age twins . . . associated with [specific pathognomonic environmental factors, including ineffective parenting behavior . . . as well as child abuse . . . harsh/aversive parenting . . . and neglect. [As well, PAPD] appears to have prevalence rates similar to other PDs in clinical and community samples, is more strongly associated with autonomy/agency than sociotropy/communion personality dimensions and [is not] considered a subtype of other PDs (e.g., narcissistic) . . . or a phenomenon that merely overlaps with other PDs."[12]

A central part of the problem related to diagnosis seems to be that too many observers rely on a purely descriptive/behavioral approach to making the diagnosis, one based almost entirely on observed, manifest (clinical) features. This approach, by overlooking the central defining, *dynamic* issues that characterize this disorder, leads to much in the way of misdiagnosis, bungled causality, and improper treatment. As Fine, Overholser, and Berkoff note, "Vaillant has [properly] focused on the underlying dynamics of passive-aggression rather than the specific [behavioral manifestations of] P-A personality disorder."[13] Yet, paraphrasing Stricker, the diagnosis of Passive-Aggressive Personality Disorder "should be made not only on the basis of the manifest behavior but also on the basis of the dynamics of that behavior,"[14] for dynamic issues tend to be more fundamental, and lead to greater pathognomonic differentiation, than do descriptive presentations.

The book to follow poses and attempts to answer three core questions, the answers to which help define passive-aggressive personality disorder, hopefully once again making it an officially recognized personality disorder, one that will reappear in any forthcoming *DSM-6*.

These three questions and their answers emphasize the underlying (suppressed) hostility that is at the heart of this syndrome. The goal here is this: to lead to what Wetzler and Jose call "internal consistency values comparable if not superior to most PD diagnoses [that] yet still apply to many patients."[15]

These questions are:

One: Why do passive-aggressives get so angry? (The answer goes to determining the specific anger triggers that release the characteristic passive-aggressive angry response.)

Two: Why can't (or won't) passive-aggressives express their anger directly? (The answer goes to why, as Potter-Efron and Potter Efron state, the passive-aggressives view "anger as an enemy, something to avoid at all costs.")[16]

Three: How exactly do passive-aggressives express what anger they can muster and feel they can reveal? (Such anger, as Potter-Efron and Potter-Efron suggest, goes into making up the specific anger styles that passive-aggressives select to express how angry they feel, however indirectly they express that anger, and however miniscule is the measure of the anger that they in the end allow to come through.)[17]

The questions themselves, along with their answers, tell us not only much about the characteristics of this disorder but also about how to help all those this disorders afflicts. (We hear ways to deal effectively with the submerged hostility that exists behind what appears to be the neutral to pleasant PAPD façade passive-aggressives manifest.)

Clinical Manifestations

Those who believe that a discrete passive-aggressive personality disorder exists mention the following as characteristic of this entity:

Passive-aggressives, in contradistinction to many other individuals with a personality disorder, such as passive-dependents, suppress their angry feelings, only to later come to express them, at least most of the time, obliquely (and only on rare occasions, directly). This oblique expression of anger generally occurs in the context of chronic hostility. Although often associated with a specific single grievance, oblique anger frequently requires no immediate provocation. In fact, the mechanism of deflection may break down in the face of direct provocation that, by acting as an especially potent trigger, opens the way to more overt (direct) forms of expression of anger.

Typical examples of oblique hostile expressions of anger include: preaching at others purportedly, but not actually, for their own good; excusing oneself by accusing others, and so making others feel guilty when the fault is one's own; killing with kindness—being especially nice to one's purported adversaries as a way to also hurt them by making them feel guilty (a variety of the Midas punishment where the passive-aggressive uses a positive gesture as a vehicle for a negative one, as did the patient who along with a Christmas card sent a letter detailing his complaints against the recipient speaking of improving relations by airing legitimate grievances); and bumbling behaviors in which an otherwise competent or well-coordinated person becomes ineffective, e.g., less than useful, or actually harmful, to another individual. In the same category, but more specifically retaliatory, are the actions of the patient who punished his therapist for the hypocrisy of demanding money in return for understanding by paying his therapy bill in meager installments, as it were, slowly starving the doctor; the obsessional passive-aggressive student who, angered by his teacher, responded not with a tirade but with a long incomprehensible essay that, he gloated, "made her writhe to read it"; the wife who replied to her husband's boast that a painting he bought many years ago for $1,000 was now worth 50 times that amount by reminding him of the many similar bargains he had turned down over the same period, and by noting that in fact the painting was in an early style that the market had subsequently disowned; and the boss who, when displeased with an employee, would announce, "I have a bone to pick with you," then keep the employee in suspense until a meeting took place, one that the boss deliberately scheduled to be a few, nervous-making, weeks away. In this category too is the man who was undergoing therapy three times a week who expressed his anger at his psychiatrist for taking an annual one-month vacation by resuming sessions with a former psychiatrist whom he had left some months before, even though the patient didn't really need the interim support, and recognized that seeking it was actually counterproductive.

Oblique anger may consist either of anger expressed by *omission,* or anger expressed by *commission,* or both. Either form of expression may be justified by error or lofty motives, for both of these make a perfect cover for secret malicious intent.

Among familiar "sins" of *omission* (justified by "unintentional" error) are forgetting, commonly an anniversary; and Freudian slips involving such behavior as not hearing or overlooking.

An example of a "sin" of *commission* is verbal accident-proneness, one form of which is another classical Freudian slip behavior where one says the consciously unwanted thing because one either fails to perceive one's (negative) motivating attitude or perceives it not in time, or mistakenly believes that attitude to have been concealable, with the individual remaining unaware of the implications of his or her actions or words—until awareness comes—only too late. Thus a psychiatrist, thanking his supervisor for helping him with an article, failed to recognize the secret death wish expressed when, his tongue slipping, he told the senior person, "I will be thankful to you until the day *you* die (italics supplied)."

Sins of commission (typically justified by lofty motives) include pseudoconcerns for the material, moral, or psychological interest/wellbeing of the victim and/or society. The subject might give disappointing gifts that however embody moral or esthetic values compatible with benevolent intentions, and dispense advice morally/theoretically unimpeachable but consciously or unconsciously clearly meant to have hurtful consequences, such as calling an author's attention to a typo found in an already published manuscript "so that you, the author, can profit by not making the same mistake again." Some forms of activism rely heavily on this form of expression and justify it retrospectively as innocent on the basis of its being philosophically and socially useful.

Some passive-aggressive behavior has cultural roots, especially in societies where inherently protest is frowned upon (the military, some bureaucracies, and some countries belong here).

In all its forms, expressing anger *obliquely* is generally motivated by a desire to wound while concealing the intention to do so, and even the existence of the anger itself from the objects of the anger (and sometimes from the angry subjects themselves). It is motivated as well by a desire to effectively provoke counteranger, and to do this so subtly that the victim, believing his or her negative response unjustified, assumes full blame and even sees the passive-aggressive individual not as the provocative agent but as the innocent victim of his or her, the actual victim's, counter-maliciousness.

The *content* of the anger displays certain specific fingerprints. The typical passive-aggressive becomes angry about such *oral* matters as deprivation, for example, the feeling of not having enough of, or of being deprived of, something he or she needs; about such *anal* matters as being under the absolute control of others; and about such *phallic* matters as those related to comparative deprivation where the anger is provoked by issues related to competition.

When the content of the anger is about such fundamentally oral matters as rejection, the patient is also likely to be depressed. When the content of the anger is primarily about such fundamentally anal matters as being controlled (policed), or such derivatively anal matters as being neat, clean, timely, or thrifty, then obsessive-compulsive illness may be superimposed. When the content of the anger is primarily about such fundamentally phallic matters as castration, or such derivatively phallic matters as competition, seduction, or sexual rage/abandonment, then histrionic personality disorder may also be suspected.

Passive aggression, to an extent depending on how it is specifically defined, tends to overlap diagnostically with other personality disorders creating "mixed personality disorder." In large measure, this is because passive-aggression and other, related, personality disorders use many of the same anger-concealing defenses. These include: turning around on the self, also characteristic of depression; and selective abstraction, also characteristic of psychopathy (where the intent is to buffalo others by eliminating information that goes contrary to a point one wants to make, omitting/avoiding certain deep yet valid truths in order to selectively refer to only one or a few of these truths, and generally to their insignificant minor valid elements. Also frequently active are admixtures of avoidance, where interpersonal removal is chosen as a primary protective mechanism; reaction formation, where one says and does the opposite of what one means, e.g., using such mechanisms of irony as "killing with kindness" as typified by oily overconcern; regression, as in becoming childish to disavow adult responsibility, say by citing so-called "can't-be-helped" developmental fixation; rationalization, as when the intellect spins to justify emotional action and reaction; the citing of social approval (PC correctness) to prove one's rationality; compromise formation where two opposing ideas are forged into one that expresses both while emphasizing neither; and denial directed to developing a "not-me, not-ever" stance in regard to one's past and likely future beliefs and actions.

Hafter-Gray, in a personal communication, suggests that the core defense is an action-level defense coming earlier in development before one has achieved a capacity to symbolize (so that the person cannot express his or her feelings in words because of developmental failure—poor constitutional endowment, inappropriate parenting, or massive trauma—especially when a current out-front situation is too dangerous to allow free expression of one's thoughts and feelings).[18]

In conclusion, because anger restraints of a defensive nature play a significant role in the psychogenesis of disorders other than passive-aggression, sneaky anger is found to be characteristic of diverse disorders, so that its presence alone does not automatically equate with the diagnosis of PAPD, or any other specific, diagnosis. Also, while all passive-aggressives hold back their anger in some way and for the same reasons, not all passive-aggressives hold back their anger in quite the same way, and so different passive-aggressives express their anger in different ways, that is, they do so by the use of different anger styles.

It is also true that whatever category they fall into, passive-aggressives treat themselves in much the same way as they treat others. It is, in other words, an error to assume that this is only an alloplastic disorder (where others get hurt), and not one that is autoplastic (where the only one to suffer is oneself). That is, patients who express anger at others are ultimately often, according to Reich, as masochistic as they are sadistic.[19]

Alloplastic or autoplastic, while the objects of the anger differ among passive-aggressives, similarity of purpose and method are retained. To illustrate, many passive-aggressives effectively express anger at *themselves* by depriving themselves via various methods of relational self-denial. This is illustrated by a patient who was a main object of his own anger. Since he felt guilty about having made too much money, he appeased his unreasonable conscience placating his sense of guilt by masochistically taking arduous subway trips instead of cab rides, which he could easily afford, to get to work. Of course, without this being his prime purpose, he also involved other people simultaneously. In his case, the public transportation in town was so bad that when he relied on it he could always expect to be late for work, that way, at one and the same time, inconveniencing not only himself but also, by his being late, annoying his coworkers and simultaneously annoying his boss.

Some passive-aggressives go contrary to the classic belief and express anger directly. This happens when what Benjamin calls an "inside ball of anger"[20] explodes as defenses break down, and do so with a great impact on individual relationships. Here the mechanisms of indirect expression of anger become invalidated, as subtle defiance no longer suffices. When defenses break down and the patient gives way to rage, then overt rage, which may be verbalized, or with difficulty controlled by transformative acting-out, is more likely to occur than the characteristic oblique anger (associated with specific external provocation). The rage can also occur seemingly spontaneously, taking the form of verbalized temper tantrums that are essentially releases, sometimes pleasurable, of a general sense of pent-up aggression. If the object of the behavior retaliates in kind, so much the better, for now the victim's response is used to go back to justify the initial attack (diminishing the patient's guilt), and in any case results in a set-to which subsequently affords the patient the fullest scope for expression of what anger remains to be verbalized.

In many instances, patients express and control their anger simultaneously leading to "seething." Seething is one form of the many *anger styles* that, as discussed further in Chapter 6, characterize one of the different types of passive-aggressive expression of anger (the different anger styles).

Finally, passive-aggressive behavior is normal under some circumstances. This, however, doesn't mean that PAPD should be diagnosed only when it is manifest in certain contexts and there should be so many stipulations that one seems to warrant eliminating the diagnosis entirely. When the technique of deflecting anger is consciously used as a means of sparing another, the usage, being largely empathic, is also less passive-aggressive than normative, and may not even be indicative of a personality disorder.

Personality Traits

The above discussion of PAPD doesn't fully apply to what are called "passive-aggressive traits." The *trait* of passive-aggression describes a behavior without referencing a full *disorder*. As a trait, passive-aggression is universally accepted as a formulation describing a discrete behavior/behavioral constellation, and few if any observers deny that passive-aggressive personality traits exist in the real world, where they become manifest as interpersonal transactions of a given specificity. These disturb life, and on occasion even end it prematurely. An example of a passive-aggressive trait might be obstructionism. Here too, important dynamic considerations apply, for obstructionism due to OCPD vacillation resulting from uncertainty is not the same thing, and so doesn't have the same diagnostic implication, as obstructionism due to suppressed anger toward others. As Bowles notes, the trait of "'stubbornness' [can be put down] to either a lack of effort [or] to purposeful sabotage."[21]

Therapy

There are many viable diverse approaches to psychotherapy with passive-aggressive patients. What these all have in common are: welcoming, encouraging, understanding of the (passive-aggressive) process, the imparting of hope, the relieving of guilt, helping with organizing and restructuring one's schedule/life, and therapeutic/empathic enhancement (of affected others) to help them avoid setting off a hair-triggered passive-aggressive emotional response on their own part.

As much as possible, the specific therapeutic approaches taken should be geared precisely to the psychological complexion of the passive-aggressive individual in treatment. Some passive-aggressives (masochistic and OCPD passives-aggressives among them) respond to approaches that emphasize guilt reduction, while others (psychopathic/hypomanic passive-aggressives) may benefit the most from approaches that emphasize the institution of self-control. Some passive-aggressives respond effectively to insight therapy while others, perhaps those less intellectually oriented, respond better to behavioral (action-oriented) approaches. All approaches that emphasize understanding and improving interpersonal relationships with the goal of helping one feel less lost, alone, and afraid, are potentially helpful.

Many passive-aggressives do better with a noncritical therapist, one who avoids putting the patient down by emphasizing the more positive elements of the passive-aggressive patient's thoughts and actions—e.g., you are not a bad person even though you are too anxious and afraid, seemingly for your own good, to be anything but too nice in many or all of your relationships.

Unlike those many other forms of therapy which are intentionally meant to be self-enhancing, therapy for passive-aggressives should, at least sometimes/partially, be focused on *discouraging* the free expression of aspects of the true self. This is because for the passive-aggressive patient, self-realization often works against self-improvement. Indeed, the reverse of this approach pertains for the many passive-aggressives who do best with therapists who tell them to keep negativity inside and display only their more socially acceptable, less peevish, sides, as, for example, to as much as possible reduce displays of anger and resentment that distract from their basic nobility.

Too many passives-aggressives, having become overly eager to sacrifice togetherness on the altar of the satisfaction of immediate emotional discharge, willingly relinquish being loved just in order to be triumphant—via allowing themselves to accept and validate all their knee-jerk (instinctual, e.g., angry) responses. They willingly gratify their need to express their anger sneakily as they refuse to alter spontaneous responses out of appropriate concern for what might happen next. As a result, for this, more than almost any other kind of patient, self-mastery, not self-expression, often involving the conscious installation of self-control, is for them the royal road to self-improvement, especially in the important realm of the enhancement of their relationships with others.

Also, for passive-aggressives, some forms of therapy are problematical because they are manipulative, and as such perceived to be excessively trivial. In the realm of the excessively trivial, passive-aggressives generally disfavor as possibly ineffective such manipulations as "get a watermelon and thinking of it as your mother hack it up into little pieces." For such individuals, seriously intellectually oriented approaches such as cognitive therapy tend to hold the most appeal, and so stand the best chance of being effective.

PART 1

Description

CHAPTER ONE

Making the Diagnosis

It was a War Department technical bulletin that first described passive-aggressive personality disorder as long ago as 1945. Also early on, Berne described a phenomenon akin to PAPD without however actually naming it as such. In 1964, in speaking of the antithesis to his game of Corner—a marital game where the husband tempts the wife to provoke him and then becomes moody and goes "out with the boys, leaving [his wife] at home to nurse her injured feelings," he provides striking discussions not only of the passive-aggressive interaction itself but also of a therapeutic way to avoid perpetuating vicious cycles of sadomasochistic psychopathology. Thus according to Berne, "All [Mrs. White] has to do is . . . take her husband by the arm, smile and go along with him (a shift from Child to Adult ego state)."[1]

Unfortunately, more recently, after an almost unprecedented run of interest and popularity, the concept of passive-aggressive personality disorder has peaked in general interest and popularity. Very recently it has actually come under unfriendly fire from many sources. Presently as a diagnosis, although not at all neglected in the self-help literature, it has in the scientific literature been reduced to being the subject of an ongoing rich but diversionary and distracting debate about whether or not it is a discrete, identifiable personality disorder with inclusive and exclusive features constituting boundaries sufficiently distinct to make it a predictably recognizable syndrome. This debate has provided refinements that strengthen, deepen, and broaden the concept. At the same time, it has also confused the issue and paradoxically ultimately dampened interest in its subject, leading to a number of unfortunate results. Currently, too often those who ask, "Is passive-aggression in fact a discreet personality disorder?"

in response hear different and at times even fully contrasting viewpoints, leaving all concerned confused about what to think and where to go to be further enlightened.

The Classical View

Fine, Overholser, and Berkoff in 1992, concluded in their review of the literature about PAPD that there is no inherent consistency between different clinical descriptions of passive-aggressive personality disorder. They believe that in great measure, this is because "various authors emphasize different features"[2] thus making it hard to identify passive-aggressive personality disorder and pin it down as being a true syndrome reproducible from observer to observer. In a typical, inconsistent response, different observers emphasize different predetermined triggers each deems to be characteristic of passive-aggressive personality disorder. Some dismiss passive-aggressives as "mere narcissists," while others dismiss them as overly perfectionistic OCPDs.

In the camp of those who believe that PAPD represents a discrete reliably identifiable syndrome are the flowing two observers:

Gunderson, who believes that passive-aggressive personality disorder is a "useful diagnos[is]" characterized by a tendency to "appear inept or passive . . . covertly designed to avoid responsibility or to control or punish others [and] to deny or conceal hostility."[3]

Hopwood et al. who say that the results of their study, "The construct validity of passive-aggressive personality disorder" suggest that "the construct is unidimensional, internally consistent, and reasonably stable."[4]

Some experts reserve the diagnosis of passive-aggressive personality disorder, or any other PD diagnosis, for individuals who are afflicted with the relevant problem under most circumstances and with most people. For them, passive-aggressive *traits* (see below) must continuously prevail and be constantly employed, having become both fixed and broad-based, while occurring across many situations, with a significant number of maladaptive traits strung together into a homogeneous seamless construct with few mollifying attributes, giving the personality a fixed, new, distinct, hard-edged, pathological identity characterized by a (passive-aggressive) pattern that is not only repetitive but is also a predictable and widespread, chronic, unremitting, immutable, and troublesome matter. For example, a man who did not return borrowed books was considered to suffer from a passive-aggressive personality disorder because he behaved in a (similarly) passive-aggressive way on many occasions. The manner in which he refused to return the books and his motivation for keeping them generally defined him as a person, as his selfish, unreliable, covertly angry behavior in turn affected most if not all his important actions and relationships. In particular, it affected his relationship with his wife—from whom he was later divorced. (as she put it, "We tried and tried but we just cannot get along"), and his relationships with his coworkers, with whom he developed a reputation for being stubborn, opinionated, and unreliable. It also adversely affected his professional judgments, which others characterized as pigheaded, as he tenaciously held opinions that were the opposite of those that knowledgeable others embraced, as he expressed these in a contentious manner with punitive intent, and especially in a way that he became famous for: one that poignantly failed to take the human dimension of his victims into account. Clearly, in his case, not returning books flagged the presence of more severe, more widespread, underlying problems in no way limited to one or two, intermittent, characteristic manifestation.

The Dimensional Diagnosis

In contrast, there is a camp of authors who only recognize the disorder in a dimensional sense. They believe that if passive-aggressive personality disorder does exists at all it does so only in a certain limited way Thus Fine, Overholser, and Berkoff, speaking of this dimensional viewpoint, suggest that passive-aggression can best be retained as a "useful construct [only] when viewed from a dimensional rather than from a categorical perspective," one they define as an entity that, to be recognized, only requires that the clinician, rather than having to make a dichotomous (present vs. absent) judgment, finds it "enough to acknowledge . . . that many people display the quality of passive-aggression in some situations or [only] on certain occasions"[5] and to recognize who specifically these people are. Wetzler, too, sometimes seems to make the diagnosis of passive-aggressive personality disorder specifically using dimensional criteria, that is, he makes it in individuals who display passive-aggressive behaviors only at certain times in their lives and only on certain occasions. For example, he still makes the diagnosis of passive-aggressive personality disorder in men who "act in an extremely passive-aggressive manner at [their] companies from nine to five, but show no signs of it in any other area of their lives."[6] Many experts make the (dimensional) diagnosis in individuals who are passive-aggressive on some days but not on others, or at work but not at home. They apply it to successful entrepreneurs whose passive-aggression is limited to their inability to make a commitment to relationships/marriage. They make it in a boss who at home is a happily married woman who loves her family and treats them kindly, but at work is a feared tyrant who treats her employees harshly; just as they might make it for the father who, seeing men but not women as the competition, is passive-aggressive with his son but not with his daughter. Commonly a dimensional diagnosis is often made in individuals who confine their passive-aggressive response(s) to their relationships with authority.

I had the opportunity to observe and treat a large number of World War II veterans—individuals presumably not dissimilar from those for whom the diagnosis was originally conceived. The personality of some of these individuals seemed to me defined by resistant behaviors especially manifest by a need to control and direct certain aspects of their medical care: complaining about it but without taking available steps to solve potentially resolvable problems with their treatment. However, not all these patients acted equally passive-aggressively outside the clinic. Rather their passive-aggression seemed confined to their relationships within the Veterans Administration, which they saw as a system that mistreated them. The clear implication was that any changes that were necessary should be made not within themselves but in the VA bureaucracy they had to deal with, for to them it was the system, not their interaction with it, which was giving them their problems.

Other Approaches

Some observers are reluctant to make even a dimensional diagnosis. They view partial or intermittent manifestations of PAPD marked only by some passive-aggressive features not as constituting a partial manifestation of PAPD but as merely manifesting a certain expressive style where negative affect rather than specifically suppressed hostility prevails, but no symptom disorder with full and intact boundaries exists on any level. They merely note that some individuals react in a certain predictable way under certain circumstances. Just because they are highly sensitive to such factors as their mood of the day; their present environment; and with whom they just now happen to be interacting does not mean that they are simply for these reasons alone suffering from PAPD. Key rule-ins and rule-outs are missing, whereupon some individuals, those who possess but a few key passive-aggressive traits, are best categorized as having another disorder, for example one that Millon might call a "Negativistic Personality."[7] Such individuals in some ways and in certain contexts look passive-aggressive, but in other ways and in other contexts look as if they might belong to another primary diagnostic constellation, so that the same traits may be best classified not as part of a passive-aggressive indirect anger problem, and hence a manifestation of a passive-aggressive personality disorder, but as contributing to an entirely different personality disorder, perhaps OCPD, or paranoid personality disorder.

Reasons for Underdiagnosis

Passive-aggression being routinely hidden from its victims is also routinely hidden from those who observe and treat emotional disorder. Typically victims are abused so subtly that they figuratively (and unfortunately sometimes even literally) do not know what has hit them. Not surprisingly, as a result, victims of passive-aggression succumb to the passive-aggressives in their lives. Next, instead of acknowledging what is happening, and treating all concerned with dynamic understanding that breeds gentleness toward and compassion for the emotionally troubled people that passives-aggressives in fact are, victims provoke their victimizers further, often to the point that the passive-aggressives and their victim(s) become enmeshed in a sadomasochistic struggle, a relationship that is both inherently troublesome and leads to some of the major (but unrecognized) complications of passive-aggression such as road rage and spousal abuse.

A good way to clarify the concept and properly make the diagnosis of passive aggression involves avoiding the following dangers relative to conceptualizing and diagnosing this personality disorder.

One: Overlooking how characteristics of passive-aggression are not limited to how passive-aggressives treat others. Many passive-aggressives themselves take the brunt of their passive-aggressive psychopathology. For example, Reich, focusing on how passive-aggressive mechanisms can be self-directed, emphasizes the masochistic elements in passive-aggression.[8] (I find it helpful to conceptually divide the personality disorders into garlic, onion, and red pepper disorders. In the first others take the brunt of the psychopathology; in the second the individual him or herself suffers the most; while in the third both the individual and his or her target victim are sufferers. And passive-aggressive behavior can be found in all three categories.)

Two: Overlooking how victims abet passive-aggression by covering-up the passive-aggression of others via adapting, sometimes too readily, to the passive-aggressives in their lives.

Three: Refusing to make any diagnosis that requires too large an amount of inferring or supposedly completely unscientific mind-reading, of others' (often negative) motivations.

Four: Denial of negativity, an approach that is both very common and entirely understandable. Denying that a man could not commit to marrying her, a woman excused his behavior by saying, "He is just being slow to act," even though the man's intent was actually to express hostility to her, however subtly, by constantly postponing their engagement. Victims often excuse others' lateness by citing the unreliability of the other person's car when the real problem is the failure to make needed car repairs precisely because they secretly relish keeping boyfriends or girlfriends waiting, and even enjoy stranding them in a dark lonely place. Too often, victims of such behavior will instead think, "This is not worth fighting, or even thinking, about," and simply go around what is happening, doing so "for the sake of my relationship." Under such circumstances, everyone simply misses what is actually going on.

Victims of passive-aggression, overlooking that even loved ones can be angry people, and, even more troubling, specifically angry with them, deny that they should in fact attribute angry/aggressive motives to people they know and love. They deny the possibility that such people might be angry with them because they do not want to admit that others are taking advantage of them because they think that feeling they are being taken advantage of is a projective reflection of their own irrational hostility. Too many of us, if only out of empathy for individuals with an emotional disorder, refuse to face the fact that other people can, and do, have emotional difficulties of their own and that these can, and do, frequently impinge on us, and affect us deeply, as the negativity specifically affects us in specifically negative ways.

While nonacceptance of others' anger avoids an immediate confrontation, it ultimately obscures the diagnosis and thus perpetuates the process while turning unilateral passive-aggression into the bilateral sadomasochism discussed in Chapter 11. Still, many victims, preferring to be bullied over being abandoned, settle for taking what good they can get from a relationship. As a professor of psychiatry once said, quoting a patient, "For some, it is better to be wanted by the police than to never be wanted at all." Unhelpfully, family and friends as well as therapists trying to be kind and keep all concerned, their loved ones, friends, and patients, coming back to them deliberately try to spin passive-aggression into normalcy just so that the passive-aggressives in their lives can remain in a relationship of some sort with them. The diagnosis PAPD may, under such circumstances, never even come to mind.

Overlooking/downplaying the diagnostic importance of *subtle* interpersonal actions, all concerned give overt violence most of their attention even when it is covert violence that does most of the damage. Victims focused on the importance of the blackened eyes and broken bones of spousal abuse tend to downplay the importance of *silent* (but deadly) emotional/psychological abuse and battering: their own hurt feelings; their compromised or destroyed relationships; their stifled initiative and creativity; and such disorders as reactive depression and writer's block, and such psychosomatic physical sequelae as hypertension and sexual impotence—all of which they ignore as being potential complications of passive-aggression and the interactions with passive-aggressives in everyday life situations. They accept being bombarded by fresh salespeople, picky or abusive spouses, critical mothers/in-laws, lay reviewers who condemn a work doing so by writing their reviews in all caps, angry professional critics, thankless daughters with teeth sharper than a serpent's, and unsympathetic bosses—people all of whose hostility is as devastating in deep effect as it can be un-dramatic in its superficial manifestations.

Passive-aggressive individuals themselves obscure their own intent (of being anger avoiders) by defensive reaction formation and denial often installed so that they can view themselves as being the nice, altruistic, empathic, concerned, caring people they want to be known as. And they do this in part because, as Millon, quoting Small, suggests, they want to maintain "enduring relationships [with others] over long periods of time."[9] They also do it to convince others that *they* themselves are the ones who are innocent victims, the ones being abused. Passive-aggressives know how to make all concerned, their therapists included, believe that their actions are second, not first, strike, provoked not agented, the "I didn't misspeak, you misheard me" routine. As for making oneself look innocent, we can anticipate that the man who does not return books, although the lender asked him several times to do so, would say, "I was busy" or "I forgot," not that, "I wanted to make you writhe in order to make you uncomfortable in retaliation for your intrusively pushing me to give them back," and might even add that, "You are paranoid, which is why you get so upset about such little things." Passive-aggressives, good at making excuses for themselves, excuse their tardiness by routinely blaming the victim for overly emphasizing the urgency of keeping a certain commitment on time. Real intents are entirely overlooked in favor of offering legions of rationalizations (excuses) for those who deny service, including the patently rationalized, "Most people take a few days to do what they say they are going to do."

Making passive-aggressives' hostile actions look like second and not first strike, a passive-aggressive individual, angry because his mother talked too long to him when he made a routine phone call to her, terminated the call by generously offering "to let you go because I know you must be busy," his subtle way of deflecting the blame for his desire to terminate the conversation from him onto her. When others reacted to his hostility, he told them, "You should be less upset about such minor things." As a result, others never deviated from their belief that: he is a nice guy, I cannot fault him for much, if anything at all.

Overlooking ingrained negative therapeutic resistances leading to therapeutic failures, therapists view many of their passive-aggressive patients as merely slow-learners, or as patients merely, and understandably, somewhat *reluctant* to participate in, but not technically speaking resistive to, the therapeutic process. Many such therapists are hesitant to identify passive-aggression in their psychotherapy patients lest they simply, by criticizing the patient for something minor, cause him or her to somehow feel bad, and then quit treatment.

Five: Failing to study the passive-aggressive as a whole. That at the very least requires taking an adequate outside history, one that includes or emphasizes others' reaction to the presenting so-called passive-aggressive behavior. Taking a full history is admittedly difficult to do in these cases, because victims' accounts are too often somewhat unreliable due to victims' underreporting the passive-aggression of others by rationalizing that the passive-aggressives around them are not really angry at all. Thus victims put themselves in league with the passive-aggressive individual who already considerably rationalizes and seriously downplays his or her own angry interpersonal interactions.

Six: Accepting the current unpopularity of psychodynamic explorations/formulations. With psychodynamic theories no longer in ascendency, such concepts as "instinctual desire leading to superego prohibition and thus a specific (compromise) resolution of the conflict between the two via the use of such specific defense mechanisms as the reaction formation of passive-aggression are considered to be retro even though they do adequately reflect what is in actuality going on.

Seven: Allowing one's own passive-aggression to interfere with making a proper diagnosis. Almost everyone has passive-aggressive traits, and that makes virtually everyone, therapists included, reluctant to identify these same traits in others as being of a pathological nature.

Eight: Allowing the passive-aggression to be obscured by other associated disorders. The patient seems less passive-aggressive if his or her passive-aggressive traits are only an insignificant feature of a mixed clinical picture. This was the case for a patient who was passive-aggressive only with people who worked for her, avoidant on dates, and obsessive-compulsive in her relationship with her husband leading to her being diagnosed as having a mixed personality disorder. While most observers agree that in such cases multiple diagnoses can be appropriate, too often when there is a mixed picture like this, clinicians overlook passive-aggressive features entirely as they fully attribute what passive-aggressiveness does exist to other disorders, so that they might come to see passive-aggressive "blaming" as "paranoid," "whining" as "depressed," and/or "brooding" as "obsessive-compulsive."

Nine: Accepting how society affirms passive-aggressives for covering their hostility with a polite façade—while simultaneously punishing those who are honest and direct about what they think and how they feel. Too often, society deems suppressing one's anger as admirable, a way to be a morally upright individual. Society therefore views passive-aggressive anger suppression as being in the realm of that which is nonpathological.

Ten: The diagnostician's failure to recognize the passive-aggressive nature of behaviors other than the ones considered to be classic for the disorder. Professionals tend to accept only certain behaviors as pathognomonic. So in attempting to make the diagnosis they overlook those that are rare, hard to classify, and seemingly of a nonspecific nature. Therapists who follow tradition and look only for obstructionism, negativism, and defiance of authority (long considered to be among the most prominent and pathognomonic features of PAPD) will overlook other, just as pathognomonic behaviors, such as whining and teasing.

Here is a sampling of (commonly overlooked) forms deflected hostility can, and often does, take:

The *passive-aggressive question*, the familiar question that hides hostility within research consisting of a search for truth in the form of a supposedly honest answer, like the question asked of a political leader, "Do you think it is your policies that have created all the divisiveness rampant in this country today?"

Irony and sarcasm. It would appear that Wilde's character in *Lady Windermere's Fan* passive-aggressively means the opposite of what he says when he avers, "I have met hundreds of good women. I never seem to meet any but good women. The world is perfectly packed with good women."[10]

"*Constructive criticism*" that comes uncomfortably close to an invalidation of sincere and valid efforts. For example, an editor tells an author of a text, referring to her use of a certain word the editor considered obsolete, "This ancient term you use is known only to those who picked up some out-of-date surgical text—or one of your newest books." A comment about one of her books is: "she has written other books, meaning that she is not an expert on this one topic."

Hostile associations/quotations. When a man told a friend how upset he was that his contractor left a job half done, the next words out of the friend's mouth were a reply that supposedly was a quote from the friend's own mother, a woman who purportedly always said, "Never show a fool something half-finished."

Insincere retractions and apologies. This is exemplified by the innocent-appearing, "All I said was . . ." or "I only meant that . . ."

Nonverbal behaviors. These express anger indirectly, in a form that can be subsequently denied by saying the equivalent of, "What, are you some sort of a mind-reader?"

Familiar examples of expressing anger nonverbally include: rolling of the eyes to indicate disapproval; shrugging of the shoulders to indicate disbelief; making the shame sign to express embarrassment and disgust; extending the third finger to humiliate and violate; and expressing a hostile superiority in dress that involves the rejection of social values. Smiles can be sardonic, haughty, or humbling, as can stomping about to suggest frustration. As Potter-Efron and Potter-Efron put it, "You've seen the little smile of the boy whose parents can't get him to clean his room. It's the same smile on the face of the woman who just can't balance the checkbook and the man who can't even get home on time. It's the smile that says 'I've got you.'"[11] Uncovered fantasies can in certain instances of sputtering and stuttering suggest that these ways of "speaking while at the same time holding back" are crafted to make others squirm due to never getting to hear what presses to be said—a teasing disappointing of those who request/want/need another's performance, one reason why asking stutterers to "come out with it" can make their stuttering worse.

A man's sexual dysfunction can be a nonverbal passive-aggressive behavior when it is a vehicle for expressing hostility subtly, but still effectively. As Wetzler says, "the two sexual dysfunctions most often related to passive-aggressive personality conflicts are an inability to get and maintain an erection and premature ejaculation."[12] Impotence, frigidity, and dyspareunia can reflect a refusal to perform on demand. However, equally passive-aggressive can be the insistences of a partner who longs for and demands the perfect orgasm with the perfect timing from the perfect mate every night and refuses to accept anything less. Temporomandibular jaw joint pain and periodontal disease associated with enamel loss can occur from bruxism (grinding of the teeth) motivated out of suppressed hostility. Tension due to anger associated with resistance to performing one's job as the boss requests can contribute to the formation of, or exacerbate an already present, carpal tunnel syndrome. Clinicians have in the past connected tics, torticollis, ulcer, obesity, and alcoholism, among other disorders, to covert aggression, and physiologists suggest that the vasoconstriction of Cannon's "fight" can lead to hypertension, while autonomic expressions such as a flush of suppressed anger can predispose to such skin diseases as hives and acne rosacea. A colleague's chronic fatigue syndrome was, psychodynamically speaking, his angry attempt to control other interdependent workers, along the lines of "you do it, I'm too tired to budge."

Once in place for other reasons, such primary disorders as skin or eating disorders can be harnessed secondarily to send negative interpersonal messages. One patient expressed hostility to others by not covering up an infectious skin disorder on her legs—instead continuing to wear shorts at the gym.

Characteristic of such nonverbal behaviors are that they stop just short of actions that can be perceived to be out of control. Passive-aggressives generally desire to give the impression that they are in complete control of their behavior. They wish to provoke irritation, but know that acting overtly hostile, and certainly acting deranged, would defuse the irritation they want to inflame, in part because then their victims could discount this behavior as the product of a mind too disturbed to send any meaningful/coherent message.

Eleven: Failing to understand what exactly a personality disorder of any sort is. This often lies in the elusive nature not only of passive-aggressive personality disorder but of all personality disorder. This elusiveness makes it as difficult to identify, describe, classify, understand, and cure passive-aggressive as it does to understand and cure any other personality disorder. Some personality-disordered behavior defies classification because it does not readily coalesce into full disorder (and is not even well-served by the making of a dimensional diagnosis). Much personality disordered behavior is tentative, disorganized, multifaceted, or paradoxical. The term only designates, and does not define, a conception. Definition requires elaboration, and elaboration can lead to formulations that are no better than, as definitions of definitions, products of circular thinking.

Overdiagnosis

Overdiagnosing occurs due to the failure to distinguish a trait from a syndrome, and thus a failure to distinguish a passive-aggressive trait from the full passive-aggressive personality disorder.

Differentiating Normalcy and Personality Traits from Personality Disorder

Making the diagnosis of PAPD requires a full understanding of the role played by passive-aggressive personality traits and, what they consist of, the defense mechanisms that constitute passive-aggression.

The mildest and most normative of character mechanisms called "personality traits" are generally less intense, although more diffuse and widespread, than symptoms of a personality disorder. As mild thought-constellations/behaviors they involve a fixed style of relating to oneself and others, resolutely propelled by fantasy (in the passive-aggressive often of a paranoid and narcissistic nature). Mostly they originate in infancy or childhood, and are dogmatically retained throughout life—often simplistically, because circumstances and common sense indicate that these rigid, armored attitudes be abandoned—due to their being a set way of viewing things that come from within, are weakly and only with effort influenced/determined from without; and so, being overly rigid, fixed, repetitive, predictable, and inappropriate, are barely subject to the rules of reality, and generally not influenced by the regulations associated with common sense.

To the individual, the passive-aggressive personality traits, like other personality traits, may or may not feel foreign. Thus some hair-trigger annoyance is often believed to be "justified as such" and so is accepted by the individual into the person. So is most narcissism. The quality of being either "ego-syntonic" (acceptable) or "ego-dystonic" (ego-alien or unacceptable) refers to this quality of self-acceptance or nonacceptance.

In subject and style, traits are so like proverbs and overvalued ideas that they can seem less like symptoms than like phenomena properly conceptualized as a lifetime, personal, overvaluation and realization of a familiar saying. Thus the formulation "love thy neighbor" may be a maxim or proverb; and/or an overvalued idea; and/or an apt pithy summary of the attitude of a subject with the prominent passive-aggressive personality trait of piteous reaction formation (to one's anger).

In turn, because personality traits are like proverbs, proverbs can serve as headlines to the narrative of one's personality type, as is the case with the personality trait of empathy, well-defined by the admonition to "do unto others as you would wish others to do unto you."

Traits, like symptoms, may consist of pungent positive as well as negative constructs, such as the excess of empathy that lurks behind masochism. Still, in many passive-aggressives, Mr. Lowdown predominates over Mr. Loveable, as the passive-aggressive launches an interpersonal attack couched as a sweetness that, whatever its superficial positive virtues, is in fact the product of negativity held back and covered up by its opposite.

While most passive-aggressives become excessively kind to suppress cruelty (to "undo" cruelty, undoing being a common defense mechanism here), it is conceivable that there are passive-aggressives who at least from time to time become excessively cruel to suppress the opposite tendency: to be kind. In many cases, traits commonly point to/represent the individual's internal struggles with any issues that elicit self-disapproval related to guilt.

Traits are closely aligned with certain specific defense mechanisms. Thus the trait of excessive kindness appearing where one would expect just the opposite is closely aligned with the defense of reaction formation. In fact, personality traits, and so personality, much like neurotic and psychotic symptoms, can often be precisely characterized by the defenses that go into making them up. Conversely, specific different traits represent the operation of different defense mechanisms. To illustrate, deflecting anxiety over anger via using the defense mechanism of reaction formation can lead to the development of the trait of excessive passive-aggressive false kindness, and insincere sharing/caring.

With a "return of the repressed," feelings, which are often unkind, break through, coming out of reaction formation because the individual, having failed to completely conquer them, now requires the even greater, but still persistently ineffective, taking of counter-instinctual countermeasures.

Certain specific defense mechanisms are in turn closely aligned with the presence and manifestation of certain disorders. Thus reaction formation is closely aligned with passive-aggression. But most defense mechanisms are shared by a number of disorders; e.g., the same defense of reaction formation belongs not only to passive-aggression but also to obsessive-compulsive personality disorder, and to, as Prout and Platt (1983) suggest referring to Donald F. Klein's observations, anyone who "wishes to behave aggressively and is blocked from doing so either by external circumstances or by internal inhibition."[13]

Traits are not invariably formed for reasons that are entirely internal. Traits may also contain elements of responding (being reactive) to what is happening in the external world; e.g., "I have already seen enough suffering in my life to warrant my becoming as charitable and kind as I can possibly be, and to all persons, even those who, truly making me mad, are thus deserving of my being nasty to them."

Moreover, passive-aggression itself can be used as a healthy coping mechanism, as such constituting an effective defense mechanism that represents a way to deal with internal anxiety. Passive-aggression is found in almost everybody under certain kinds of stress, making it a possibly healthy, justifiable, self-protective response, e.g., a way to handle implacable hostile authority, or a method that can constitute an effective way of self-expression by understatement or by the use of sarcasm, humor, or irony.

As Millon suggests, passive-aggressive activity is present in all of us at least at sometime in our lives. For many individuals passive-aggression is a "personality pattern"[14] not constituting a full syndrome. That is in part why passive-aggression is often seen as nothing more than a trait/defense mechanism found in many people who are essentially normal or merely have mild personality problems.

As a general principle, certain behaviors are universal under given situations, and behavior that is abnormal under some circumstances may be rationally deemed to be normal under others, e.g., when the individual is on vacation or at a special time of the year. For this such terms as "spring fever," "midsummer madness," and "winter doldrums" remind us that cultural allowance is regularly made for some deviation from year-round norms.

Passive-aggressive thoughts and behaviors approach normal the more a given situation seriously requires them. The same thinking, or doing, when required, is not nearly as abnormal as it is when it is not in reality specifically called for. For example, holding back hostility and expressing it in a roundabout way is a good idea, not an abnormal stance, when fishing for a good grade in a bad class.

All this suggests that a great deal of allowance, cultural and otherwise, is, or ought to be, made for some deviation from "some norms." However, such distinctions are elusive, being largely relative. As we know from the political arena, placing personal gain in importance above truth or the collective good in considering winning the only thing worthwhile may be normal, at least socially approved of, behavior—until and unless logic is so twisted for personal gain, and the facts are so skillfully selected and/or misrepresented that even the sufferer believes in the truth of his or her manipulative distortions to the point that the outlines of abnormality, in this case of psychopathy, become distinctly discernible. Even here, some forms of psychopathy are so prevalent that one might consider introducing the (admittedly cumbersome) term social-antisocial personality disorder ("seminormal psychopathic personality disorder") to cover behaviors that look like dishonest spin when these are but part of a (normal) political campaign to win. Similarly when it comes to passive-aggression, there are times when subtly fixing another's wagon is appropriate retaliation for harm that is potentially to be, or has already been, done.

Societal variation is of additional importance because what is defined as normal behavior varies from society to society. This suggests that there are multiple "normals" depending on individual differences, or "types." For example, there is normal extroversion versus normal introversion depending on whether one is a Type A or a Type B personality, both of which are themselves variants of normal. In some societies, passive-aggression is so common and accepted that any other possibility is unthinkable, perhaps because it is impossible to carry off in a given sociocultural context.

CHAPTER TWO

Differential Diagnosis

Of the many observers who question whether or not passive-aggressive personality disorder really exists as a discrete entity, some agree with Sprock and Hunsucker's (extreme) view that "Passive-Aggressive Personality overlaps to such an extent with other personality disorders that it is seen almost exclusively in patients with other personality disorders."[1] For many of these observers even certifiable passive-aggressive *behaviors* e.g., universally accepted passive-aggressive *traits*, such as stubborn withholding, do not represent unique phenomena that define a special category of emotional disturbance.

The following are commonly found admixtures where behaviors overlap creating the appearance of "impure" or "mixed" personality disorders often confounded with and having to be differentiated from PAPD.

PAPD and AVPD

Individuals suffering from passive-aggression are like individuals with avoidant personality disorder in ways sufficiently significant to create what Millon calls an "avoidant-passive-aggressive mixed personality."[2] Thus both PAPD and AVPDs get angry under similar or the same circumstances, and both desire to restrain their expression of anger.

In both disorders not only are many of the anger triggers the same; but also many of the same defenses are used to handle what anger does get through. As a result the styles of handling (expressing) what residual anger spills over seriously overlap. So, as it turns out, central to both PAPD and AVPD is that instead of getting openly mad both PAPDs and AVPDs subtly and quietly, defensively, distance themselves from those with whom they feel uncomfortably angry, with both using, according to Millon, specific "detached patterns"[3] to deal with their anger. As a result, both by pulling back from what are often uncomprehending victims leave a trail of wounded rejected people behind them, people unaware of what if anything they have done to cause the relational shift/rift. Have they provoked the other person to become annoyed? For both, the disorder's goal is to reduce interpersonally provoked anger by inhibiting, via distancing, one's tendency to feel anger in specific, if not in all, close active interpersonal encounters.

Thus as Beck notes, in both disorders, AVPD as well as PAPD, "dysphoric thoughts and . . . negative feelings consisting of sadness and fear [as well as of] anger"[4] toward others occur. In both there is, as Benjamin says, an inner "ball of anger that both do not openly express,"[5] so that both become full of "great indignation."[6] As Benjamin also says, here speaking specifically of avoidants, "Usually [these individuals] restrain this aspect [of their behavior] but there are times when it breaks through and these individuals tend [like passive-aggressives] to become indignant about alleged humiliations" and so "become quite commanding and judgmental themselves."[7] In short, Sullivan, possibly speaking of the commonality of anger in avoidants and passive-aggressives, poetically opines that anger accounts for] the disjunctive nature of "malevolence," the feeling that "once upon a time everything was lovely, but that was before I had to deal with people."[8]

Also in both an important issue is not what you did to provoke others; e.g., how others may react to you, but how you assess yourself, such as the role played by unacceptably hostile impulses from within you, directed toward yourself.

As for some *differences*, while motivationally speaking, avoidants bind anger so as not to have to feel humiliated in relational dyads, passive-aggressives bind anger not only to protect their self-image but also to protect what they hope will amount to currently satisfactorily ongoing relationships, ones they don't want to lose.

Also while in the first case, that of avoidants, there is a fear of and so anger in relationship to getting close; in the second case, that of passive-aggressives, there is more in the way of retaliatory anger, that is, anger meant to get back at someone for having done the passive-aggressive person wrong, and in any one of a number of ways.

Thus two patients routinely cancelled dates at the last minute saying the likes of, "I am so sorry I can't make it tonight, can I have a rain check?" seriously inconveniencing their date. On the part of the AVPD, the distancing was motivated by the avoidant fear that accepting a first date was a harbinger of trouble to come. In contrast, on the part of the passive-aggressive individual, aspects of the angry distancing were primarily motivated by a basic wish to make others feel uncomfortable, hopefully driving them away by getting under the person's skin—with the indirectness of the negativity here as elsewhere a safer proposition than behaving in such an overt way that a permanent rift might come about.

Also as for the differences, in AVPD, anxiety is more the motivator for pulling back than is anger. Sullivan might describe such anxiousness as follows: there is a "somnolent detachment called out by . . . severe [relational] anxiety."[9] Also, in AVPD, the inhibition is much more extensive and selective than it is in PAPD, where it tends to be partial and highly selective.

Passive-Dependent Personality Disorder

Both passive-aggressives and passive-dependents fear being assertive because they believe that being assertive necessarily entails being *aggressive* and any aggression challenges the very existence of a relationship.

However, passive-dependents keep most of their anger in to avoid *any* risk to their relationships while passive-aggressives, willing to take at least some risk, allow themselves to express some anger, so that they likely become less the angry-clinging person than the pest who expresses his or her anger by instead becoming annoying. Thus passive-dependents, but not passive-aggressives, keep all, if not all, of their anger to themselves out of fear that any assertion/aggression, even of the indirect kind, will prove fatal to a relationship they absolutely need to retain.

Also, while PAPDs fear and rage about many and varied things, passive-dependents primarily get angry about the possibility of their being rejected, which means feeling lost, or minimally somewhat, relationally speaking, at sea.

Narcissistic Personality Disorder

Passive-aggressives are like narcissists in their self-centeredness, that is, as Yeomans and Caligor put it, "the sense of self in NPD is based in the individual's attribution to the self of all characteristic affect states that are desirable and good while relegating to others all that is devalued."[10] Not surprisingly then, both passive-aggressives and narcissists become angered when they sense others are overly preoccupied with their own self-interest and self-importance.

Passive-aggressives differ from narcissists in that they are open to some degree of negotiation, that is, they sustain the hope that a compromise can be reached and some mutually satisfactory resolution achieved. Resolution of differences can happen with passive-aggressives but not so much with narcissists for the latter are most unlikely to accept any compromise achieved via the exercise of mutuality. For narcissists tend to feel that they cannot get enough out a relationship unless *all* their needs are met, and met by others who recognize that they, the narcissists, are entitled to be fully satisfied, no questions asked, and no gratification withheld, or for any reason.

Borderline Personality Disorder

As Fonagy and Campbell note, passive-aggressives and borderlines alike manifest a relational problem in the arena of object constancy. But passive-aggressives become hostile in such a discreet way as to maintain their relationships as much as possible and at all times. They maintain a degree of desired object stability because they need to hold on to their relationships. In contrast in BPDs, emotional lability and impulsivity prevail and tend to create a specific problem characterized by alternating and thus cycling between dependent merging and full independent emerging, then back again, creating periods in their relationships where breakups prevail with relationship solidity being the casualty.[11]

Sadomasochistic Personality Disorder

Many individuals simultaneously fall into two diagnostic categories: PAPD and sadomasochistic personality disorder.

Both PAPDs and sadomasochists act in a self-defeating way that is the ultimate product of their being hurtful to others. As Reich puts it, there is a "compulsion to torture others which makes the patient suffer no less than the object."[12] Consequently, both passive-aggressives and masochists self-punish through provocative behavior towards others whom in turn they try their best to provoke to become abusive toward them.

Both sadomasochists and passive-aggressives choose objects who demonstrate their willingness to participate in mutual abuse. Hence, they both need to find and stick with a troubled relationship, one they know will not likely work out along predetermined lines.

As for the differences, unlike with sadomasochism, where the relationship starts with hurtful enmeshment as one of its prime formative purposes, with passive-aggression the relationship starts off with being unilateral only later to develop into a dyadic problem as behaviors predictably interlock and tensions predictably escalate. Thus sooner or later most passive-aggressive relationships become sadomasochistic-resonant interactions in which all concerned participate actively and fully, making it difficult to determine who started what, and so who is fundamentally the abuser and who is the abused?

In conclusion it follows that serious conceptual errors occur when an observer with preconceived notions, personal bias, or sexist viewpoints attributes the responsibility for lateness, foot-dragging, nagging and the like exclusively to one member of a dyad when two individuals are in fact actively intermeshed in the process. The wife who won't clean the house the way her husband wants her to may be a unilaterally bumbling housewife; or, more likely, she may just be the victim of a sexist husband, with each, husband and wife, devaluing the other, and with typical passive-aggressive sulking as a way to attack others, here provoked by others' attempts to provoke a vulnerable victim.

To anticipate therapeutic approaches, here coping requires identifying and understanding what is going on with *both* participants lest self-sustaining vicious cycles take over, where friends and colleagues stay away or ultimately leave; spouses file for divorce; and family relationships deteriorate to the point that both the passive-aggressive and the sadomasochist become lonely and depressed individuals abandoned by those no longer able to tolerate not only all the hostility coming in at them from another person but also the strong, unpleasant feelings their own (counter) hostility evokes within themselves.

Violence is too often the final escalation point of sadomasochism. For this reason, successful intervention in abusive sadomasochistic relationships can often prolong or save passive-aggressives' lives. Sadomasochists must be kept from becoming casualties of road rage, child abuse, spousal abuse, alcohol and drug addiction, reckless sexual activity, or other actively or passively self-destructive behaviors that can considerably disrupt the days of all concerned, and, in those increasingly common cases where one picks on the wrong person to be first passive-aggressive to, then sadomasochistic with, even end one or both lives prematurely.

Depression

It can be difficult to distinguish passive-aggression from clinical depression due to the presence of the chronic, negative mood in both disorders. Also in both disorders there is a tendency to put the mood, already in place, to use in order to antagonize others, a process which a professor of psychiatry once called, "Beating others over their heads with one's bloody body." And, not surprisingly, in both, revenge soon becomes an important motivator of the micro-aggressiveness of each.

In both passive-aggression and depression, moodiness is typically triggered when someone does not support them adequately emotionally, either in subtle or obvious ways. In the absence of daily praise, e.g., where there is stroke deprivation either real or imagined, sufferers from both disorders experience partial or full dysphoria associated with feeling hopeless about ever winning in their (ill-considered) relationship games. What develops is the pessimistic view that when it comes to relationships there is no sense even trying to form and keep them going since there is little chance of ever succeeding adequately in that realm. This feeling is partly due to catastrophic thinking, where both passive-aggressives and depressives alike come to believe that any sign of disinterest in them constitutes a turndown, a turndown a rejection, and a rejection an event of tragic proportions.

Depression itself often begins or is intensified when passive-aggressives, unable to express their anger openly at others, instead turn their anger around on themselves and hurt themselves much as at other times and in other ways they might desire to hurt others. Thus feeling depressed can be viewed as a passive-aggressive way to treat oneself, with depression's casualty profitably understood as being the equivalent of a moralistic negative self-attitude that affects oneself the same way it represents a weapon directed toward others.

A significant difference between the two disorders involves the degree to which self-blame is present. Self-blame is higher in depression than it is in passive-aggression, where, blaming others is generally more the fundamental issue than blaming oneself.

Hypomania

Passive-aggressives and hypomanics alike challenge others who don't treat them as they expect to be treated. They feel that because others don't give them the things they want, they must therefore take revenge on them by depriving them, which they do by making others' lives difficult.

Passive-aggressive mood is also far more negative than that of hypomanics, in part because hypomanics tend to deny how negative they feel, whereas passive-aggressives are more likely to show their negativity to others thence to use it in the service of their being aggressive toward them.

Passive-aggressive are also more prone to be able to negotiate when interpersonal requests seem to be, and are, appropriate. They also respond if only weakly to rational social constraints. This contrasts with hypomanics where mood and hence behavior seems at times immune to external challenges and hard to revise/correct because the individual in question cannot be profitably reasoned with.

Passive-aggressives are likely more guilt-prone than hypomanics who if they feel guilty at all suppress this feeling in favor of the feeling that others, not themselves, are the ones doing wrong and so are the ones who should be chastised.

Paranoid Personality Disorder

Both passive-aggressive and paranoid individuals are preoccupied with fantasies in which they blame others for having mistreated them. Like PAPDs, paranoids perceive bland statements about aspects of themselves not as neutral comments but as extremely negative remarks, and so believe that in many interactions they must get back at others quickly, at least before they give others a chance to harm them, or harm them even more. Both conclude that I am not at fault, you are, and so, convinced of their own innocence, without insight into their own negativistic elaborations, feel "I don't provoke what you say and do, you, by having initiated things, have provoked me to respond the way I reacted." Not surprisingly then, paranoid relational anger is believed to be appropriate because it is considered to be retaliatory, along the lines of "you started it."

Passive-aggressives are often misdiagnosed as paranoids because like paranoids they turn any seeming lack of support into full personal chastisement and abandonment. They then retaliate by taking vengeance on others for having chastised them, although mostly others' wrongs are imagined, or at the very least overblown.

A difficulty both have with basic trust leads both passive-aggressives and paranoids to become highly skeptical of everyone, convinced that no one will show them any good will whatsoever, and certain that either they will trust everyone and get burned, or trust no one and get abandoned. This difficulty leads both to become highly skeptical of the motivation of all concerned. Convinced that because they can trust no one they must always be on the alert to defend themselves and to retaliate before they are themselves destroyed, they self-protectively read between the lines, whence they predictably discover meanings that aren't there in what others say and do.

To some extent, the content of the anger distinguishes the anger associated with passive-aggression from the anger associated with paranoia. Passive-aggressive anger generally seems more reactive (from without) than projected (from within).

Another distinguishing point between the two disorders is that para-noids, taking themselves more seriously than passive-aggressives, are usu-ally more determined in their beliefs than are passive-aggressives, and are as such much less likely to perceive and respond in the main to what they believe to be challenges. So along these lines, paranoids become more liti-gious than passive-aggressives. The latter generally content themselves with simply annoying others, say, being prissy as their way to express their hostility. This is in contrast to the former who go all the way to indulge in verbal attacks and like to start lawsuits when no law has actually been broken.

Obsessive-Compulsive Disorder/OCPD

Both OCPD/OCDS and passive-aggressives show effects on their victim that can be remarkably similar. This is in part because the dynamics of the two disorders are so clearly aligned.

For both passive-aggressives and OCPDs, the core psychological prob-lem can be similar: hair-trigger anger sugarcoated to allow the angry individual—the passive-aggressive person or the OCPD—to disavow responsibility for his or her anger and its "innocent" effect on others' psy-chological state. The expressive patterns may also be very much the same. Thus both share the methods by which they express their anger towards others, as both fiendishly come late to appointments, the more important the appointment the later they appear. But the mechanism by which they achieve their similar expressive ends may be different: suppression in the case of passive-aggressives, uncertainty in the case of OCPDs. That is, the pathway by which they achieve their similar ends seems to differ in the two cases, as the passive-aggressive plans to be late in order to be annoying, while the obsessive compulsive also can't make it on time but that's because he or she needs to do rituals before starting out on one's special journey.

Also, passive-aggressives settle into and maintain a difficult relationship more than OCPDs do, who tend to do and undo a relationship to the point that ultimately it becomes unworkable. Attempting to relate, becoming anxious about doing so, pulling back with an apology that supposedly makes everything all right, and then trying again, either with the same person or with someone different, is more characteristic of the OCPD than is the slow and steady relational erosion often culminating in the sado-masochistic interlock that ultimately characterizes PAPD. In the latter, it is more characteristic for a relationship to start with only one member of the dyad only to end up with both actively participating.

Bigotry

Sometimes passive-aggression takes the form of homophobia and other forms of bigotry—with the bigotry a way to express anger indirectly, and so to appear reasonable. In both passive-aggression and bigotry, anger is expressed indirectly in part because society demands that it must not be otherwise—since open bigotry nowadays can be a criminal offense. In both, to some extent anger is expressed indirectly in part out of guilt; for even the most well-endowed bigots unconsciously feel a twinge of regret about the kind of inhumanity they are, or are not, displaying to others.

Unfortunately, like much that is passive-aggressive, this less overt bigotry is more pervasive and widespread, and thus overall more damaging to its victims and society, than openly, and so fully known, violent enmity. It is more toxic just by nature of its greater invisibility and therefore presumable ideological acceptability. For as with passive-aggression in general, victims often take subtle wounds more to heart than wounds obviously intended to be hurtful. They then go on to treat themselves as shabbily as the bigots in their lives treat them. At least, although it hurt or killed them, victims could once dismiss violence that was overt as "not me, but them." Covert, passive-aggressive violence, when done cleverly, and subtly, tends to come across as deserved, and so, being taken to heart, incorporated into one's self-image and heartlessness to the self.

CHAPTER THREE

Anger Triggers: Reasons Why Passive-Aggressives Get So Angry

Question One: Why Do Passive-Aggressives Get So Angry?

As Reich has suggested in another context, characteristic "traits [that] are found, individually in other neurotic characters [have become through a definitive arrangement] the key to the [passive-aggressive personality] and its typical reactions."[1] That means that passive-aggressive personality disorder can be considered to be a distinctive compound consisting of "individual traits that while possible manifestations of other disorders, have been here selected out to be combined in an idiosyncratic way so as to form a new, independent, entity that is special by virtue of what has been borrowed and how the borrowings have been pieced together, e.g., which have and which have not been adopted, and given or not given prominence."[2]

One borrowing requiring our scrutiny relates to "What makes passive-aggressives so angry?" What is involved here involves seeking specific sensitivities, what many observers call passive-aggressive "anger triggers." Here are some of the commonest anger triggers that figure in arousing passive-aggressive ire. I classify them according to the *familiar syndromes,* such as paranoia, to which these anger triggers are most closely related.

AVPD Anger Triggers

Passive-aggressive anger often erupts when vulnerable individuals feel others are cornering them, that is, invading their space by getting too close, in effect threatening to engulf them.

Masochistic Anger Triggers

Masochistically inclined passive-aggressives often become angry at others whom they feel are forcing them into a position of being too successful—actually winning when they, the passive-aggressives, in fact want, and need, to be a loser and a failure. Freud, in his 1924 paper "The economic problem in masochism" (published in 1957), spoke of individuals who need to be punished and to suffer due to "an unconscious sense of guilt which plays an extensive part in [their] social life."[3] Such individuals are angered by those who promote them, encourage them to act in their own interests and become successful, and even offer to accept them into their peer group thereby enabling them to become a part of, and overly dependent on, that group—to form loving relationships therein, and maintain them, even when those threaten them with excessive commitment and even though they frighten them with unbearable closeness.

Histrionic Anger Triggers

Status issues are among the most central matters for histrionic passive-aggressives. Thus histrionic passive-aggressives get angry at others whom they perceive to be more successful than they themselves are. Among these passive-aggressives are "playahataz": people who dislike, or actually hate, those other people who are actually accomplishing things, and so rage at anyone in authority, or an equal or a subordinate who has as much talent as, or more talent than, they have. For such individuals, another's success has become for them proof that they themselves have become failures.

Such histrionic passive-aggressives find that being put down is the problem, with the solution involving their taking vengeance in the form of push-back consisting of putting others down in turn so that they, the passive-aggressives, can themselves now become, or still remain, the ones on top. In this group are those where anger arises when they feel they are actually losing out in competition with someone "bigger and better," someone who by successfully competing with them threatens their status by doing better than they, due to being more talented, or held in higher repute in a world that, devalues that passive-aggressive person. They particularly rage at those they feel are keeping them from rising to the top in an organization or, if they themselves are already on top, those whom they suspect are trying to dislodge them from the lofty perch they stand on, even though there is room at this particular top for more than one. For them, anger is not only principled but also tactical: the means by which they can challenge/kill off the competition.

These histrionic passive-aggressives become the angriest at those whom they feel have unfulfillable expectations of them, and are using those to control them by having expectations of them that are too big. I once told a cab driver with a distinctive bass voice that in my opinion he could parlay that into a million bucks. To this he responded, "Don't mess with me man, I am a modest person."

Paranoid Anger Triggers

Paranoid passive-aggressives are especially hypersensitive to criticism. As "The Quality Assurance Project" (1991) puts it, "An extreme interpersonal sensitivity to perceived rejection and the need to interpret ordinary [or slightly negative] human interactions as rejection leads these [passive-aggressives] to see all developing involvement with others as [potentially] hazardous."[4]

According to the *DSM IV* "much [of the] paranoid anger would be based on hypersensitivity to what other people think, partly in turn based on their proneness to exaggerate the dangers of a negative evaluation. [Passive-aggressives] carefully avoid taking personal risks because they fear being exposed, ridiculed, and shamed, e.g., for crying or blushing. Suspiciousness leads to imaginations of attack."[5]

Their hypersensitivity to what other people think is often based on a projection. That is, they feel criticized by others due to projecting what they themselves feel guilty about onto these others, something they do to the point that they believe that they are being accused of the very same thing that they already feel guilty about (and are accusing themselves of, and dealing with, by accusing others along similar lines). As both the *DSM-IV* and *DSM-5* state in their criteria for paranoid personality disorder, passive-aggressives anger often involves "minutely scrutiniz[ing others] for evidence of hostile intentions." They are prone to respond to "minor slights [that] arouse major hostility,"[6] here consisting of blaming others for mistreating them, although the perception of mistreatment does not align with the reality but is rather a projection of how they feel about (mistreat) themselves, causing them to both look for and find reasons to feel annoyed about how others are presumably treating them. Coming to believe that their personal feelings of inadequacy are actual products of others humiliating them for being inadequate, they blame others mostly for the same thing for which they blame themselves. If they feel guilty about their own passivity they rage at others for attempting (as they see it) to force them into a passive role. They attribute their own harsh punitive conscience to others and as a result, again projecting, feel that others are judging them harshly, according to the exact same, and equal, degree of, harshness by which they judge themselves.

Clearly such passive-aggressives like to set others up as adversaries, people toward whom they can express an inner anger already in place. This antagonizes others, who predictably come to be seen as/grow into legitimate adversaries. The passive-aggressives have now come to believe that their original improper, passive-aggressive stance is in reality justified, e.g., "I am right to feel that you are my adversary, and here's the evidence."

Due to having projected their own inadequacies onto others, they develop a sense of low self-esteem based on the belief that others have turned against them. Having now turned against themselves, they imagine that others are right to have turned against them, to the point that they imagine that they are being attacked, criticized, and thwarted, and in areas where they feel unable to adequately defend themselves.

Cognitively speaking, paranoid passive-aggressives thinking in a dichotomous fashion illogically come to believe that incomplete affirmation of them is the same thing as total disregard of them, so that if the feedback they get is not all positive then it is all negative. Then they jump to the conclusion that "You don't like me at all" and next, making a further illogical/unwarranted leap, come to feel "You persecute me." They then seek revenge for their having been thusly treated—with their passive-aggressive behavior the preferred medium by which they retaliate.

Much paranoid passive-aggressive expression of anger is also tactical. Paranoid passive-aggressives antagonize others so that they *can be* the aggressor to them. They perceive their hostility to be justified because it is manifest toward some blameworthy victim. For example, playing Berne's game of Corner, a man eager to have a fight with his wife has no problem antagonizing her so that she snaps at him, justifying his storming out of the room and leaving her for the night.[7]

A paranoid passive-aggressive individual actively looked for reasons to be passive-aggressive toward others. He was eating dinner with three other people at a restaurant when the bill for the entire party came to $92.01. This meant that, since they were splitting the check, one of them had to pay an extra penny. Secretly delighted that he now had a ready-made reason for complaining, something he could blame for his anger at the world, he grudgingly paid the extra penny then groused, in an angry tone of voice, "I always get stuck with that." As with most passive-aggressive triggers, the penny counted less in reality than it counted emotionally, having aroused his suspicion that others were out to get away with something, both literally and figuratively at his expense, along the lines of "friends like these always know how to be your enemies."

Others' innocent questions meant to gather information become attacks, e.g., "how old are you?" becomes a declaration that "you are behind the times," as "where are you from?" becomes an accusation that "you are from one of those low-rent places where losers live."

Once, a patient's husband said to her about a restaurant they were eating in for the first time, "This place is cleaner than my own home." She, overlooking that he was just using their home as an admirable standard of comparison, became angry with him for condemning her abilities as a housekeeper.

One individual unconsciously even set animals up so that he could complain about their being antagonistic to him. For example, he left the tops of his garbage cans open just so that he could curse at the raccoons that feasted on the garbage within; left his eyeglasses out on a low coffee table just so that he could complain about how his dog chewed them up; and kept restocking his fish pond just so that he could plan his revenge on a rare blue heron that hovered overhead looking for, and occasionally finding, a meal made up of his goldfish.

To anticipate how paranoid passive-aggressives express their anger circuitously, a topic discussed further in Chapter 5, paranoid passive-aggressives display their anger indirectly in blaming terms. They angrily blame these others for being unjust to them or causing them to fail. They angrily blame others for what they themselves feel guilty about and are trying to disavow in themselves. A boss, herself a frequent absentee, blames the failure of her business on the employees who "never do anything right when I am away," or who "refuse to give up a vacation to which they are entitled even though the place is short on help and about to have severe financial problems."

Using the defense of identifying with the (fantasized) aggressor, paranoid passive-aggressives typically express their anger indirectly by vengefully getting back at others by maltreating them in the same (passive-aggressive) way they feel they have been mistreated by them. If they feel devalued, they sneakily devalue back. If they feel attacked, they attack back. If they feel spied upon, they pursue others in order to spy back.

Paranoid passive-aggressives seek retaliation rather than remedy. They complain about others and the world instead of trying to change it for the better. Dwelling on others' incompetencies, which they deem to be both significant and fixed, they make little or no attempt to prevent or remedy what they believe to be a bad situation. As Beck (1999) puts it, they fail to "apply [their] problem-solving skills to difficulties before hurt or psychological damage occurs."[8] They seem to prefer complaining about injustices to actually making things right once again.

Passive-aggressive paranoia takes a social form in the persecution industry. Here, whole groups are blamed for being destructive to society and consequently in reality ought to be shunned and/or condemned. Demands are made for reparation *now* to make up for early disregard *then*; but by definition these demands are nonnegotiable, having no real possibility of ever coming to be satisfied exactly. Here the passive-aggressive technique involves stickiness characterized by not letting anything go and moving on when it makes a kind of sense to finally do so.

Narcissistic/Borderline Anger Triggers

Anger over deprivation plays a central role in the genesis and maintenance of anger in passive-aggressive patients who simultaneously suffer from *Narcissistic* and *Borderline* personality problems. In one case, a neighbor asked to move into the apartment of a man next door while she was redoing her kitchen. When refused she rapped her neighbor's knuckles for being a selfish person who needs to think of himself first, and others only next. In another case, a women expected a doctor, who although he lived down the hall was still basically a stranger to her, to come over and attend to some recently self-inflicted wounds of hers; and when he made himself unavailable she decided, "If you won't do this for me, there is nothing more I will ever do for, or with, you."

These passive-aggressives become especially angry due to what Beck (1999) calls the "egocentric perspective"[9]—one where they feel unappreciated, e.g., not treated specially, such as when they feel others aren't paying enough attention to them, and so, as they see it, are depriving them of what they need, want, and should have. A self-centered doctor would not budge when a nurse asked him to leave a room that had been assigned to her for giving a lecture. The doctor, who had his newspapers and his lunch spread all over the conference table, refusing to comply, instead "politely" suggested that the nurse seek a therapist and get treatment for being a hostile and pushy woman who should take both her students and her mouth elsewhere. He reacted this way because he felt she was picking on him, did not appreciate his true worth as a physician, was trying to evict him from a symbolic home where he felt he deserved to live, was attempting to control him, and, since she occupied an inferior status as both a female and a nurse, had no business pushing him, a male doctor, around.

A patient getting angry when her son-in-law asks her to measure her coffee and make it stronger, the way he likes it, in response, says, "I never measured coffee in my life, and I won't start now, just for you." She gets angry because she feels her son-in-law does not recognize that she is a talented individual, and so all of her decisions should prevail; and because she believes that his asking her for something that he likes is a criticism of something she likes, and does. She is sufficiently narcissistic to actually believe that "my narcissism is normal; yours is self-centered."

Narcissistic passive-aggressives feel that their own position and importance is too exceptionally great to be challenged by just anyone, especially by "big-nobodies," which is "everyone, for everyone is smaller than I am." A patient really believed that as a child he had stopped World War II singlehandedly. On his seventh birthday he closed his eyes and, as he blew out the candles, said to himself, "I want the war to stop when I am eight years old." When it did—and on that very day—he became convinced that he had everything to do with it, another reason why he saw himself as a very special person. Today, he is not someone whom just anyone can get away with challenging, at least not without in the process asking for trouble for their assumption that they are a big enough shot to rightfully feel like they can devalue him.

As selfish individuals, narcissistic passive-aggressives get angry when supplies they want and need are not immediately forthcoming, especially because they do not like being called upon to suffer delays or make sacrifices. Most prefer to get without giving, then flare when others expect something from them first, or in return.

In some ways like individuals with an antisocial personality disorder, they get angry not only when people hurt their egos but also when people hurt their chances—by getting in their way. A good part of the problem is that they, lacking empathy for others, and not being particularly altruistic, do not care that others have needs of their own. A well-known psychotherapist hired other therapists to see her patients in exchange for a salary. After years of employing a certain therapist, she offered her a $5 raise, but, needing the money, she, the salaried therapist, asked for a $10 raise. Instead in reply she was told, "You can have your $10 raise—I just won't refer you any more patients."

The assumed superiority of the narcissist often takes the form of that hypocrisy where they become convinced that, being special, they do not have to be consistent. In fact, other's expectations that they be consistent make them angry. They especially don't like it when others want them to apply the high expectations they have of others to themselves. Inconsistency was a particular feature of the behavior of a patient who felt no compunction at all about continuing to run an unlicensed day care center at home—even after she married a man who was a convicted pedophile.

Narcissistic individuals get angry when asked to carry their weight in a given situation, even one in which they have a big personal stake. A patient, a tenant who believes herself entitled to better air conditioners, took her landlord to court for not providing them. He was willing to replace the old ones, but she, thinking he would disturb her peace, would not let him into the apartment to inspect the old air conditioners and measure so that he could order the right replacements.

As I will explain more fully in Chapter 6, one way narcissistic passive-aggressives typically express their anger indirectly is by double binding others (one of their "anger styles"). They put others in no-win situations by making excessive and contradictory demands upon them and insisting that to keep them happy, and the peace, others must meet these demands, and do so both immediately and exactly as requested. People put others in a difficult position by giving them him only two unpalatable alternatives: such as saying yes and steaming over losing control of one's possessions, and saying no and fearing a loss, e.g., of one's friendships.

Narcissistic passive-aggressives make excessive demands on others and feel slighted when these are not fully met. When a patient was a child, his parents catered to his every whim. Later in life, feeling entitled, he expected professionals to be "in" even when their offices were closed. He relied for much of his medical care on knocking on physician-neighbors' doors when he had an acute medical problem. A cab driver, he asked any doctor riding in the cab he drove for emergency medical advice. Several times, he even announced to anyone who said he was in the mental health professions that he was about to make a serious suicidal attempt, then asked "What should I do now?" Those doctors who were not professionally forthcoming, however concerned for his health they might personally be, got a bumpy ride, unnecessary detours, or a radio tuned in between stations and turned up loud enough to be annoying. He also discovered ways to uncover specialists' privately held cell phone numbers. Then he would call up the doctors and demand a consultation for himself and for his children—right then and now. Attempts to turn him down were met by guilt-inducing begging and crying about how "you are my last hope." When he was still "refused," e.g., when told to "make an appointment with my secretary," he complained that "all doctors want is your money, anyway."

When he was running on a treadmill at the gym, he reserved the machine next to him for a friend, not yet arrived. Once a woman came over and tried to use the reserved machine. He became annoyed, feeling that she had no right to take "his" machine away from him. So he rebuffed the new arrival by ordering her to find another treadmill.

Because of the inaccessibility of a particular part of his house to the road, he wanted to use his next door neighbor's driveway to bring heavy construction equipment down to his own property. His neighbor, citing possible damage to the driveway and uncertainties about insurance coverage, politely refused to allow him access. The neighbor then found himself the victim of the patient's petty spiteful retaliatory acts. For example, the patient held noisy dinner parties as close as possible to his neighbor's house, ordered his neighbor to remove twigs he falsely accused the neighbor of deliberately piling up on his property just to make an ugly mess, and called the police when he saw his neighbor cut down a few reeds in a wetland that was supposed to remain a pristine area. Property rights were for him, as they are for many homeowners sensitive in this arena, not a source of self-protection but an excuse to make demands on others and threaten to sue those who fail to comply exactly.

Affective/Depressive Anger Triggers

Affective depressive type triggers involve anger which arises out of feeling rejected; feeling guilty and ashamed over something one presumably did or is about to do; and feeling aroused due to believing one is being criticized, however mildly, and especially when others criticisms resemble one's own self-criticisms.

Anger triggered this way typically manifests itself in feeling hopeless, as when there is the existential belief that nothing will ever work out as planned, and the worrisome conviction that if all is not already lost, all will soon be gone.

Affectively depressive type triggers are especially likely to be active in individuals who tend to be exceptionally idealistic people. As exacting individuals, these people demand that situations and relationships meet certain strict-to-impossible criteria. Only they are soon led to conclude that their irrational, impractical, and overly perfectionistic standards are, disappointingly, only partially, or in no way, achievable.

Affective/Hypomanic Anger Triggers

Affective/ hypomanic type anger triggers are set-off when feeling/being thwarted occurs and seems irrational. Hypomanic sneaky hostility is manifest as living well as the best revenge, and is characterized by oral, anal and phallic sadism consisting of symbolic biting; soiling/defecating on; and castrating others retaliatively respectively.

Obsessive-Compulsive Anger Triggers

These individuals worry that even others' mildest corrections of them are criticisms directed at them, as did the individual who saw any attempt in the course of an ordinary conversation to correct his grammar as a defiling of him personally.

As hypersensitive individuals, OCPD passive-aggressives interpret off-the-cuff expressions like, "you've just got to be kidding" not as a statement (= "Unbelievable! You just have got to be making a joke)," but as an accusation that they are foolish souls for believing in, and promoting, something so outlandish.

OCPD passive-aggressives particularly dislike feeling/being told what to do. They become angry because they feel others are saying that "I know more than you do," meaning that they can no longer perceive themselves as being superior to all others currently in the room.

OCPD passive-aggressives are often themselves judgmental people. As such they always know what's best for others; and so fail to consider and respect others' diverse opinions. Instead they find legitimate different opinions and varying moralities to be unacceptable simply because they don't match up exactly to the way they themselves see things. Those looking for a partner fail to recognize that when it comes to relationships sometimes it's "opposites attract" and sometimes it's "birds of a feather flock together." They forget that there are differing ways to see things, themselves all ethically valid, decent, and honorable, and that early to bed and early to rise is a good thing, but so is burning the midnight oil—staying up late working, and the next morning getting up even later. When others' MO differs from their own it's not a matter of each approach being reflective of an individual's often private and sometimes idiosyncratic personal preferences/rational beliefs systems however appropriately competitive they may be. Instead in their preoccupation with who is going to win in some ideational conflict, failing to respect the other person's opinion, they learn little to nothing new and so don't grow, as instead they get angry at others who try to interject their beliefs. Their own standards are the only ones worth embracing, even though those are not necessarily the ones all others personally choose to subscribe to. When serious negativity results it can disrupt relationships, sometimes permanently as philosophical struggles become bitter arguments.

Obsessive-compulsive passive-aggressives like their routines. So they become angry when they feel some steady state of theirs has become disrupted. When others cause them to deviate from some (often unnecessary procedural) routine they have established, they feel insecure, and imbalanced, and rage in an attempt to condemn insecurity and reestablish stability. They don't like their schedule interrupted, as when a friend calls and interrupts them in the middle of something minor that they are doing and feel compelled to finish, although that something could easily have waited.

As stubborn individuals, they get angry when asked to cooperate in joint endeavors, because they see a request as a demand, and cooperating as yielding.

Miniaturists, they tend to argue over things that are of only of little value being merely representational and figurative. They respond in anger to something small that a partner did wrong, after overlooking the other things that the same partner did right. They even "celebrate" finding minor blemishes as if these are major flaws, and even though others might find these things to be merely annoying not fully engaging. Insignificant omissions become significant commissions, for they themselves lack the ability to comfortably concede and compromise. For them compromise would involve recognizing, understanding, and buying into others' contributions to an engagement, and cooperating would mean that they have to admit that they themselves are imperfect.

Their rigid preoccupation with details means that they are a stickler for minutiae, as they overlook recognizing the big picture in their overconcern for minor rules, making lists, keeping order, and imposing organization. They come to favor paradigms they don't permit to ever shift, as they study timetables and schedules, and relish classificatory abstractions which for them are inherently of such pressing concern that the real purpose of an endeavor gets lost—diminishing functionality thereby freezing progress and stalling process.

They become intolerant of others' positions and viewpoints, especially about matters of politics or religion, as they focus on angrily blaming others for forcefully keeping them back by these others being rigid in their own turn. This makes them highly contentious individuals whose views others must hold, and whose commands others must obey lest subtle passive-aggressive attacks on others begin and get pursued.

Perfectionistic, obsessive-compulsive passive-aggressive individuals tend also to be rigid, inflexible, unbending, unyielding, and tightly disciplined people who feel uncomfortable (angrily disappointed) when their own activities are not fully structured—because as they see it others are interfering with their rigid routines. Following tightly woven rule systems that have for them become of life or death significance turns out to be more important than any actual goal that might be part of, or lead the way to, true achievement and useful accomplishment. They demand others be similarly inclined, and rage when others try to insert their own, more relaxed, agendas into the picture.

Predictably, such individuals turn out to be serial dating website aficionados or Internet trolls, always looking for that perfect partner after having found everyone who previously came their way wanting in some (often realistically unimportant) respect. When already in a relationship they deal with their search for perfectionism by making backup plans just in case something goes wrong. Only the other individuals involved in the relationship sense their ambivalence, virtually assuring that something will in fact go amiss. When as frequently happens their partners make them angry, they take their aroused anger out on their partners by becoming restless, often to the point that they begin to actually question the value of a given relationship/marriage. Hurting their old relationships by subjecting them to constant questioning, they are always thinking, "Can my old (comfortable) relationship be the only right one for me?" with their answer always being a resounding, angry, "Not really." So they look for something better, and, not finding it as hoped, start affairs, part of their plans of escape.

Mixed Anger Triggers

Rarely is one anger trigger found in isolation, as the following two cases illustrate.

A patient stubbornly refused to return borrowed books because, feeling somewhat paranoid, he thought the lender in demanding them back was indicating that he did not trust him; feeling depressed he believed that without them he would be deprived of something he needed, leaving him feeling and being further depleted; did not like being rushed and otherwise told what to do; being competitive he poignantly felt his masculinity threatened if he yielded to others' "whims"; and because being a sadomasochist he enjoyed torturing the lender of the books by not giving him what he asked for and what was rightfully his, and had been so for a long time now.

A patient who hated commitment because to him that meant being controlled teased a woman who loved and wanted to marry him first by promising to marry her and then by backing out at the last minute. He felt that doing what a woman wanted him to do was surrendering, and that surrendering meant being feminine. Also, feeling somewhat paranoid, he suspected she was not only after him, but his money and his body too. His narcissism flared because he believed himself to be too good for her; his obsessionalism came to the fore as a revulsion about dirty thoughts, something that showed as his dislike for her stubbornly putting "dirty sexual ideas" in his mind, and because sadomasochistically he saw disdain for her needs as more enjoyable than cooperating and making a good marital choice. Sadistically he savored her pain as he imagined her waiting, forever, tension mounting, for him to come around and ask her for a date, and then request her hand in marriage, a process he would start only just so he could enjoy never finishing it.

CHAPTER FOUR

More Reasons Why Passive-Aggressives Get So Angry (More Anger Triggers)

In Chapter 3, I discussed some reasons why passive-aggressives get so angry and do so so readily. I classified these according to their affinity with such familiar syndromes as OCPD and paranoia to which the angry feelings seem to have affinity. Here, I look closely at some other, non-syndromal, anger triggers, specifically those related to:

1. core emotional conflicts
2. distortive cognitive mindsets, typically associated with self-destructive behavioral patterns
3. specific interpersonal misunderstandings
4. (poor) tactical planning
5. biological issues with components related to the genetic basis of anger

Core Conflicts

Core conflicts, often first formed in childhood, continue essentially unaltered into adulthood to serve as characteristic anger triggers. In passive-aggressives, these are typically related to dependency, control, and competition/status conflicts. These issues often come together to form a conglomerate—a characteristic group of feelings which becoming simultaneously aroused readily reach threshold to form a characteristic passive-aggressive "vulnerability complex" leading inevitably to an escalating increase of anger.

Dependency Issues/Conflicts

Many observers mention/emphasize the central role played by unfulfilled/thwarted dependency needs as a source of anger and note that these are a special problem for the more passive-dependent passive-aggressive cohort of patients.

A patient said he always got very angry with his wife when he felt she was being inattentive to him, even though he knew she had only become momentarily so. He became angry in part because her transient inattentiveness reminded him of how when he was a child in the supermarket with his mother she just looked away and would not even acknowledge his presence when he pleaded with her to buy him a certain item, in particular one kind of candy bar he felt he could not live without.

Benjamin notes the importance of anger-inducing "abrupt loss of nurturance" as it leads to feelings of "unfairness."[1] Millon notes that many passive-aggressives go through life repeating the early experience of having been "replaced by a younger sibling [in] parental affections consequently withdrawn and redirected to a newborn child."[2] Fine, Overholser, and Berkoff note that passive-aggressive individuals are "easily annoyed by signs of indifference."[3]

Passive-aggressive individuals typically feel as threatened by too much as by too little dependency. Some passive-aggressives can be hostile-dependent people who fear and dislike acceptance almost as much as they fear and dislike rejection. As a result, they get as annoyed when others seem to be coming too close as they do when others seem to be becoming too remote. Wetzler notes that the passive-aggressive is "afraid of being dependent, and confused about how much dependency is too much or too little. Either way, he's angry about it."[4] Thus anger in passive-aggressives originates not only in frustrated but also in (excessively) gratified dependency. As Malinow suggests, passive-aggressives have an "original conflict of hostile dependency" because, as Millon puts it, they are individuals who "struggle between being dependently compliant and assertively autonomous and so fear both being abandoned and being overwhelmed."[5] They dislike being rejected but they also court it. They angrily demand being cared for yet they drive others away when they sense all concerned are getting too intimate. They have become like Freud's porcupines who, when too close to each other, move away from each other for fear of being pricked; whereupon, too far from each other, they move closer to each other to relieve the discomfort attendant upon getting cold, so that they angrily complain both that they are being rejected and that they have become more dependent than they might like to be.[6]

Hence, their dependency conflicts are ambivalent enmeshments marked by alternating between separation "anxiety" accompanied by separation "anger" with a fear of emerging and losing one's identity marked by anger over being devoured. This conflict is partly responsible for one of passive-aggression's most notable features: the passive-aggressive's putting others in a no-win situation in which getting too close to, threatens the passive-aggressive, while remaining too distant from, rejects the passive-aggressive. Consequently, the passive-aggressive appears to alternately merge and emerge with others, in each case feeling rage at potential or actual partners due to blaming these partners for the lack of satisfaction that each phase (merging and emerging) and distance calculation position brings to him or her, the passive-aggressive individual.

Similarly, as the *DSM-IV* notes, passive-aggressive *borderlines* are notable for a "pattern of unstable and intense interpersonal relationships characterized by alternating between extremes of idealization and devaluation."[7] An ambivalence about forming and maintaining interpersonal relationships leads borderline passive-aggressives to alternately love too well and hate too intensely; to develop close ties with, then drop, people impulsively— seducing then abandoning them suddenly, and with little or no provocation or warning. Now these borderline-like passive-aggressive individuals feel lonely, hunger for contact, and call and come over constantly; and now, put off by something trivial, they remain aloof. Refusing invitations to visit or be visited, they don't return phone calls, hence blaming others entirely for their relational problems though they themselves have initiated procedural difficulties due to their own relational conflicts/problems. Now they are relentless seekers for love and affection, and now, however much they unconsciously fear loneliness and abandonment, they, raging over something trivial, disrupt potentially workable relationships offered or already in progress. When they are involved in relationships, they dream of how wonderful it was to be alone, and grouse vocally that relationships invade their space and feel too close for comfort. Then, when they arrange to be alone, they dream of how wonderful it was for them to be involved in relationships as they complain that others do not get close enough to them quickly enough for them. But when they are once again involved in relationships, they, being hypersensitive or provocative, blow up over things that people concerned with relationship maintenance would at least try to forgive, and, as best they can, attempt to forget.

In short, borderline passive-aggressives first merge after overestimating others as all good and actively courting them out of intense loneliness and fear of being abandoned. Then, brought up short in disappointment, they come to underestimate others as being all bad so that they may actively break up a relationship with them. After first assigning individuals the qualities of savior wise and true, they next come to see only others' real, perceived, or delusionally imagined minor flaws, and in a rage they consign others to oblivion by awarding them unrealistic (generally overblown) qualities of villain, fool, and cheat.

In the emerging phase, they become isolated, while in the merging phase, they might get married after knowing the person for only a few days, then, shifting once again after a few weeks and claiming that "we are incompatible," file for a divorce.

Clearly most damaging is how borderline passive-aggressives catch others up in a relationship where lofty promises are made then breached as the primary mechanism for displaying relational angry ambivalence. Thus:

> Oscar avoided me through his not matching his actions to words of lofty promises, saying, "I can't live without you" then ditching me, displaying phony emotions with drama that was intense but of short duration. Characteristic phony emotions included crying and laughing which were as if rehearsed, more an obligatory wailing with a time limit as if there were a hole in the middle of a display characterized by a panoply of excuses related to actually making plans.

These included:

- I wasn't prepared to talk about making plans. You took me off guard. You jumped in too strongly and didn't wait for me to bring up the subject.
- My son Sacha is still under eighteen. I can't leave him if I am to protect him from my wife, Josette, who is crazy and I'm afraid of what she might do to him if I see you this month.
- My brother-in-law is gay, so if I leave my son now, he may have too much of an influence on him.
- Your being upset with me made me too upset to talk to you about a plan!

Conflicts About Control

Passive-aggressive individuals are often seriously conflicted about who is to be in control of whom. At times they come to view themselves as independent people who pride themselves on not running with the herd, and so as always being the ones in charge of the goings on. Often they get annoyed because they see others' perceived or actually expressed needs as demands made upon them, and others' perceived or actually expressed expectations as commands issued to them.

Fine, Overholser, and Berkoff (1992) emphasize how often passive-aggression is a "reaction to being a powerless subordinate."[8] Wetzler notes that the passive-aggressive man "fights to demonstrate his independence,"[9] and that passive-aggression is "manifesting. . . . power."[10]

Oldham and Morris cite the example of a patient who "does not accede to anyone's demands, even the smallest ones"[11] because he feels that if he did it would cramp his independent style. Like him, passive-aggressives, especially those with a paranoid streak, readily become angered by attempts to control them. However, they get annoyed not only when others actually try to tell them what to think or to do, but also when they misinterpret but modest suggestions others make as others ordering them about. Liking to be the ones on top and in authority, they coerce others as they feel coerced, and rebel in order to at least try to maintain control. Their wanting to be in control accounts for a behavior these individuals are famous for: coming too early or late to an engagement just so that they can have the final say about the arrangements. According to Wetzler, "chronic lateness and forgetfulness [are among] the most infuriating and inconsiderate of all passive-aggressive traits"[12] and are the result of a self-serving need to "set the ground rules of [a] relationship."[13]

They are also known for becoming martinets when threatened by others' potential power. For example, one colleague, who wishes to remain anonymous, putting his foot down, resisted any suggestion on my part that passive-aggressive personality disorder actually existed—the equivalent of his saying, "Passive-aggression is a behavior, not a personality disorder."

Benjamin in emphasizing issues of control and autonomy, suggests that passive-aggressives both "see authorities or caregivers as cruel [and] unfairly demanding" and complain about authority's being "neglectful."[14] So often passive-aggressives when dating toss all promising suitors aside and, selecting out those with problems, pick people they can readily put one over on, e.g. people they can put into no-win situations. For example, they readily put others into double binds where opposite responses on the part of the victim are each unsatisfactory, yet the victim finds him or herself put in a no-win position of having to respond one way or the other—or else.

However, at other times, having become excessively submissive, they rage when others refuse to take over fully and guide them completely. Now, as Wetzler says, the passive-aggressive man willingly makes others "important and powerful."[15]

It follows that paradoxically passive-aggressive individuals often beg to be controlled, so that, as Wetzler notes, the passive-aggressive man "fights to demonstrate his independence while revealing quite the opposite."[16]

So, when control is relaxed or is not available, the compliant side emerging, these same individuals who so recently complained about their being controlled, now complain about too much freedom, calling it "lack of care, concern, and absence of supervision."

This ambivalence about control makes overpermissiveness toward passive-aggressives as therapeutically undesirable for them as does too much control of them. Ambivalence helps explain why passive-aggressives complain when a therapist tells them what to do, yet bristle or even quit treatment when the therapist will not guide them specifically. It helps explain why they abdicate up to a point, and then do an about-face and refuse to budge. It helps explain why sometimes they say yes when they mean no, and at other times "no" is the first word out of their mouths, even when they mean "yes."

Developmentally, passive-aggressives may have become ambivalent about control because they came from a background where a parent (parents) alternated unpredictably between overpermissiveness and overcontrol, so that the child did not know what he or she could expect/count on. Some passive-aggressives as children seem to have been traumatized by all the uncertainty, and so are now recreating the trauma of uncertainty in the interpersonal arena in order to reexperience, and so to finally master, this ancient but still seemingly relevant problem.

The latter was the case for a patient whose constant vacillations in the here and now hearkened back to his relationship with a father who sometimes took extra good care of him, and sometimes seemed not to care whether he lived or died, was safe or got hurt. For example, the overly concerned father warned the child repeatedly never to put his head on the back of a movie theater seat lest he get a rare, incurable fungus, yet the underconcerned father let his child hold a Roman candle firecracker in his hand while it was discharging, and sat idly by as his son, then only five years old, cavorted on the beach for six hours in the hot sun, without benefit of lotion or clothing cover, and got a severe second-degree sunburn, which the lax father, paradoxically not caring to take control of a child who being so young needed the guidance, made no attempt even to have treated.

A 58-year-old woman ran across an old boyfriend who rapidly became interested in her romantically, to the point of saying that he wanted to marry her. She immediately became enraged that he was so forward; and she told him she wasn't interested because "she only wanted to do what she wanted to do, not what other people wanted from her."

This said, much controversy still exists as to the developmental ante-cedents of passive-aggression. According to Wetzler and Jose, "critics question . . . whether adults should be diagnosed with PAPD if they . . . do not have oppositional (defiant) disorder . . . in childhood or adoles-cence, and four versions of the DSM . . . suggest . . . a temporal linkage."[17] "Skepticism about PAPD due to the absence of a linkage with OD or ODD [is] puzzling. Why would *overt* (italics supplied) oppositionality in child-hood (e.g. often loses temper, often argues with adults, often actively defies, often deliberately annoys people) be related to passive-aggression later in life? If anything, we would expect that passive-aggression in adulthood would be linked to PAPD in childhood."[18]

Conflicts About Competition

A fear of competition, which may reflect Oedipal-level issues, exists. Passive-aggressive issues involve being afraid to succeed, a pattern first described by Horner in 1972 in reference to certain women, but applying equally well to passive-aggressive men. To win a competition was to set themselves up for retaliation and further competition. Due to fundamen-tal self-esteem problems passive-aggressive individuals lacked the self-confidence to engage in such competitions. They doubted they could win and, should they win, they expected success to make them even more vul-nerable. Consequently they inhibited their competitive drive and ambi-tion; they tied their own hands, and fell well short of their potential.[19]

As overly competitive people, passive-aggressives are preoccupied with issues of status. Always wanting to be the winner and number one, they dislike it when others are, or seem to be, more successful than they are. Yet, ambivalent here as elsewhere, passive-aggressives are also submissive, often masochistic, individuals who, afraid of success, want, and try, to lose, and feel uncomfortable with others who encourage them to act strong and independent, something they fear might overall be as being equally dan-gerous to their well-being.

Not surprisingly, then, much passive-aggressive anger originates around issues of status and rivalry. Many passive-aggressives want to triumph/win in all situations. Fine, Overholser, and Berkoff note that "P-A people often resent others' successes and are jealous."[20] According to the *DSM~IV*, the passive-aggressive "expresses envy and resentment toward those appar-ently more fortunate."[21] Always alert to who is number one, they are, according to Millon, "frequently critical and cynical with regard to what others have attained, yet covet these achievements themselves."[22] Annoyed with others' being successful, they condemn them as braggarts for merely reporting their triumphs, or savage them as narcissists simply for repeating a personal story of how they accomplished something good. They do not respect others' accomplishments nearly so much as they invalidate others' efforts.

A patient, a competitive attorney, without being asked his opinion, told a reporter, primarily to put her down, "I have seen you reporting the financial news on television, and I just want to ask you a question: 'What makes you think you know anything about finances?'" The same man, attempting to dominate a neighbor in the building where they both lived, put his things in the neighbor's storage bin as his way to tell him, "This is my building, and there is less room here for you than you think." This preceded the neighbor storing a large dining table and chairs of his in the hall when he realized that his apartment wouldn't absorb a dining set of such large dimensions.

On the job, competitive passive-aggressives predictably make poor collaborators. They rage when others act as, and are, more talented than they, the passive-aggressives, feel they themselves just happen to be, and they put others down just to prop themselves up. At the office, they often target one other individual to compete with, burnishing their own image in typical passive-aggressive fashion by backbiting, undercutting, or spreading false rumors about this colleague. If they are the boss, and there are two people doing the same or similar jobs, they favor one as their way to demean and humiliate the other. Here the passive aggression to one takes the shape of forming an overt bond with another, their being overtly positive to Y having become their way to be clearly, and publicly, negative to X.

Competitive individuals also have (paradoxically) mixed feelings about wanting to be on top. While as competitive individuals they want to be number one, at the same time they dislike the responsibility of being exposed as "standing out" which to them="being outstanding," which is, for them, itself problematic. Wetzler describes not only a fear of losing out to, but also a "fear of winning out over other men."[23] Fears of winning out are often Oedipal in nature. This is the case when the fears originate in a belief that competition equals murder, a feeling that regularly contaminates the passive-aggressive's actually being in the lead. A fear of success partly accounts for the reactive masochistic self-defeating that marks much of what passive-aggressives ultimately do, and helps explain why they undo and get themselves into trouble both personally and professionally—often just by their being passive-aggressive.

Developmentally, according to Rosenthal, new studies show that the "interplay between young siblings exerts a powerful lifelong force" as siblings "keep the relationships they had when they were young—such as rivalry."[24] According to Millon and Davis, competitive desires may start not only with "sibling rivalry" but also with the formative impact of the "shock and pain of being 'replaced' [by a new arrival] generat[ing] intense anxieties and strong feelings of jealousy. . . . resentment [and] disappointment."[25] When competitive anger originates in Oedipal rivalry, problems with competition often manifest themselves later in life as a tendency to make every occasion a test of who has and who will get what singly available reward. Most passive-aggressives have a zero-sum belief that life offers only limited supplies overall. Therefore they perceive everything they want as the one and only available prize, and rage in the belief that what others get they, by definition, will predictably lose.

In conclusion, as overly competitive people, passive-aggressives are preoccupied with issues of status. Always wanting to be the proud winner and number one, if only for the implied bragging rights, they dislike it when others are, or seem to be, more successful than they are. Yet, ambivalent here as elsewhere, they are also submissive, often masochistic, individuals who, afraid of success, want and try to lose, and feel uncomfortable with others who encourage them to act strong and independent—because they fear that that might be even more dangerous than being weak and dependent.

Finally, this global ambivalence about issues of competition/status combined with ambivalence about issues related to dependency and control contributes to passive-aggressives' free-floating hair-trigger anger in a general way. This is because people who have mixed feelings about most things that matter get and feel angry all the time because nothing satisfies them—since they are threatened by the opposite of everything.

Narcissistic Conflicts

Many passive-aggressives seeing everything from the "me" perspective find themselves getting angry when they feel others are putting their own, even minor, needs/preferences first. A woman who was invited over for a dinner that the host spent days cooking, wouldn't eat anything because "just today I decided to go on a diet." A neighbor once asked a friend to use a man's apartment while he was having his overhauled, which in effect would have put the man out of a space he wanted to keep open in case he needed it. When the friend said "no," the response came back in as pinched a thank-you as he could possibly muster: "OK, J."

Cognitive Determinants

According to Burns and Epstein, passive-aggression is the product of "negative cognitions or [negative] automatic thoughts" and stable underlying incorrect or partially correct assumptions. These distort and disrupt interpersonal relationships through the creation of irrational disjunctive beliefs about oneself, others, and the world. These irrational beliefs, developed and maintained in the face of much, if not all, evidence to the contrary, lead to decreased interpersonal objectivity due to flawed interpretations of often interpersonal events. These flawed interpretations feed back to firm up and elaborate the original distortive beliefs to the point that the latter become "unwritten laws—activated stable underlying assumptions such as, 'If someone doesn't like me, then that means that I am unlikable.'"[26] These unwritten laws, being irrational self-defeating attitudes and rigid unreasonable expectations not based on the reality of the situation, lead naturally on to such catastrophic thinking as, "Since I am unlikeable, all is lost" so that the passive-aggressive individual becomes angry due to having lost realistic internal guidelines about what is and what is not good and right for others to think about him or her.

Depressive (Introjective) Cognitive Errors

Here, cognitive errors lead to typical angry guilt responses characterized by the belief that one is being called a bad person for having minor peccadilloes/flaws—ones that are being identified as completely disqualifying lesions. Such individuals get angry after coming to believe that signs of commitment equal unacceptable overinvolvement. They identify their submissiveness as being unacceptable due to a complete loss of control and total, abject surrender to one's shadowy enemies; and ordinary desire is nothing more than embarrassingly desperate longing (for gratification).

Due to their hypersensitivity, legitimate questions that others ask become not queries but attacks. As an example, a salesman sees a customer's asking him how to fix a clock that broke down after she bought it from him as an accusation that he, working for a crooked store, deliberately sold her a piece of junk—and now it's payback time.

Depressive passive-aggressives often take their anger out on others indirectly by "merely" letting others know how sad they feel, generally accompanied by the implication that somehow others have a responsibility for having made them respond/feel this way.

Projective (Paranoid) Cognitive Errors

Overall, passive-aggressives who think in the paranoid mode erase the boundary line between "me" and "you" so that they become angry due to attributing their own thoughts and fears to others, thus condemning others for the very same things for which they blame themselves.

A lack of basic trust leads to a widespread suspiciousness of others' motives and so to the belief that one, the passive-aggressive, is responding appropriately to others' negativity. Now their anger at others incorrectly becomes "there is reason to feel angry for you, for you are the one who started it."

Here are some common projective assumptions about others that passive-aggressives are prone to concoct. These may be divided into errors of thought *content* and errors of thought *process*.

Examples of thought content errors are:

I feel unworthy and devalue myself. This leads to projection of unworthiness and self-devaluation to become "you devalue me" in kind. Therefore a cancellation of a date due to sudden illness becomes a personal rejection; an offer to matchmake becomes a humiliation for being so desperate that one needs to be fixed up, and the best intentioned advice, including that from a truly concerned therapist, becomes a criticism for prior wrongdoing.

I feel guilty about my sexuality. This leads to projection of sexual guilt which turns a friendly look from a stranger into a culpable come-on; and a friendly "cruise" into a hostile stare; or into "sexual harassment" worthy of a lawsuit.

I fear being controlled. This leads to a conviction that others are trying to "corner me" turning a potential partner's request to have a close or exclusive relationship into an assault on one's independence. Good advice becomes an attempt on the advisor's part to manipulate me for personal gain; and a "personals" ad on the Internet becomes not an offer to meet meant to attract, but a pack of lies designed to attack.

Examples of thought process errors, where "How I feel about you becomes what you are doing to me," include:

Reversal of cause and effect. Passive-aggressives commonly provoke others to get angry with them and then blame those others for behaving badly to them. The victim has now become the victimizer, and so a presumed legitimate target of the passive-aggressive's peevishness.

Self-reference or personalization. According to Beck, this falls under the rubric of "primal thinking," in which a neutral or ambiguous event is assumed to be directed against oneself.[27] He defines primal thinking as denoting such fundamental cognitive processes and their associated errors and distortions as personalization, in which individuals assume ambiguous stimuli are primarily directed at them; selective abstraction, in which individuals "take things out of context"; dichotomous judgments, in which situations are viewed as either black or white with nothing in between; and "thinking according to exclusive causes," where individuals get angry because they see only the dark side of others' motivations toward them. Paranoid passive-aggressives, who have a tendency to personalize, think that being at all involved in interpersonal interactions means that other people are targeting them as individuals. In addition, the self-reference of personalization can lead passive-aggressives to get upset after falsely concluding that another's anger, though in actuality directed elsewhere, is meant exclusively for them. When a husband blew up at having eggs thrown at his house, his wife flared at him, as if his anger were meant for her, saying, "Don't take it out on me."

Overreacting. Overreacting is a complex cognitive error that is the product of a combination of other cognitive errors, some of which have been already mentioned. Passive-aggressives who overreact tend to make minor into major issues, awarding them an importance they do not warrant. They overvalue the significance of little things. They attach excessive meaning to trivial utterances because they read (or really misread) what ought to merely have been seen as nuanced, and have been remarked only selectively. As a result, they react excessively to criticism. A patient threatens his wife with divorce because she asked him a question and then, before he had a chance to answer it, turned around to her cousin and asked him the same question. The husband, seeing himself as the king of the jungle, interprets that as a lack of respect then, feeling himself devalued, devalues her back because, as he sees it, what she just did is a paradigm for everything else she does, which comes down to "demeaning me" by "comparing me unfavorably to all others." A patient refused to go out with a man because when they were first introduced, he called her Myrna instead of by her right name, Myra. Innocent colloquialisms are often the fodder for this level of misunderstanding. To those who are currently called "snowflakes," the statement, "You've got to be kidding," often meant to suggest awe and amazement, often gets misinterpreted as an accusation of being frivolous or lying.

The making of false equivalencies (similar = the same thing). Passive-aggressives "think angrily" due to emphasizing the similarities of, while overlooking the significant mitigating differences between, A and B. They thus perceive a little questioning of them to be a shattering critical assault upon them; see mere disinterest on the part of others as full negativity or hatred on others' parts toward them; and misinterpret advice from others ("this is what you can profitably do") as a demand made upon them to comply ("do as I say.") They see kidding them as a complete humiliation of them; turn mild constructive suggestions about alternatives into a put-down or a personal attack for being inflexible, or stupid; and interpret others' friendliness as inappropriate sexual interest, or even unacceptable sexual harassment.

One of my passive-aggressive patients developed his characteristic sensitivity to criticism because he redefined criticism as anything sort of complete acceptance, so that if you didn't love him completely you condemned him totally. He developed low self-esteem because he viewed any slight imperfection on his part as a fatal flaw, and came to believe that if he were fingered by others as being not all good then he was no good at all. He developed a fear of losing his identity completely because he viewed closeness as merging and merging as engulfment—so that any woman who liked him would by definition keep him from completely realizing his individuality by demanding that he submerge himself fully into her, thence to have the resultant lack of individuality entirely obliterate his self-boundaries, which would readily, he became convinced, soon become fully blurred to the point that he would lose his own identity entirely.

Other cognitive errors include:

Thinking According to Exclusive (and Exclusively Negative) Causes. Passive-aggressives who think along such lines become selectively blind to alternative (positive) explanations for what they suspect. Unable to think of any positive elements in, and so other explanations for, others' presumed negativity toward them, they explain others' less than fully positive behavior toward them as strictly antagonistic and rejecting. Although they see the possibility of negativity in much positivity, they rarely if ever see the possibility of positivity in those situations that they at first perceive to be completely negative. Thus, "He didn't return my phone call yet," becomes not "He wants to get back to me, but he is busy," but "He does not like me enough to want to get back to me, now, or ever." Or, "He was talking to me when his cell phone rang, and when he picked it up he naturally temporarily turned away from me," becomes not "He had to answer that call because he saw it was business," but "Though I've been good to him he clearly prefers the person calling him over me." Harsh self-punitive attitudes originate along similar lines, so that instead of "My anxiety, showing, is somewhat off-putting toward others, so I better be careful and keep my anxiety to myself," we hear the much more self-pejorative of "I destroy anyone who wants to love me by becoming anxious and remote in their presence, and so I am not worthy of others even trying to get close to me."

Here, passive-aggressives tend to fixate on a single negative explanation for others' actions and, automatically excluding alternative explanations, see only that one. These individuals fail to see other possibilities and explanations.

Ad Hominem Thinking. As one example of thinking according to exclusive causes, passive-aggressives, without first obtaining evidence to determine whether another individual's personal life in any way affects that individual's professional performance/level of competence, use "who or what a person is," or is "thought to be," or, at least theoretically is something she or he might see as "evidence" to put him or her down. In a typical sequence, a woman's, or a gay man's, ability to practice law is judged by the "evidence" of his or his sexual orientation and he or she is then put down not openly but by "simply" and "duly" being ignored, e.g. shunned, thus being deprived of school admission, or, if he or she is in practice, of the referrals he or she needs to develop a following.

Overgeneralization (From One Specific to All Instances). Passive-aggressives who overgeneralize slide too easily from shaky hypothesis to incontrovertible evidence to irrefutable fact. For example, a patient viewing all new relationships as if they are repeats of old traumatic ones becomes effectively blind to alternative (evaluative) possibilities, so that he comes to feel that because he fell in love with someone hurtful, or unreliable, once, no one he loves now can subsequently ever be trusted again.

Parentalization. Very frequently passive-aggressives negatively *parentalize* what are in fact positive relationships after basing their conclusions on the formulaic "new nonparental=old parental" relationships. Then, emphasizing the inconsequential/inaccurately-perceived negative features of the new based on a tenuous similarity of the "new" to some less than satisfactory "old," they come to automatically believe that all those of the same or opposite sex not only remind them of an abusive father or a rejecting mother, but might as well be, or actually are, that person.

Catastrophic (Alarmist or Worst Possible Scenario) Thinking. Catastrophic thinking involves histrionic exaggeration leading to overcautiousness or to the taking of desperate (and unnecessary) protective measures, in either event leading to serious personal and professional misjudgments or even to such self-destructive behavior as the making of a serious suicide attempt. Passive-aggressives who think this way typically make "mountains out of molehills" as they indulge in "all-is-lost" or "for want of a nail the ship was lost" or "for want of a penny the kingdom was lost" thinking. They assign absolute rather than relative meaning to minor problematic events then overreact to these as if they incontrovertibly constitute major negative developments. They become unable to say to themselves, "so what," and "big deal," then remain calm and unemotional about things that don't really matter, or even about things that do matter but not that much, or, if that much, ought to be recalculated as best being overlooked for the overall good, and the happiness and peace of mind, of all concerned. For such individuals "mindfulness" becomes an impossibility because it becomes a casualty of overemphasis.

Serious perfectionism can result in relational catastrophic thinking where the passive-aggressive discards a potentially or actually viable relationship because of its perceived minor flaws, pulling back completely from a valid social/sexual interaction just because the other person has merely made a single, insignificant, transactional (interpersonal) blunder.

Selective Abstraction. Here there is a focus on small details—taken out of context—that might be indicative of a threat (but are not). Passive-aggressives often become angry after they overlook qualifiers or disclaimers to the point that they see only the negative aspects of a situation. They start in the middle of a story, proving a point of contention by ignoring what came first, then jumping out of the narrative before the end of the tale ever gets told.

Dichotomous Thinking. Here individuals feel/become angry because they see things as either all black or all white. At work, readily viewing others as all bad because others are not all good, they subtly abuse colleagues and denigrate customers. In like manner, at home, overlooking the good, they become critical of and abusive to a less-than-perfect partner. In their love lives they make for overly perfectionistic suitors who discard a qualified candidate because of a single, sometimes imagined, flaw, rationalizing their own behavior with such specious arguments as "You shouldn't get involved with someone *at all* unless you can be involved with this person *completely*," and "How can you love a man *risk free* if he has already been *divorced once*, let alone a number of times?"

In typical fashion they flare at, and retaliate against, others they view as less than completely supportive, thinking, "If you are not all for me, then you are completely against me."

Similar Things Are the Same Thing. Here passive-aggressives become hostile after failing to see important differences and failing to make important distinctions between one thought/behavior and another, conceptually overlapping, one. A man mistreats a woman who loves him because, as he sees it, getting close to her is the exact same thing as renouncing his own identity. In what should be a collaborative relationship, a woman becomes hostile toward a man instead of cooperating with him because, as she sees it, collaborating means abdicating, or capitulating, to this man, as to all men, and (she believes) all men are inherently and inevitably mentally if not physically abusive. There is an associated tendency to exaggerate the significance of others' actions after viewing, and condemning, unintentional errors as planned simply because both are errors, and true accidents as deliberately caused simply because all accidents have a spontaneous thoughtless quality about them.

Many or all of these cognitive errors are used to justify anger already in place, making the anger look rational, and inevitable. Passive-aggressives not only become angry because they selectively see only certain facts (selective abstraction), they also selectively see only certain facts to justify an angry response already there for some other reason. This allows passive-aggressives to persist in their anger in the face of convincing arguments to the contrary. For example, I here repeat the case of how Myra, already primed to feel that "all men disappoint me," used being called Myrna as proof that she was right about her contentions about all men.

Many passive-aggressives make two, or more, cognitive errors simultaneously/sequentially (cumulatively). For example, a patient's habit of taking criticism too seriously led him to feel too frightened and devastated to relate intimately to anyone. This serious fear of criticism started with "similar equals the same thing" distortive thinking, so that if someone merely requested that he do something, that request became an intended criticism that that thing was not done. Also, thinking catastrophically, he perceived merely minor criticism to be a complete personal rejection, and the rejection a warning that a given relationship was in serious trouble, and it, and his life, were going to end badly.

Cognitive errors do not develop or thrive in a vacuum. Rather, they appear, take shape, and persist within a facilitating matrix of disruptive, often traumatic, developmental events; internal conflicts inadequately handled/poorly resolved due to normative or pathological defensiveness; negative behavioral conditioning; distortive interpersonal (transferential) perceptions first formed in childhood thence to persist into adulthood; comorbid emotional disorder; misguided existential and socially influenced/socially based philosophical beliefs; and ongoing real-life stresses and questionable social standards.

A shy hypersensitive avoidant patient carrying on the "great tradition" of early parental negativity felt uncomfortable meeting new people because his parents failed to distinguish his making a minor social blunder from ruining himself completely socially. Thus a friend said, "You made a faux-pas." Mistranslating the French according to what he thought it meant (for him "faux" sounded like "fool"), he heard, "you never get anything right." He believed that others' basic feelings about him could change, without warning, from positive to negative just the same way his parents' basic feelings did change toward him when as a child he did something they disapproved of. He did not believe that adult interpersonal relationships had an inbuilt margin of error. Instead he believed that most people's basic feelings could change completely from positive to negative over something trivial (and would rarely change back again). He saw most people as being fixed in the role of an established parental clone, people who would turn on him the same way his parents did when he made childish mistakes, inevitably made at the time because he actually was a child!

As an adult, he continued to think this way in the here and now because as a child, he had *identified* with parents who thought the same way then, and he had long ago jumped to the only partly true (or completely false) conclusion that his parents were criticizing or rejecting him, with their setting firm limits on him. This meant that they were furiously criticizing him and rejecting him completely. (I could not convince him otherwise because his family actually did continue to reject him over nothing— showing a clear preference for his brothers and sisters now, as they did then, and, seamlessly, essentially from the day he was born.)

Behavioral Aspects

Speaking behaviorally, as Potter-Efron and Potter-Efron note, the rising anger found in this disorder can be attributed in part to a behavioral developmental process where the anger itself, oblique as well as direct, can become "addictive."[28] Having become "habitual,"[29] it has "become a bad habit."[30] There is enjoyment to be had from getting angry. The rush of anger is, using the term in a general sense, addictive because it is pleasurable and desirable.

As we shall see in Chapter 5, the need to *express this anger indirectly* also originates in cognitive errors. For example, the pattern of habitually expressing anger indirectly regularly arises from the belief that it is dangerous to express oneself honestly and openly because one thinks, oedipally, that competing with a rival is like, and therefore exactly the same thing as, murdering one's father.

Anger can be, and often is, learned as a way to accomplish a specific end. Anger can also be an attention-getting device. In certain ways some passive-aggressives are like the dog that attempts to call attention to itself by being annoying, say by running circles around an inattentive owner, or by barking incessantly. Some passive-aggressives are more like a feline, one that chews the telephone cord to make its displeasure known, indirectly, so as to get attention while simultaneously avoiding seriously alienating the object of its affections and the source of its gratification of important needs. Potter-Efron and Potter-Efron might call this anger when it occurs in humans "deliberate anger"—anger planned for purposes of "power and control."[31]

Passive-aggressives also suffer from anger buildup. Passive-aggressives get angrier than most and stay angry longer because, being passive-aggressive, they not only have a great deal of difficulty discharging their anger directly but also, due to their passive-aggressive approach to problem-solving, have a great deal of difficulty resolving the realistic issues that created the anger in the first place.

Interpersonal Reasons

Passive-aggressives are very sensitive, hyperalert, individuals with one eye always open to the possibility that they are being picked on. They also actively look for hidden meanings in the words and actions of their so-called persecutors and, routinely finding them, respond accordingly (as they believe).

According to Berne, individuals who resemble passive-aggressives "sulk"[32] like "a man who is angry at his mother"[33] and tend to be "overly sensitive to parental influences."[34]

Passive-aggressives are particularly sensitive to rejection and humiliation of the kind that can in turn provoke game playing. For example, Berne's game of Blemish is mostly about resentment arising within the depressive sulk "I feel I am no good because of the way you treat me."[35] The idea "I am no good" gets protectively transformed into "you are no good"[36] (e.g., for having treated me this way). The transformation takes place in order to ward off "insecurity [with the aim of] reassurance,"[37] The goal is accomplished by putting others down as second strike, that is in a defensive, critical, way.

Opportunistic/Tactical Reasons

I emphasize two tactical reasons for feeling/getting angry:

Anger is sometimes engineered for purposes of secondary gain, that is, anger creates opportunity, as when anger is a way to cow authority so that one may get ahead in a specific situation, or in life in general.

Anger can be sadomasochistic fun. Passive-aggressives can be somewhat sadistic. Their anger at others, and their desire to hurt them, can be a primary, pleasure-giving, force within. They can also be somewhat masochistic, for their anger is an invitation to others to abuse them. As Perry notes, "in the psychodynamic literature, passive aggression is discussed under the topic of masochism," with masochists dealing with their aggression passively—by "inviting harm and abuse, turning [the anger] against the self."[38]

Biological Reasons

While it is quite a leap from discerning a genetic component in anger to discerning a genetic component in passive-aggression, the close relationship between anger and passive-aggression as revealed via a study of temperament makes an exploration of the biological basis of anger potentially fruitful. Temperament, which some observers believe to be biologically determined, generally plays a role in determining how angry people get; why they get angry; as well as how exactly they express their anger in the (idiosyncratic) anger styles they choose to adopt.

A nurse calls up an on call technician in the middle of the night to make an inappropriate request—a request that one of the nurse's patients put the nurse up to making. The technician's wife seethes with anger about having been awakened. She calls all concerned "stupid." The technician himself, who is the one on call, is not quite so upset. His disposition is phlegmatic, and so he takes the position that "How was she (the nurse) to correctly evaluate the request?—she got tainted information." The same technician, who works 9 to 5, tells his wife, "I have to call a patient at 10 p.m. tonight. His wife, my patient, doesn't speak any English and her husband, who does, doesn't get home until late in the evening." The technician's wife counters, "Don't call—you aren't getting paid for working the late shift."

To quote Meissner, "innate biological predisposition plays a role in character formation in both its instinctual and ego fundaments."[39] For example, among the clinicians who believe that passive-aggressives are born angry, or at least angrier than most, Millon and Davis speak of the "Biophysical Level [of passive-aggression as manifest in an] irritable mood."[40] They note that these individuals are "frequently touchy, temperamental, and peevish, followed in turn by sullen and moody withdrawal. Petulant and impatient, [they unreasonably] scorn . . . those in authority and report . . . being annoyed easily or frustrated by many."[41]

Possible support for postulating the biological basis of temperament and so the possible biological basis of passive-aggressiveness in its anger dimension is to be found in common expressions that seem to allude to how passive-aggressives in some ways act almost "animalistic." Thus we say of passive-aggressives that "their feathers have been ruffled, they lock horns, they are stubborn as mules, they hog machines at the gym, and they will do anything to stay on top of the pecking order and fight not to be at the bottom of the food chain." As anyone who has wandered too close to an active bird's nest knows, controlled anger, in the form of buzzing heads without actually attacking the people attached to them, is an innate protective response that in animals and passive-aggressives alike seems to arise in reaction to turf invasions. That may be why some people in that controlled road rage as exemplified by giving other drivers the finger remind some observers of territorial dogs barking at someone who merely passes by without their being any real threat to the dog's well-being/ personal rights.

Also, according to Millon, clinical identification with, e.g. modeling one-self after, others, a process that contributes to a child's being like his or her (passive-aggressive) parents, can be not only a product of shared experience and learning, but also be a product of a "biological substrate for affective irritability. . . . transmitted by genetic mechanisms."[42]

Finally, in the realm of prevalence according to gender, as is evident from the title of Wetzler's book, *Living with the Passive-Aggressive Man*, some authors focus on passive-aggression in men perhaps because they have found that passive-aggression is found mainly in men. Millon expresses the opposite view, suggesting that "the negativistic or passive-aggressive personality pattern is judged somewhat more prevalent among women than among men."[43] However, Millon speculates that the reason for this is that "negative and obstreperous traits among men are judged as 'tough-mindedness,' while these very same characteristics among women are viewed as 'bitchy' and 'passive-aggressive.'"[44]

Some endorse the possibility that passive-aggressive anger origins, core dynamics, cognitive errors, and the like are not discriminatory based on gender, and that the same passive-aggressive dynamics, with minor variations, are present and exist in equal measure in both men and women. Perceived differences then might be the product of something in the evaluative process.

CHAPTER FIVE

Reasons Passive-Aggressives Can Only Express Their Anger Indirectly

Question Two: Why Can't Passive-Aggressive Individuals Express Their Anger More Directly?

This chapter discusses why passive-aggressives get angry then can't express their anger directly but prefer to, or must, express it in roundabout ways. (Chapters 6 and 7 discuss the anger styles that characterize/transmit this modified expressions of anger, e.g., the paranoid anger style where it's "I am not basically antagonistic to you, I am only getting back at you because you were the one who started it, having sorely antagonized me first.")

Passive-aggressives hold back and deflect their anger for a number of reasons and in a number of ways:

Comorbidity

Many individuals suffer from mixed disorders creating *comorbidity*. To illustrate, many suffer from mixed OCPD and passive-aggressive personality disorder. If so, they might express their anger indirectly as a reflection of their tendency to vacillate about all things, and especially about feeling/being angry. Individuals suffering from passive-aggression along with depression find fear of the consequences of their anger, particularly loss, to be an especially poignant issue for them. Passive-aggressives who are also masochistic are highly relationship dependent, and so for them object-constancy, dependent on restraint of anger, is key. As Small et al. emphasize, such passive-aggressives have learned to *suppress* their anger to maintain "enduring relationships."[1] As Reich referring to *masochism* in terms equally applicable to passive-aggression, suggests, "the masochistic character cannot tolerate giving up an object (hence the masochistic sticking to a love object)."[2]

As Wetzler notes, for many, anger expressed passive-aggressively feels "safer. . . . than direct aggression."[3] Thus passive-aggressives erect a complex defensive structure to safely moderate both the anger itself and the way it gets expressed. It is this defensive structure that comes across to the clinician as passive-aggressive personality problems intermingled with another symptom disorder, e.g., Millon's "Avoidant-passive-aggressive mixed personality."[4]

Developmental Factors

Various plausible developmental explanations have been given to account for how and why a child gets to be an angry adult who expresses his or her anger indirectly. The precise role that childhood development plays in shaping this specific aspect of adult behavior, although conjectural, is still worth exploring.

General Developmental Problems

Stricker presents general developmental reasons for passive-aggressives being afraid to get openly angry. These appear to consist of firmly embedded poisonous introjects originally resulting from "parenting which is so [overall] threatening that the child does not dare to express feelings directly."[5]

Parentally induced introjects leading to guilt, shame, fear, and confusion over one's anger, and so what is and what is not acceptable for a child to be angry about, contribute to the pattern of indirect anger expression in the adult, as follows:

Guilt. Guilt about expressing anger directly can be induced by a parental authority figure who tells his or her children that it is bad to be angry, or who actively or passively punishes his or her children for their angry thoughts, words, and deeds.

Parents who generate guilt over a child's complaints about a new sibling about to be or just having been born, e.g., by responding punitively when the old child complains "the new baby is usurping my unique position as the only one" by reprimanding the child for being selfish, may create a child who feels unsafe expressing any anger directly to his parents. Such a child may go on to become a resentfully deferential child-to-adult in many or all sectors of his or her interpersonal relationships. In one case matters became even more difficult for a son when his mother lost the unborn baby, an event for which she blamed the son, even more than he blamed himself.

Shame. Parents embarrassed by their child's instincts overall often shame the child, encouraging him or her to suppress all his or her instincts, anger included. However, children rarely buy in completely to parental views about what they should think and do about their anger. At first they do, but then, rebelling against the parental philosophy, they cast off parental constraints because they recognize that their parents are being excessively and arbitrarily suppressive, or flat-out wrong. As adults, such children typically vacillate between letting their anger out, feeling sheepish, and holding it in to avoid feeling as if they are saying and doing the wrong things.

Fear. Children often suppress their anger out of *fear* of no longer being autonomous. Such children when they become adults follow orders up to a point whereupon they angrily rebel about what they fear the most—which is a kind of enforced dependency.

Simultaneous resentful compliance and angry rebellion characterized the emotional life of one soon-to-become-passive-aggressive, who would say yes to a request and then drag his feet about complying with it. When this man was a child, his father put him to bed for days and sometimes weeks to treat an imaginary illness, or to prevent his getting a real one by "making certain he got enough rest." For example, during a raging flu epidemic, the father happened to hear that bed rest increased the strength of the immune system and hence the ability to resist disease. So he ordered his perfectly healthy son to bed for two months so that he would become immunologically strong enough to be able to fend off any viral attack. The child, becoming himself fearful of getting sick, followed orders—all the while, however, dreaming about his eventually growing up and thence being in a better position to rebel when, after becoming of age, he would realistically become less dependent on, and so far less vulnerable to, his parents' ideological whims.

Confusion. In the realm of *confusion*, some passive-aggressive adults are less innately ambivalent about their anger than they are truly mystified about how to express it. They say the wrong thing/do things wrong because they do not really know how to do things right. Because they long ago found that they can't know in advance exactly how their anger will go over with others, they try different forms of anger expression to see what works best, e.g., is in their best interests.

Constant bickering within the family makes it difficult for children to know what is the "right way" to feel about, and the correct way to do things. Is the mother right to criticize the father for never wanting to do work around the house, or is the father right to criticize the mother for constantly nagging him to do that work himself although he would prefer to pay to have it done, and could afford that. "What is right to get angry about?" now becomes the pressing question in the lives of such children, and, unable to answer it definitively, they answer it in a different way each time, and as a result vacillate in their own attitudes about getting angry, so that they might look as if they are behaving oppositionally when they are in reality merely uncertain about how to think and what to do.

Phase-Specific Developmental Factors

A simplified version of psychoanalytic theory presumes that a growing child traverses three main developmental phases on his or her way to adulthood—the oral, the anal, and the phallic/genital. A child can thus become an excessively angry adult who favors expressing his or her anger indirectly when problems on one or more of these three levels occur then, the problems never being adequately resolved, instead parlay themselves into trials of the child becoming an adult:

Oral Phase Difficulties

In this realm, fears of rejection/disengagement prevail as early and excessive needs for nurturance that persist from childhood into later life go virtually unchanged, leading to the adult's fear of being rejected over some minor deviance. Parents with internal agendas that early on ignore the child's (shifting) personal needs frustrate the child's longing to have someone stable to always depend on, someone to love and be loved by, and someone to take care of him or her—not someone to frustrate his or her longings—in a way that persists virtually unaltered from childhood into adulthood.

Issues of early rejection are expectedly the most persistent for passive-aggressives who "remain orally fixated." Thus Benjamin[6] stresses that anger might only be expressed in an indirect way lest one wind up replaced by a younger sibling or some other competitive interloper. The older child, as Benjamin suggests, is fearful about being back "down on the farm" after having "been to Paris."[7] Terrifying feelings of loss appear as the child becomes afraid to express rage out of a fear of making things worse—as Stricker puts it, specifically out of a fear of "losing whatever little [e.g., support] he or she has been [to date] able to gather."[8]

When parents are habitually openly rejecting, the adult passive-aggressive's habitual suppressing anger can be a continuation of a child's master plan to, by being good, rescue at least something from his or her relationship with his or her parents. Such children are in effect forced to decide between avoidance (mostly an unacceptable option), and (the far more acceptable compromise of) restraint.

Many parents of passive-aggressives are neither completely rejecting nor completely accepting of the child. Instead they are ambivalent about loving the child—sending him or her double messages. Now the child, becoming distrustful, him or herself becomes ambivalent about loving his or her parents. Here suppressing anger can represent an indication that one has become resigned to one's circumstances. With such parents, children learn and apply lifelong methods consisting of being both somewhat loving and somewhat hostile at one and the same time, their personal compromise, their way to maintain a safe distance from mother and father—without either openly rejecting or abandoning *them*.

Intrusive parenting—involving parents having gotten too close—can generate anger that is expressed indirectly as the adult's difficulty with commitment (generally consisting more of hesitancy than a full inability/ refusal to commit). Here, what takes over and persists is the fear of one's individuality being seriously threatened. With his or her identity and individuality potentially stifled, the adult, having felt overwhelmed and encroached upon as a child, goes to some lengths to maintain boundaries so that he or she becomes an individual who first lovingly relinquishes a degree of individualization to others, and then, when others respond positively to all of the closeness, panics and resists that, exactly out of a fear of winding up in a painful merger.

Anal Phase Difficulties

An adult passive-aggressive's anger/anger issues can stem from early conflicts about autonomy versus control. These often start with matters surrounding toilet-training, so that adult passive-aggressives feel angry in the here and now at contemporary people who, as their parents were, somehow manage to be disinterested in them yet at the same time manage to become overly enmeshed with them. As a consequence, such children, persistently overly concerned with rational relational stability, learn to enhance their ongoing relational safety by always carefully, when it comes to getting close, watching their step to avoid making the wrong distance decision.

Phallic-Oedipal Phase Difficulties

As adults, some oedipally fixated passive-aggressives can be thought of as psychologically speaking being the equivalent of oedipal assassins. These individuals at least in their fantasies first become preoccupied with the oedipal fantasy of killing the father, then live to regret it. For them, as Jones suggests in discussing Freud's *Totem and Taboo,* ambivalence is about rage over competitive issues subsequently challenged head on by remorse. There is a prominent aggressive admixture of "contumely" and "awe" in relationship to authority, the child's "rulers," which shows up and asserts itself almost routinely in important relationships, leaving the passive-aggressive individual vulnerable on almost every front where important human interactions are currently being transacted.

Defensive Factors

Passive-aggressives employ a number of defense mechanisms to rein in their anger. For this reason the clinical picture of passive-aggression is created in part out of specific psychological defenses maladaptively employed to handle anxiety and guilt originating in forbidden hostile feelings. These are forbidden because they abrade on an overly harsh conscience often, but not entirely, reflective of what one's society believes is, or ought to be, taboo.

Characteristically, passive-aggressives undo the negative with the positive through the defense of reaction formation. Passive-aggressives commonly go from being angry to becoming defensively saccharine sweet—a way to salve their consciences by protesting their having felt and even acted in an angry, often bitter, and perhaps close-to violent, fashion.

Different defenses tend to show specific (pathognomonic) affinities for given specific instinctual patterns. In particular, doing and undoing and reaction formation as defenses show a special affinity for unacceptable hostility. While preserving the original passive-aggressive goal—of expressing hurtful anger indirectly, also preserved is a mechanism for the partial abreaction of anger in the form of an indirect expression of hostility, as passive-aggressives simultaneously take the anger back, only to render it even more hurtful and harder for others to bear than an air-clearing outburst of rage (one that other people soon get over) might have done.

Often even basic defenses, including compromise formation and reaction formation, fail, sometimes explosively. When this happens one might see momentary dysregulation, e.g., rage attacks due to the ball of anger bursting (a very temporary occurrence in the truly passive-aggressive individual). This is called "the return of the repressed" and it often undoes what at first appears to have been satisfactorily done. For example, reaction formation directed to hostility at first gives the appearance of making the hostility more gentle. Only ultimately the aggressiveness breaks through, and possibly as enhanced, as can happen when the anger returns in the form of obsessively torturing others with protestations of one's goodness/altruism.

The aware observer can understand how social protests that literally block traffic "for the ultimate good of society" often themselves hint at the hostility that drives such behavior, just as individuals who present as a paragon of punctuality are in many instances surprisingly unpunctual as they defeat their intention to be exactly on time by (apologetically) being unable to leave the house before straightening and cleaning up "just one more time." And the seemingly cleanest person can in some curious respects be underneath astonishingly dirty, like the neighbor who keeps a spotless house by washing his dogs' urine off his balcony—onto the balconies of the residents below.

Conflict between hurting and sparing loved ones is often present and is closely associated with moral dilemmas, and in particular those of a religious nature. These moral dilemmas often consist, in the words of Wicks, of a cover for the goal of "elimination of anger as an emotion."[9]

Specific *defensive* anger disguises include the following.

Projection of Anger (The Paranoid Defense)

Paranoid passive-aggressives disavow the responsibility for their anger. Instead they blame others for making them angry. Via projection, "I am ashamed of myself" becomes "you shame (persecute) me, an innocent victim of your negativity." Now when their anger emerges it takes the form of second not first strike, and so appears to consist of appropriate retaliation.

Retroflexion of Anger (The Depressive Defense)

In retroflexion of anger, a defense generally associated with depression, after the anger first appears it gets turned back on the self, only to reappear in the form of beating others over their heads with one's own bloody body. Here complaints along the lines of "see how I suffer" are meant to be anger equivalents. The anger is still directed at others so that "how bad I feel" really is a statement of "how bad you make me feel."

Doing and Undoing (The Obsessive-Compulsive Defense)

Passive-aggressives take back commitments they themselves have made to avoid potential blame for having made them, only, coming to feel as if they have acted cowardly, they soon step forward again, and the process repeats itself.

Passive-aggressives modify their anger by doing and undoing it. Some-times they take it back in the very act of expressing it. An example of this simultaneous doing and undoing is how they smile as they say something very hostile, or ask a hostile, passed-off as a rhetorical, question, hiding their annoyance behind the inserted question mark as second thoughts lead the passive-aggressive individual to take one fearful step back to undo every bold, positive/potentially creative step taken forward. A man asked a composer why he never wrote with a particular audience in mind, why he kept writing for a second-rate music publisher, whether he had to pay to publish his compositions, and who was his ghostwriter for the orches-tral parts.

Exemplifying those who do and undo sequentially are people who ask pointedly hostile questions and then take them back with an apology by saying, "It was only a question"—a request for forgiveness that is their way to dilute their hostility—however insincerely and after the fact. A shopper asked a patient she saw carrying mothballs in the supermarket, "Is that brand any good?" The patient started to give a yes or no answer, only to then, leaving the person who asked the question at sea, avoid committing herself to the right answer by saying, "I was advised by a friend that these are wise to purchase." This way she blamed someone else for a recommen-dation she herself grudgingly gave—her way of avoiding responsibility should the neighbor buy and use the mothballs only to have something go wrong. (She was afraid that they would stain the neighbor's carpet or the neighbor would inadvertently ingest them and be poisoned.) "Do what is right for you," she said, a common hostilely noncommittal response to others, however demonstrably in need of guidance these others might actually be.

When entrenched and prolonged the process of taking back thoughts and feelings to neutralize/reverse angry ideas and actions becomes, tech-nically speaking, a "reaction formation" against that which has been, or that which one believes to have been, thought/done. Thus, according to some analytic theorists, prolonged excessive cleanliness which undoes an underlying wish to contaminate others might be a passive-aggressive "reac-tion formation" against certain (possibly anal) hostile wishes—consisting of wanting to hurt others directly by "smearing them with dirt."

The process of undoing and reaction formation may refer either to the taking back of badness with goodness, or to the taking back of goodness with badness. However, the process usually, although not exclusively, goes in the direction of the positive's taking back of the negative, as in "killing with kindness."

Compromise Formation

One often remains angry and suppresses one's anger simultaneously by using a defense called *compromise formation* as the chosen form of conflict resolution. In such a case a given thought/action is hedged by its conveying two opposite meanings at one and the same time. Since opposing trends predictably produce ambivalence, the victim cannot always accurately fully determine the primary thought in play/motivation. Thus he or she can rarely answer the question: Is being compulsively early primarily submissive or, when it inconveniences another, disruptively rebellious, or both?

Reaction Formation

Passive-aggressives in reaction formation use expressions of concern to cover expressions of hostility. "I am only trying to be helpful because I am worried about you" is a familiar alerting phrase passive-aggressives use when they really mean to say, "You need the help because something is seriously wrong with you." Whether it is an adolescent kindly offering his seat on the train to someone in her thirties, or a reparative therapist "kindly" extending himself to offer to cure gays and lesbians of being homosexual, these individuals by "killing with kindness" disguise their true (hostile) intentions under the mantle of so-called altruism, empathy, and pity.

Parents favoring reaction formation often hide their controlling agendas for their children by discouraging self-realization for the "child's own good." This they do on what appear to be the safe/rationally determined grounds of "practicality," as they "helpfully" explain, "I am only trying to give you good advice—to warn you that you cannot make a living doing what you love, no matter how much you love it." (In contrast, a non-passive-aggressive parent might encourage the child to succeed in his chosen beloved profession while simultaneously recommending backup plans in case of actual failure. The latter behavior is not passive-aggressive because the motive is not primarily to reject or control, but to assist.)

Unctuousness is a characteristic reaction formation, exemplified by the oily way telemarketers have of saying, "Have a nice day" after having been rejected for a sale—using a tone of voice that colloquially speaking "could kill"—disguising their death wishes toward others (who have not complied) but doing so only just barely, so that others can still simultaneously feel guilty and injured, yet, no matter how much they suspect it, cannot prove that they have been victimized in any way, and certainly not by having been told off in no uncertain terms.

Rationalization

While projectors costume their anger in, "I did nothing wrong, I only blame you for provoking me here," and those in reaction formation mask their anger as something good that disguises something bad, rationalizers hide their anger by finding ways to justify it after the fact, that is, after it has become manifest. This justifying simultaneously reduces their own guilt and titrates the blow to others to some desirable lesser degree of harshness. As parents they are not abusers but strict disciplinarians—who mete out harsh parental discipline, which they call not "hate" but "tough love," not because they are controlling, or sadistic, but because they are lovingly concerned with all concerned doing the right thing.

Rationalizers, ignoring the dynamics of human interactions, and using selective abstraction to emphasize a (partially) positive over a (prevailing) negative motive, argue that they are entirely motivated not at all by hostility but only by reasonable caution, as they merely follow unimpeachable (positive) social convention.

Many rationalizations are offered by critics to excuse savaging behaviors as instances of altruism put forth not as admonitions but for the good of the victim—for example, "so that you do not repeat the errors of your ways." An acquaintance told a man, "for his own protection," that people were only being nice to him because they wanted to meet his beautiful wife. Then he asked him, as if innocently, "Why else do you think that people would pay any attention to you?" Then he called the man up to tell him that he knew about his wife's infidelities, doing so "only" so that the man could take protective measures. In another example, hospitals overwork their students to save money, then justify their actions by referring to the benefits of continuity and of being baptized by fire—in their proclaimed scheme of things these being the best possible ways "for you as students to learn through continuity, and as well to build character through hard work."

Many rationalizations are narcissistic as when "hate" is rationalized as "free speech" overlooking the oppressive effects "my freedom" has on others. Narcissists often justify their cruel and malicious intent in terms of higher, lofty, transcendental motives. "It's not my fault" rationalizations proceed along these lines of "I cannot help myself, I am natively temperamental," as for example in, "I cannot help seething at you because I was born labile" (the excuse of "my temperament"), or because "I was traumatized as a child." In my field, legitimate psychiatric diagnoses can be used, really "misapplied," to make excuses for one's indirect hostility, as when pathological obsessionalism is blamed for verbal cruelty ("I just can't stop asking you if you have contaminated me"). Claiming emotional/physical disability can be equally absolving, as in "I express as much anger as I do because of my overactive hormones." Also belonging here is a focus on a "not-me" origin of anger as being due to some (merely theoretical) "chemical imbalance."

Youth and inexperience also offer what some passive-aggressives consider to be satisfactory excuses for being difficult, as does society's being presumably to blame for all one's personality problems. Some such claims can be pertinent in given instances. However, with passive-aggressives they are often overused "explanations" advanced to obscure the real truth—to cover the actual motivation for an individual's passive-aggressive behavior simply as a way to avoid true accountability.

Denial

Denial, typically accompanied by isolation of affect (discussed below) enforces reaction formation and rationalization, with both helping passive-aggressives remain unaware of the often cruel implications of their passive-aggressive words and actions. (It also helps them hide their true motivations from their victims.)

Passive-aggressive individuals are often surprised at the responses they provoke. They deny the fact that anger as they express it may evoke a response, perhaps directly expressed counter-anger. When it does evoke such a response, they typically deny having given cause, as they accuse the other of overreacting. Perhaps merely letting others know how we feel is not aggression and therefore it is okay to say what one thinks as long as one does not express oneself emotionally simultaneously. According to Wetzler, Tavris, citing the positive advantages of expressing anger this way, calls this a "feelings report."[10] In some cases this amounts to the making of a nice legal point, but it often does so only at the expense of taking too little account of the dynamics of specific human responses. Many patients will endure growing isolation rather than give up what they see as their right of free expression, especially because they believe that they use that right with restraint, although in reality they use it with cunning. But in some cases "merely" reporting feelings, although not openly aggressive, is close to being quintessentially passive-aggressive. Instead of dispassionately telling a lover that one is angry, then detailing "why" in numbing detail isolated from feeling not as altruistic as one believes it to be, one might better come up with ways to be less angry in the first place.

It is always wise to keep in mind what Keating says: "Recent studies suggest that, contrary to popular opinion, it is not always helpful to express our feelings, to strive for a catharsis or to 'talk them out.' Sometimes such efforts only intensify feelings. It may be best to distract ourselves with other interests. Hostile feelings, at least, can seem to dissipate more quickly this way."[11]

Isolation (of Affect)

In isolation of affect, the passive-aggression consists of trying, generally successfully, to wrest emotion from thought, that is, to isolate emotional charge (emotional "cathexis") from ideational content (belief). As a consequence, many passive-aggressive individuals seem to be cold, abstract, and emotionless as if what they say and do doesn't really matter on all levels. Now their ideas appear in consciousness, and so to others, as bland due to having been stripped of naturally occurring, and so expectedly anticipated, associated emotions. The displacement of affect generally follows the isolation of affect. Through this process of displacement, the relevant emotions, continuously felt, become relocated and so are still to be found, although elsewhere, where they likely present in an incongruous fashion.

Passive-aggressives commonly employ two forms of displacement of affect. In the first, they use third parties as vehicles for expressing their own hostility, and therefore as part of their plan to express their hostility indirectly. In that way they do not have to take responsibility for their anger or directly face their victims with it. They can instead send messengers, quote others, or reveal themselves to others hoping (knowing) the information will get back to the intended victim. A husband watching his wife head for a riverbank "jokingly" tells his son-in-law, whom he knows will repeat to his mother-in-law what was just said about her to him, that he hopes she drowns. A physician expressed his hatred of a colleague by repeatedly quoting a patient, one who disliked the doctor, to that doctor. Sometimes the victim hears something really meant for him or her in the context of a complaint about a third party, as when a man, angry with his wife, tells her about a coworker in terms clearly applicable to the wife herself. A formerly common form of displacing anger to one by expressing it directly to another was "kicking the dog," a method for "safely" abreacting anger by attacking others instead of the intended target. Such passive-aggressives might "kick the dog" in the presence of the person they are really angry with in order to tell the real victim how angry they are at him or her—one step removed. Sophisticated victims know from the kicker's behavior, and subsequent verbal associations, that the anger is really meant for them.

Pets can be enlisted/trained to become messengers of annoyance, as can one's children.

Sometimes such behavior looks innocent, but it is so only on the surface. For example, one patient said he brought his very young children to restaurants primarily frequented by adults because he could not find babysitters. However, his true motivation was revealed, and underscored, when he went on to describe his reluctance to contain the children after all arrived. As he put it, ignoring how they were running amok among the startled diners, "My kids have rights too, and others have to learn to accept these." He also relished bringing his wife and children to gay restaurants deliberately to annoy the "stuck-up queers" and show them the wonders of heterosexual life. Sometimes more serious offenses are involved, as when homophobic parents who are on the surface accepting of two gay men as neighbors, egg their children on to literally egg the side of the gay men's house, put dents in their new car, or hit their mailbox with a baseball bat.

In another form of displacement, passive-aggressives complain about a minor matter to refer to a major matter in order to both focus on and (partially) blind the victim to the depth and significance of that anger that the passive-aggressive actually feels. A boss, in conflict about her desire to tell an employee how angry she is that the employee went on vacation and left her with all his work, instead criticized him for breaking a rarely enforced rule—to tell people where he was going whenever he left the immediate area.

Passive-aggressives who detach a feeling from one thing then reattach it to another typically move affect from a matter of greater importance to a matter of lesser importance, allowing freer access to the first, more significant, topic—since now the passive-aggressive no longer appears to feel so strongly about that. The overuse of this defense contributes to the appearance of blandness of feeling that characterizes the affective tone of many passive-aggressives.

Expectedly, such affect redeployment will on the one hand lead to underresponse (in relationship to the first, major, thing) and to overresponse (in relationship to the second, minor thing). Clinically, the tendency to overrespond emotionally—to magnify by making much of little, seems to have less import for passive-aggressives than the tendency to underrespond emotionally—to minimize, that is, to at least seem to be making too little of much. Thus the passive-aggressive with hostility about threatened intimacy first encapsulates intimate emotions and then moves them on—to instead feel them in relationship to touching, further displaced onto "togetherness" such as "being on one page" (cooperativeness), which now becomes of significance due to the resultant symbolic enhancement of familiarity. The benefit accrued is that the original emotions can now be more easily managed/displayed because, having been diluted, they have become less striking and so more likely to yield themselves up to attempts at self-control/denial.

Many passive-aggressives can, using these mechanisms, think horrific thoughts and contemplate horrific deeds without experiencing excessive personal guilt or substantial revulsion—because, having severed original thought from emotion, and having moved the emotion itself on, they now "don't feel that all strongly about this or that." The loss is that the passive-aggressive comes to appear extraordinarily "picky" about things that theoretically at least ought not to count that much.

Displacement (of Idea)

Displacement of idea from a whole to a part, occurring with some frequency, is exemplified by a lawyer's not only regularly raising her fee but doing so in an amount that reflected the cost of living index exactly, so that instead of rounding out the numbers she winds up with a fee that ends in an odd number, such as $300.72 per hour. This reflects her own secret wish to overcharge while seeming not to charge too much. For she can now think, "I am not overcharging you, for, as you can see, I am just raising my fee based on an official Government index of inflation."

Displacement of Emphasis

Passive-aggressives allude to a central, but for them not fully expressible, matter by citing and highlighting only one of the matter's (often peripheral) facets, e.g., the fearful belief that touching=groping=sex=rape, so "we should keep our distance from one another."

Passive-aggressives also displace what alarms them, such as personal humiliation, defeat, and rejection, onto an abstraction. Thus they might displace their critical feelings about others' forbidden sexual desires onto such an abstraction as a complaint about another's poor hygiene, or the belief "gay sex is dirty" may be displaced to a complaint that gays are defiling the true sacred meaning of marriage.

In therapy, passive-aggressive patients tend to be particularly prone to resist by displacing from significant to trivial matters as their way to divert themselves from important issues at hand requiring insightful exposure. Thus, in therapy, passive-aggressives often discuss an insignificant aspect of a significant symptom; or discuss an acceptable symptom (for example, a somatic complaint) to avoid discussing an embarrassing dynamic (for example, forbidden erotic wishes) or a shameful symptom (a nasty recurrent thought). They disguise what they think by withholding via changing around the object of their thoughts, so that a man disappointed with his doctor instead hides this disappointment by fixating upon, and talking only about, disappointment with his boss, and with his wife.

Many passive-aggressives in therapy disguise their intentions by changing the object of their attention as they displace transference feelings toward the therapist onto feelings about a family member—or vice versa.

Passivity/Inaction (Foot Dragging/ Withholding/ Slow-Walking/ Oppositionalism)

Although not formally classified as a defense, passivity and inaction are included here on clinical grounds, because passive-aggressives use these behaviors to reduce internal anxiety and deal with external frustrations and threats via inaction. Passive-aggressives do this in ways that range from being late to, to entirely forgetting, an appointment, or an assignment. That allows them to be, and act, angry by implication so they can now get mad with less anxiety, and to express their hostility effectively, or more effectively, with less guilt. A coworker returning another's borrowed cellular phone leaves it in the desk drawer of the man she borrowed it from, "forgetting" to tell him she did so, in effect saying to him, "I will give you your phone back, but I won't let you know I did so, so that you don't actually get it." Not talking to him, not telling him what he needs to know, is her version of the passive-aggressive silent treatment. Forgetting is her way to handle anger and its expression by "withholding remembering," with leaving out aspects of communicating an important part of the process.

The board of a cooperative apartment, angry because a couple was behind in their maintenance payments, expressed their anger by putting an incomplete statement in the minutes that circulated to all the tenants. They simply stated that these tenants were in arrears on their maintenance, making the tenants look like deadbeats. The board "forgot" to mention that the couple had a reason to be "late in paying"—they had placed the funds in escrow, on their attorney's advice, pending the resolution of a serious internecine building dispute.

Tangentiality and verbosity are in some ways the equivalent of passive-aggressive withholding. When talking to a doctor, the patient might begin the story of his or her case history at some superfluous starting point then move too slowly forward, thus never getting to the end of the tale in the time he or she knows to have been allotted for telling it. Boring others is another form of indirect hostility. Here one simply fails to make an effort to be interesting and knowingly continues to be dull despite requests to cut it short—passive-aggressively continuing business as usual in spite of nonverbal feedback from others like their coughing or looking at their watch repeatedly as a way to say, "Get to the point and get it over with." Being bored oneself, especially when manifest as the withholding, or the understating, of a deserved positive response, can also be a passive-aggressive defensive action. What Mahrer calls acting in "ways which are passively complicit"[12] is another (withholding) defense, a way to let others self-destroy by not stopping others from doing something that likely won't be in their best interests. Belonging here too are friends who do nothing when cries for help are directed to them about intended suicidal or homicidal activity—as they respect being sworn to secrecy/honor a pledge "not to talk," thus assuring an individual seriously and obviously in need of assistance doesn't get it.

Acting Out

Acting out is defensive because it reduces anxiety and guilt, however irresponsibly, by bypassing ideation. As any boss who recognizes the hostility in a worker's constantly calling in sick will attest, for many passive-aggressives the expression "actions speak louder than words" holds a special truth.

Some passive-aggressives act out by referring to, supposedly only in order to solve, other people's so-called problems—even before these problems have become manifest. They offer suggestions ostensibly to condemn others "in case" they might transgress, when actually the intent is to give others big ideas they might use to promote the transgression in question.

In another common form of passive-aggressive acting out, a passive-aggressive partner selfishly takes action on his or her own without waiting for requisite input from his or her partner. One example of this is the just-mentioned partner who, while cleaning up, secretly puts things away where the other partner cannot find them when she needs them. This person relishes hiding shoes (e.g., under the bed, where they can only be found when and if the partner flags them), and he or she can only discover the hiding place too late in the morning to be found in time for their being worn that day, as intended. A husband, wanting accolades from his daughter, agrees to take her dog so that the daughter can go on vacation, only he does so without first consulting with his wife, who does not want the dog because she knows that she, not her husband, will be the one to have to take care of it. One professional colleague undermined another by doing things on her own, going over her colleagues' heads. A doctor, her colleague, refused to prescribe a certain medication to a patient without first obtaining consultation with a specialist. The patient turned for the prescription to that doctor's colleague, and she, even though knowing that the first doctor had refused to write the prescription for now, wrote it anyway, doing so when the first doctor was busy doing something else. Then she responded to the first doctor's expected complaints of "you're going over my head" by calling him hypersensitive, to hide the abusive nature of her own insensitivity.

So often, sex outside of a committed relationship/marriage is less sex than it is acting out: an indirect expression of hostility to one's partner. Cheating on a steady partner certainly has a hostile component to it when it is meant to be discovered. When some passive-aggressives cheat and it is exposed, they are not so much getting caught as they are being fulfilled. Making it worse is the adoption of the patently self-serving theory that "cheating is good for my marriage."

Passive-aggressives may act out by humiliating their victims publicly—sometimes, but not always, without mentioning them by name. A teacher criticizes a student's behavior in front of the whole class, making an example of him in the so-called valid guise of teaching the rest of the class an important lesson. A woman who was grieving publicly that her cat had died appeared to all concerned to be a kindly person who loved animals—until her partner embarrassed her by announcing to a room full of people, "All you did was complain about the cat when she was alive." A patient was trying to impress a former professor about how studious he was. "I very rarely watch television," he said. This patient's wife, in the presence of the professor vocally disagreed and emphatically reminded her husband that always after he came home from work he promptly went over to the television set, turned it on, and sat there all night, as if entranced.

The board of a cooperative published in the minutes circulated to the whole building things one tenant said about another although they were entirely false accusations. Thus they were fusing libel with slander.

Identification with the Aggressor

Passive-aggressives often express their anger about being abandoned, controlled, humbled, and/or annoyed by abandoning, controlling, humbling and annoying others in their turn. As Mahrer suggests, the person who identifies with the aggressor becomes the "active one who controls the controller or rejects the rejecter."[13] For example, a man asked his neighbor to please turn down the sound on her television set. Instead of complying, she reminded him that he slammed the door when he left in the morning, disturbing her peace. Identification with the aggressor often starts up or soon becomes part of a sadomasochistic skirmish in which it becomes very difficult to know who started what, and who is in turn now doing what to whom.

Sublimation

Passive-aggressives can manage to turn even sublimation, ordinarily a healthy defense, into a vehicle for managing anger by expressing it indirectly. Healthy people use sublimation to change anger to humor, pity, concern, or other forms of interpersonally desirable and socially acceptable behavior. Passive-aggressives use sublimation to convert anger into sarcasm, or into anger displayed as "corrupted nice gestures" as, for example, a mother pushes good-tasting but fattening food on a child, although he has told her over and over again, "I am on a strict weight reduction diet." (When he complains, she reminds him of how she worked all day creating good-tasting recipes, and did so just for his delight.)

Passive-aggressives favoring refinement tend to transition primitive wishes and fears, especially those of an instinctual nature, into a more socialized expression of those wishes and fears. Now the passive-aggressives can come to express their anger in a, as they see it, more acceptable, more socially approved of, way. They might express resentment for anything that at all resembles being told how to think and what to do not by arguing their case specifically but by sublimating their specific resentments into some general campaign, such as one to promote freedom of speech and self-expression in their world. Many passive-aggressives express anger politely via the use of socially approved methods for expressing hostility indirectly by referring not in detail but in only a general, often sublimated, way to the exact content of the (hate) speech (their own) that they wish to protect. To illustrate, for many passive-aggressives extremes of pity can be a form of sublimated (passive-aggressive) sadism. At times (hardly always), pity for animals can be a sublimation of one's pitilessness directed toward humans, e.g., "You can't adopt that dog because your outdoor area is too small for the space he needs."

Avoidance

Here deflection of anger is accomplished by staying out of a situation, e.g., "staying out of the fray" in order to (indirectly) tell the other person "I don't want to have anything (more) to do with you, and your stuff."

Symbolization

This involves dealing with uncomfortable thoughts/emotions by displacing them onto substitutive thoughts and feelings, and so expressing oneself only by "mere allusion" to the (inexpressible) original. The passive-aggressive merely selectively hints at some fundamental thought or emotion, instead using subtle or gross substitution to stay away from it exactly. For example, for the OCPD passive-aggressive arranging objects nicely in a row can symbolize wanting one's home to be a warmer loving place than you, my wife, make it. Oneself squirreling all joint funds away can be a way to tell a partner "I will be leaving you soon." Having a lot of money can be a way to reassure oneself "you can't harm me by abandoning me in the poor house"; or having saved a million can mean, "I have it all, and more than you." Stand-ins are employed to make a negative original into something manifestly more positive/to be negative in a nonspecific way, one way to keep the target from adequately defending him- or herself. Those who are compulsively late are possibly being symbolically provocative by testing others to see how they will react, and more specifically determining whether or not others will reject the passive-aggressive person if he or she is not there on time as promised ("you only had to wait for me for a few minutes!"). Fussy passive-aggressives may be criticizing others who fall short for not having what it takes as their way to convey to these others indirectly that they are being perceived as being obviously worthless and defective.

Fussiness

Other fussy passive-aggressives such as OCPD passive-aggressives have rules and regulations on "timetables" they follow assiduously. They carefully run their lives as if they are writing a table of contents for a book entitled, "My Existence." Their perfectionism is a plea to be loved, if not for themselves, then at least for the (symbolic) adequacy, admirableness, and wholesomeness (efficacy) of their words and actions. It is also a way to act superior to indirectly express annoyance with friends, and/or colleagues, or to the entire company for which they work.

Regression

Regression involves a return to an earlier, more infantile, era of psychological development where individuals had once been comfortably free from anxiety and guilt (the era of "fixation"). Nirvana is attained at the expense of adequate functioning in the here and now. Thus some adult passive-aggressive withholding can be understood as comfortable, if childish rebelliousness to avoid being submissive, a miniature war fought by the passive-aggressive refusing to budge and yield even when, or just because, others' expectations and requests are forthcoming and happen to be legitimate.

Manneristic (Nonverbal) Behaviors

Here antagonism is expressed nonverbally. Somatic mannerisms like clenching the teeth; gripping the hands to make them into fists; slowness (symbolic freezing); or clearly looking restless when a speaker is talking, can all be effectively employed to avoid overt expression of hostility while still getting one's hostile points across

Maximization

In maximization, lofty principals are applied to trivial matters leading to a skewing of priorities often in a way to assure one gets one's demands gratified. One patient put forth deep philosophical explanations for his reducing a waitress's tip for inferior or poor service, and another patient advanced an overarching scientific approach to air conditioning: refusing to allow her family to turn on the air conditioning until she heard the weather reporter telling her whether the relative humidity had reached a predetermined level making for a certain "desirable ratio." So often, lofty abstract principles are applied in a way that almost deliberately disregards/ harms the wellbeing of real people and even actual pets, as when we see the passive-aggressive preferring to allow a baby to live in an orphanage over adopting him or her out to a couple whose lifestyle one disapproves of, possibly due to their not being married, or being gay; and when a rescue group refuses to give a dog up for adoption to an individual because this individual failed to neuter another one of her dogs; or, as in another case, refusing to adopt out a German Shepherd to a couple because they had a declawed cat, and not even a cat they had had declawed themselves, but a cat they had adopted already declawed—itself supposedly indicating their philosophical acceptance of the declawing process.

Here a preoccupation that ought to be of secondary concern, however valid (or invalid) in and of itself, is inappropriately installed to become a matter of major interest and involvement in a way that can make the passive-aggressive into a cruel person due to his or her condemning others for complying with some fetish, fixation, or other idée fixe, as when one's orderliness becomes more important than one's humanity. Such a patient, typically looking to enhance his or her self-esteem, might accept making public fun of/humiliating instead of correcting others compassionately, although the latter would be both doable and a much better idea. I still cringe when I remember how a history teacher humiliated a classmate in front of the whole class for confusing the word "occidental" with the word "accidental." Like many passive-aggressives, her job, to teach, got lost in her devotion to matters of correctness, here partly for the purpose of distorting the importance of reality just to find some reason to debase someone, and to do so subtly, as well as in the guise of being helpful. Once a patient, running out of money through little fault of his own and having no funds left to pay for his train ride home from his therapy hour, asked his therapist for a loan for the carfare. The therapist, citing transference considerations, wouldn't give him any money, saying, "Better that I don't give it to you, for doing so might contaminate the transference." The patient had to walk; and to this day the therapist doesn't know what fate befell the patient—because after he left his therapist's office he literally walked, indeed. That is, he never returned. In a parallel interaction, a patient wished his therapist a happy holiday, to which the therapist, as usual purportedly seeking enlightenment over humanity and inclusiveness over the exercise of common sense—replied, "What I really need to know is, 'What exactly did you mean by that?'"

Some examples of "the principle is more important than the (humanitarian) practice" apply to some political matters of a PC nature, such as changing a diagnosis to make a patient seem less ill in order to spare his or her feelings and those of the family, doing so however in a way that neglects or aggravates the real underlying problem due to the potential for neglect arising out of the misdiagnosis.

Minimization

A hostile skewing of priorities is often due to minimization which can additionally seriously affect the exercise of good judgment. This happens should an individual ignore major problems in relationships in favor of a preoccupation with minor concerns leading to a diversionary failure of prioritization as when, according to the *PDM*, we find an off-putting attack on others created via a preoccupation "with issues of self-definition [over issues surrounding forming and maintaining relationship[s]."[14] Here instead of loving another and being "us," passive-aggressives cavil due to a fear of losing their identity to the point of "no longer being me." I once advised a patient to put self-realization below maintaining his relationships, which were in serious trouble. He shot back that, "If I did what you suggested I would cease to be me, becoming a Mr. Blandboy instead." But what ceased, due to his "being me," were each one of his, to that date, potentially viable love-affairs.

Minimization, like any other defense, is not so passives-aggressive when it is socially sanctioned, or when the practical consequences of the minimization and the resultant skewing of priorities, although that can be potentially destructive over the long term, is not immediately obvious even to the most insightful of observant individuals, and is not immediately detrimental to some important cause.

A patient refused to visit his father when the old man was dying. He had shut him out of his life because he was afraid that the father would take advantage of his appearances at the father's house to learn his address and phone number and so to at a later time intrude upon his privacy.

The tendency to de-emphasize/overlook important matters can lead to results opposite from those consciously intended:

A man cared too much that the neighbors might dislike him or find him deficient in some unimportant respect. His solution was to avoid them by hiding in the halls, running back into his apartment if a neighbor emerged at the same time as he, while speaking to the neighbor only when spoken to, and then only in monosyllables. Also, when he couldn't avoid passing someone, he at least avoided touching them by plastering himself against the wall, thus getting away from them by getting as far away from that person as he could get given the structural circumstances of the environment. As a result, he became an object of gossip and morbid curiosity—viewed in exactly the same negative way he most feared being seen.

Repetition and Excessive Elaboration

Much passive-aggression is composed on an atomic level of normal thoughts and behaviors which only become molecularly pathologically hurtful due to the exaggeration of repetition.

Passive-aggression can take the form of obsessing consisting of the tendency to say or do the same thing over and over again, perhaps, but not necessarily, with minor variations. The fear "I left something out" creating a push for completeness can torture a listener as problems get not solved but rethought. As ruminators, some passive-aggressive individuals to look like innovators constantly repeat their own inventions (or those of others as if they were their own), and continuously rediscover what they have already learned—the same thing anew every day, each time with an unmerited but unmitigated intensity/sense of freshness for the passive-aggressive psyche that is in fact intended only to be a way of getting under the skin of a victim. Examples include well-worn jokes told as if entirely fresh, the use of trite and hackneyed statements as if they were original, the overuse of clichés such "at the end of the day" or "the bottom line," and fervid tweeted complaints about nothing much, such as rage over a radio station's playing only the top 40 hits. The excessive elaboration usually actually involves verbosity, but that is not the same thing as loquacity, the chatterer's horror of a verbal vacuum. Rather for the passive-aggressive, verbosity is often the product of this march toward completeness, the product of a feel-good need for unquestionable cloture, certainty and clarity. Often passive-aggressive individuals keep adding things, the same thing over and over, due to a wish to annoy others. Thus the speaker instead of amplifying a point sticks to the same point piling on superfluous details that do not make for a good argument or clarify an important assertion. Instead he or she is motivated to reduce his, the speaker's own, anxiety, even though that means enhancing the listener's discomfort.

Repression

Fears of being emotionally flooded drive the passive-aggressive patient to be restrictive of his or her emotions. Now he or she puts others off through boring them with the same emotions displayed over and over again, to the exclusion of the expression of meaningful, or any significant, emotion at all.

In short, passive-aggression may profitably be conceptualized according to its defensive aspects, as if it is the product of one or more simultaneously operative, maladaptive defense mechanisms employed to handle anxiety due to guilt, which anxiety in turn originates mainly in the perception of inner hostile thoughts and feelings that the passive-aggressive needs to quash both in the thoughts' and feelings' perception and expression. Narcissism prevails secondarily as the speaker reveals how his or her passive aggression feels better simply omitting how the listener is now made to feel that much worse.

Common defenses meant to alter/hide and also express hostility include symbolization, which involves allusion to thought and emotion by stand-ins (these may be positive or negative in their connotations); isolation and displacement of affect, where passive-aggressives detach a feeling from a matter of importance and reattach it to an unimportant matter both hiding and expressing the feeling at one and the same time (mostly affect is detached from the momentous and reattached to something relatively insignificant constituting a changeover from the impressively meaningful to the annoyingly inconsequential); sublimation, where passive-aggressives translate primitive wishes or fears of an instinctual nature into scrubbed-clean, socially acceptable, expressions of nonsocially acceptable but true, passionate, desire allowing the passive-aggressive individual to him-or herself behave (and demand others behave) in a more socially approved of, holier-than-thou, way; minimization, where in a diminishment the individual bypasses major issues in favor of a preoccupation with minor concerns creating a deliberate (defensively diversionary), and often dangerous, failure of prioritization; maximization, where something neutral becomes a source of unnecessary worry; and intellectualization, where anxiety reduction is accomplished by placing thinking over feeling, humanitarian feelings rendered unimportant in the hierarchy of what counts, thus to disenfranchise something that would and should otherwise be of great emotional importance and impact for others.

Cognitive Behavioral Factors

Cognitive-behavioral factors include faulty cognitions that are responsible for many mistakenly drawn beliefs about becoming angry and why anger should be expressed using indirect means alone. Behavioral determinants are conditioned by the expectation of specific reward for expressing anger circuitously, aligned with the fearful expectation of punishment for expressing anger openly and honestly.

Perry and Flannery also suggest that expressing anger directly and effectively is a skill that has to be taught, and the inability to do so may be the default,[15] with the passive-aggressive patient never having learned to express anger in a healthy, wholesome way.[16] In addition, Perry and Flannery quote Wolpe as suggesting that "the patient usually does have appropriate assertiveness skills but is inhibited by anxiety from using them."[17]

Specific pathological cognitions not only help account for why passive-aggressives get so angry in the first place (as discussed in Chapter 4) but also account somewhat for the inability passive-aggressives have to be able to express their anger directly. For example, thinking dichotomously (exclusively in terms of black or white) passive-aggressives believe that expressing anger directly is *never* safe but *always* extremely dangerous. Also, thinking in terms of some=all, passive-aggressives feel that anger is not to be expressed directly because a little anger is the same thing as a violent rage.

The literature offers a number of *behavioral* explanations to account for why passive-aggressives express their anger indirectly. For example, according to some experts, the tendency to express anger obliquely can be conditioned by significant others offering reward for expressing anger circuitously and punishment for expressing anger openly and honestly— the "punitive consequences of assertion."

Also, behaviorally speaking, identification/modeling within the family tends to be a powerful force in the development of passive-aggressive personality disorder, that is, identification with, or modeling oneself after, one's passive-aggressive parents likely contributes to favoring expressing adult passive-aggressive anger indirectly. As Brody suggests in a reference to Heinz Kohut's theories, "Clinical material shows that in most cases it is the pathogenic personality of the parents . . . that account[s] for generating unsolvable inner conflicts that persist when the child becomes an adult."[18]

When children learn to be indirectly angry by being resentful, critical, chronically late, or inconsiderate via coming to do things just the way their parents did things via a process of identification, this process makes passive-aggressives' use of indirect anger effectively into a family pattern.

Tactical Factors

Tactical (interpersonal) reasons pertain, e.g., there are realistic advantages presumably to be gained from indirect anger over and above anger expressed directly, for here the passive-aggressive self protects from feared retaliation at others' hands, constituting one of the most effective ways passive-aggressives have to avoid definitively hurting the significant others in their lives, not for altruistic reasons, but so to get them to do exactly what they want them to.

Anger expression that is indirect can also be a tactic, a device, or an expedient for accomplishing a specific end when it has become tied in with the passive-aggressive's wish to torture a victim for the passive-aggressive's personal gratification. Perhaps there is a challenge to be met here: how to be angry with and cruel to others without feeling overly guilty about it and without destroying the relationship in the process.

Social Factors

Another important reason for preferring indirect over direct anger involves primarily social factors. Most people in reality disapprove of people who get angry. Certain segments of society discourage what they perceive to be direct expression of hostile thoughts and see hostility in what they believe to be misguided attempts to be kind; e.g., don't call an expectant woman "mother" because of the possibility that she is not personally identified as being a source of fecundity (such as a motherly type).

CHAPTER SIX

Anger Styles

Question Three: What Are the Different Ways (Anger Styles) Passive-Aggressives Use to Express Their Anger Indirectly?

In Chapter 4 I discussed the main reasons why passive-aggressives get angry and flare. I emphasized how the source of their anger originates in multiple pathways, including those that are syndromally related (e.g., the product of paranoid beliefs, or OCPD indecisiveness) and also including those that are biologically determined, e.g., issues originating in temperament. In Chapter 5 I discussed some of the reasons why passive-aggressives can't or won't express this anger directly. In the following two chapters, Chapters 6 and 7, I focus not on the nature of the anger itself or on the reasons why passive-aggressives can't or won't express their anger directly, but on the different indirect ways passive-aggressives do express what anger comes through, e.g., their *anger styles*. Some of these, like the reasons for withholding anger, are also syndromally derived, such as the paranoid anger style, while others are more profitably classified according to other, nonsyndromal, paradigms such as:

- the main defenses employed (for example, the anger style is heavily imprinted by reaction formation);
- the main interpersonal mechanisms deployed, e.g., avoidance;
- the main tactics brought into play, consciously or unconsciously, that is, the specific *purposes,* often retaliatory or manipulative, to which the indirect anger is put, such as the psychopathic anger style meant to extort something tangible from others, e.g., geared to win in a competitive situation by defeating others via double binding them.

Potter-Efron and Potter-Efron say that the overall anger style of passive-aggressive individuals involves being "anger sneaks."[1] Wetzler, speaking generally of the passive-aggressive man's anger style, suggests that, "Anger is at the core of passive-aggression even when it is denied, submerged or called something else. . . . Passive-aggressive guys *contain* their anger (italics added), but their message . . . comes through loud and clear."[2] In the opinion of many observers, "steamy" anger, referring to how passive-aggressives express their anger in a kind of seething, is a common indirect, oblique, circuitous, anger style employed by passive-aggressives as a way of showing and simultaneously disavowing their anger, resulting in anger being expressed via compromise formation. Walking this back, sneaky/steamy anger is as characteristic of passive-aggressive patients as expressing anger in the form of persecutory ideas (I don't hate others, others hate, and are against, me) is characteristic of paranoid individuals, and as expressing anger as retroflexed onto oneself (I don't hate you, I only hate myself) is characteristic of passive-aggressives who are depressed.

In short, clearly different passive-aggressives get angry in different specific ways, that is, different passive-aggressives employ different anger styles. Classifying these patterns—the particular ways they handle their anger, according to the style passive-aggressives choose, and show, in turn helps answer Potter-Efron and Potter-Efron's core question, "What do [passive-aggressives} do when [they do] get angry and express their anger?"[3]

Here are some subtypes of indirect anger expression (anger styles) classified according to their main interpersonal, tactical, defensive/defensive breakdown, biological and syndrome-related characteristics:

Interpersonal

Games Passive-Aggressives Play (Passive-Aggressive Gambits)

Both Berne[4] and Bonds-White[5] discuss passive-aggressive anger style terms in the playing of such games as *Blemish*, *Schlemiel*, *Look How Hard I'm Trying*, and *Why Don't You—Yes But*. To illustrate, the annoyance central to the game of Blemish originates in the angry depressive feeling, "I am not as good as you are." Then the actual game is played by expressing that anger indirectly, as Berne suggests, by avoiding "intimacy"[6] after deeming someone, like a husband, so unworthy that one should not become seriously enmeshed with this person for a lifetime. A woman who wants to avoid intimacy with her husband can, as Bonds-White suggests, play Blemish to turn a child against the woman's own husband, solidifying dependency between a child and the mother, thus excluding the father by "bind[ing] the child to her [the mother] by making him [the child] discount and look down on [him, the husband]."[7]

The anger central to the game *Why Don't You—Yes But* is mostly triggered by issues involving interpersonal *control*. In a typical case, the patient asks to be controlled or dominated, then fears and dislikes it and avoids what is perceived to be surrender. The associated annoyance is expressed indirectly in the form of asking for advice then refusing to take it, instead torturing someone who means to be helpful by sequentially rejecting all the suggestions given, ultimately, as Berne suggests, "engineer[ing] the crestfallen silence which signifies . . . victory."[8] The target throws up his or her hands in a gesture of defeat, as if to say to the victor, "No matter how hard I try, nothing you came up with helps."

In a masochistic game, "poor little me," a significant motivation for being passive-aggressive is "having a pity party for one."Ascendant is the pleasure that one gets in complaining about a renegade boyfriend/husband/girlfriend/wife to one or more friends/companions. The goals here include reducing individual anxiety and deflecting personal guilt by sharing it with caring listeners, and in particular asking the listeners to offer what one is looking for, which is more pity than advice (hopefully, in a torrent of support meant to soften the impact of loss).

What Berne calls "sulks" are, speaking dynamically, often passive-aggressive expressions of anger over being controlled using rebelliousness as a way to achieve one's ends, e.g., to recapture one's freedom. As Berne says, a sulk "is not so much concerned with arriving on time as in collecting excuses for being late. Mishaps, badly timed lights and poor driving or stupidity on the part of others fit well into [the game-player's] scheme and are secretly welcomed as contributions to [the] rebellious[ness]." And he also says, "Fears of sexual intimacy often take the form of a hostile unaccommodation to a problematical sexual partner, one who is 'playing the game of Frigid[ity].' "[9]

Defenses/Defensive Breakdown

Passive-aggressive anger styles incorporate, and so are reflective of, defensive action. For example, a close conceptual relationship exists between the defense of doing and undoing and the anger style of inconsistency and unreliability. As with any other defense, the passive-aggressive defense can break down spontaneously or as the result of intense (external or internal) pressure. The anger ball can burst and the anger break through to become overt. When this, a return of the repressed, occurs, individuals may have verbal rages, display temper tantrums, or even become violent—behaviors that are essentially releases, sometimes pleasurable, and often self-destructive, of pent up aggression.

Biological

Many authors have emphasized the role played in creating oblique anger styles by the guilt associated with expressing anger directly. It is reasonable to assume that constitutionally quick-tempered people can have more intrapsychic and experiential reasons to feel guilty than those with a more phlegmatic disposition, and therefore such people can be more motivated to make amends by becoming less openly angry, for example, in the case of histrionic passive-aggressives, by playing being seductive/coquettish.

Syndrome-Related Anger Styles

The rest of this chapter discusses the core passive-aggressive *anger styles* as they are related to primary syndromes of origin such as masochism, paranoia, and others which underlie typical aspects of the passive/aggressive personality

Thus Sprock and Hunsucker (1998) suggest that it is common for passive-aggressives to manifest a "degree of Paranoid and Narcissistic Personality Disorder symptoms [and] comorbid depressive disorders."[10] According to Millon and Davis, "There are notable similarities between depressive personalities and negativists."[11] According to Malinow, "the passive-aggressive personality overlaps with the compulsive personality."[12] Again, according to Millon and Davis, we often see the combination "Passive-aggressive histrionic mixed personality."[13] Steckel, throughout his text, calls individuals who clinically resemble passive-aggressives "sadistic,"[14] while Reich instead throughout his text calls them "masochistic."[15]

In the rest of this chapter, I focus on six syndromally related passive-aggressive anger styles as classified according to the syndrome-infused way that passive-aggressives have of expressing what anger they do allow themselves to express:

1. *Paranoid*
2. *Narcissistic*
3. *Affective depressive* type
4. *Affective hypomanic* type
5. *Obsessive-compulsive*
6. *Histrionic*

These will seem familiar because they overlap almost exactly with the anger styles discussed throughout (in different contexts).

The Paranoid Anger Style

Paranoid passive-aggressives feel suspicious of others whom they regularly identify as "the world's blameworthy ones." Typically what they express blame towards others for is something they disapprove of in themselves, as, for example, self-disgust for having sexual dreams leads to disgust with others for much the same (disgusting) reasons. They might become pathologically jealous of a partner based on a projection onto him or her of their own wish to cheat on him or her sexually. Disloyalty fears about others become others being disloyal to them. This way they can view themselves as innocent victims merely bedeviled by another's malfeasance towards their own (personal) self and its notable (innocent) positions. A characteristic of the way they tell others how they feel ("tell others off") is via their blaming others along the lines of "it's not me, it's you. Since you started it I don't hold myself responsible for what happened next." In such a formulation the passive-aggressive individual's contribution to events is either passively overlooked, or actively denied.

The Narcissistic Anger Style—Selfishness

Narcissistic passive-aggression involves feelings of entitlement, a belief that "I come first, and well before you." Feelings of superiority are also present and expressed in disdain for others along the lines of "you are a second-class citizen compared to me." Such passive-aggressives put others down by proclaiming that "no one, least of all you, compares to me"—in looks, knowledge, being up-to-date, rewards achieved, and the like. Such passive-aggressives also become unempathic individuals due to being self-centered people who manifest an absence of altruism that contributes to their habitual way of formulating and sneakily indirectly expressing negative feelings about others. Such passive-aggressives tend to gravitate toward becoming harsh professional critics/Internet Trolls—people who hide their anger under the guise of the supposed reality of the realistic content of their negative evaluations, as they, knowing it all, have been divinely impressed into service to impart their knowledge to those less adept, and to expect/demand change from those others of whom they disapprove.

Selfishness is a special vehicle for the expression of narcissistic anger. This selfishness often takes the form of an angry disdain for others' rights and needs, including, or especially, the rights of members of one's own family.

The supposed legitimacy of their protests covers another aspect of their microaggressions: the belief that others have no right to defend themselves by citing their own values, and demanding that these values, not those of others, be the only ones recognized.

A patient, who lived in the town where an out-of-town man owned a second home, persuaded the homeowner to let her house-sit for the winter in his second home. When the homeowner arrived to do a spot check, he found that to save money the house sitter had turned the heat down so low that the pipes were in danger of freezing. The reception he got upon arrival was equally chilly. For example, when the homeowner turned on his favorite radio station, his long-term houseguest changed it to the station she wanted to hear. Instead of offering sympathy when the homeowner was hurt in an automobile accident, the house-sitter complained, "You hurt yourself on purpose: you did it so that you didn't have to pick up my child and take her for the day, as agreed," adding, "if you were really concerned about me and my baby, you would have taken better care of yourself."

Once she made disapproving noises at another woman in a checkout line, her way to complain that the other woman was not collecting her groceries fast enough after they were logged in. "I am in a hurry," she said, and added, by way of explanation, that she had an emergency. The woman first in line in the beginning of this "transaction" began to comply and step aside, but then stopped complying when this person went on to describe the exact nature of her emergency: "My niece had a baby yesterday, and I just can't wait to see them both."

An author, she savaged a colleague for not buying a book she wrote, saying that the colleague was a millionaire who could afford something that cost only $19.95. She overlooked that no matter how much money the colleague had, he preferred not to buy something he did not want just because it was something that she wanted him to have, and something he could easily afford.

Narcissistic passive-aggressives use honesty to serve a purpose other than truth-telling: being hurtful by being painfully honest. Concerned about themselves more than about others, they express "my honest opinion" without bothering to ask themselves if their being painfully honest with others makes these other people actually feel bad.

For narcissists, the anger itself is an ego-booster, based on a self-validating circular belief that, "If I choose to abuse you it must mean that you deserve it, and that I have the good judgment to tell you all about how I feel."

In conclusion, narcissistic anger is triggered by mostly perceived, because less than actual, devaluation by others. The anger can't be expressed directly because that would make the angry person look bad, e.g., less than "kindness incarnate." So instead, the passive-aggressive individual employs a passive-aggressive anger style, one that involves openly overvaluing oneself—expressing one's cherished self-inflated self-assessments as if they were, being spontaneously concocted, to be simply, as expected, a given.

An aide routinely complained about the homeowner for whom she was working. She groused that he didn't have what she liked for lunch in stock in his larder. A typical complaint was that she liked flavored decaffeinated coffee, and a certain flavor of coffee cream to top it off, and wanted those things in his refrigerator. She sent this message to him by angrily reiterating her basic point whenever she could: "I, having been deprived as a child, am now, as an adult, entitled to nothing but the best."

The Affective Anger Style

There are two affective passive-aggressive anger styles: the *depressive* passive-aggressive anger style, and the *hypomanic* passive-aggressive anger style.

The Depressive Passive-Aggressive Anger Style

Depressive passive-aggressives, as almost anyone who has been named in a depressive's written complaint can attest, characteristically express their anger by taking it out on themselves while simultaneously making certain that their self-immolation spills over into figuratively beating other people over their heads with their own bloody body, "sulking," as Millon suggests, "to provoke discomfort in others."[16] According to the *DSM-IV* research criteria numbers (3) and (6) for passive-aggressive personality disorder, these individuals are especially "sullen and argumentative" and "voice exaggerated and persistent complaints of personal misfortune."[17] Here the victim's reaction is a particularly useful, even pathognomonic, guide to understanding the passive-aggressive's intent, as well as the actual presence of passive-aggression in the brew. For example, we can correctly infer that suicide is an act of criticism directed toward not only oneself but also against a victim when the victim is specifically mentioned in a suicide note in such a way as to make the victim feel guilty about what he or she did (wrong) to cause the (suicidal) action of another in the first place, e.g., "I don't mean to imply that you caused me to hurt myself, but . . ." as depressive passive-aggressives express their anger by criticizing others, by implication, in the very act of criticizing themselves, with their self-criticism a criticism of another, for it is an implied "You brought me to this," a self-humiliating/self-excoriating statement that is pointedly vengeful to others by at one and the same time being hostile to themselves.

Just as depressive passive-aggressives go back over their own lives wondering what they did wrong, they go over others' lives to determine where others went astray. Then when they find something they don't like/approve of, this becomes the only thing that captures their attention. They then do not let up but instead focus on it exclusively.

Depressive passive-aggressives are often also sadistic along the lines of "here's a funny story" whose telling is a way to humiliate its subject(s). When he was just two years old, a patient soon tired of his playmate's mother's telling him that he could not touch her child because he might contaminate her. So the boy, as he remembers it, got back at the mother by throwing dirt in his playmate's carriage. Forty years later he went to a party given by this playmate, now a grown woman. When he entered the room, she greeted him by announcing to all present, as if the act were just yesterday, "This is so and so—you know, the person I told you about, the one who threw dirt into my stroller."

The Hypomanic Passive-Aggressive Anger Style

Hypomanic passive-aggressives express their anger by "living well as the best revenge," doing thusly to bring someone else down. They also favor hostile intrusiveness couched as helpfulness, including actually stalking another to make certain they, the other person, is "adequately protected from harm," which really means, "sufficiently tortured." As Fenichel says, they use intrusive high-jinks in order to *deny* "painful sensations and facts."[18]

Obsessive-Compulsive-Anger Style

Obsessive-compulsive passive-aggressives behave in ways that are associated, and considerably overlap, with OCD and OCPD. OCDs and OCPDs who are not especially passive-aggressive, to the extent that there are any, express rage and guilt mainly internally, that is, directly to themselves, via private ruminations and rituals, that is, their ruminations and rituals have a self-punitive aspect as they take on the form of self-torture. In contrast, obsessive-compulsive passive-aggressives are mainly interested in, and committed to, assuring that there is a significant (negative) interpersonal impact to their ruminations and rituals. As such, they keep one eye wide open to the effect their ruminations and rituals are, or are not, having on others. For example, while for obsessionals who are non-passive-aggressive a primary motive, first doing, then undoing what they have just done—is to relieve their own inner tension, for obsessive-compulsive passive-aggressives a primary motive of undoing what they have just done is to annoy, really to torture, their victims by not being steadfast, e.g., by not keeping promises and not letting others know where they stand. Or they mess up and then apologize. "Screwing up"[19] (Wetzler's term), they alternately transgress and attempt to make amends as they cycle between sin and absolution, deed and apology—less out of inner guilt and more to leave their victims "ready to scream." The hostile contrition of multiple apologies is, for the victim, usually as bad as, or worse than, the original insult. (Berne's game of "Schlemiel"[20] describes this process.) Victims suffer mightily when, uncertain about what is happening, where they stand, and whether they can, as they had hoped, rescue the relationship, they willingly come back for more, however much it hurts, just in the hope of the attaining of relief in the form of closure. But that never comes. Instead, coming back for more makes things worse, for although meant to create gain it instead creates loss by virtually setting the stage for a likely, or guaranteed, ad infinitum repeat performance on the obsessive-compulsive passive-aggressive individual's part.

Acting less like the fire that guts, and more like the rust that corrodes, many OCD/OCPD passive-aggressives tend to be stubborn foot-draggers who passively, and annoyingly, resist demands for adequate performance— the *DSM-IV* research criterion number (1) for passive-aggressive personality disorder: "passively resists fulfilling routine social and occupational tasks."[21] They thwart and sabotage others as their way to tell others how angry they are (and how mad others made them, mad enough to account for everything that comes next).

An important method an OCD/OCPD passive-aggressive used was to express hostility to proclaim his own (if somewhat excessive) morality in order to devalue the morality of others. Testimonials to himself that attested to his basic goodness and personal moral transcendence took shape as his way to tell others how evil *others* were—in comparison to him. He put others down by propping himself up, doing so mostly not by actually being good but by verbally detailing how good he was, and had been throughout his life—doing this in numbing detail. Indirect microaggressions also often took the forms of condemning a victim by complimenting the victim's rival, and by loudly proclaiming his own fidelity to some personal altruistic causes to condemn those who had other, different causes these others were being, supposedly rationally, super-faithful to—while simultaneously condemning others for not directing themselves to causes he felt ought be the center, and guiding force, of, their own lives. This individual routinely asked a certain person if he was of a specific religious faith in preparation for holding him to celebrating his own holidays, e.g., "non-Christians like you shouldn't even think of celebrating my Christmas." He routinely criticized others for joining a political party which he disapproved of, and for planning to vote for a certain candidate he himself despised. He criticized others, only later trying to undo his hostility by in turn criticizing himself for being so critical, doing that by heavily favoring the use of jokes made at his own expense. On the job, he simply refused to understand what his clients meant and wanted when they asked for something when they phrased their question in inexact terminology, so that he didn't get some job done because he took no practical action due to his getting bogged down in terminological exactitude. Within his company he attempted to achieve superstar status, as Murphy and Oberlin put it, "by stepping over or on anyone who threatened his own status within the pecking order of the company."[22]

He frequently used conversation stoppers, really killers, such as, "If you would only wear black you would look 30 pounds lighter." He dismissed others by belaboring the obvious in a patronizing way, in one case repetitively warning this person, a mental health worker, to "not allow one of your patients to have his guns back because your patient had been committed to a mental hospital for having threatened to shoot his wife."

The following are some examples of typical OCD and OCPD obsessive-compulsive-passive-aggressive anger styles/behaviors. (Due to considerable overlap, the units in the following disorders have indistinct boundaries.)

Always Being Right/Dominating

For some obsessive-compulsive passive-aggressives being right becomes a vehicle for domination. These passive-aggressives tell others how wrong they are even in situations where there is no absolute right and wrong. Even with their own partners they commonly struggle about minutiae such as where some decorative items should go around the house as the husband moves them to where he thinks they ought to be, and the wife sneakily puts them back.

Foot Dragging/Refusal to Cooperate/Stubbornness

Obsessive-compulsive passive-aggressives can become negativistic, stubborn, and oppositional as their way of expressing their anger. (These passive-aggressives form the nucleus of Millon's "negativistic personality,"[23] individuals widely known for their oppositional behavior.)

A patient refused to buy a set of dining room chairs to go around her dining table. Although the family pleaded with her, "We need a place to sit down for dinner," she continued to pull out the piano bench and the stepstool for each evening meal, or, on special occasions for large groups, to borrow chairs from the funeral home where her husband worked, secretly relishing how everybody would during the repast think of their mortality, ruining festive occasions. Once she even refused a free offer of a good set of dining room chairs, saying that if she took them she would no longer be motivated to buy her own.

As stubborn individuals they "clam up" whenever someone makes a request of them, doing so because they perceive it to be a demand that they do what they are being merely asked to do. Often their stubbornness involves actually asking for advice or assistance and then refusing to accept it. Stubborn OCPD passive-aggressives, defying others by doing precisely what they were asked not to do, show what Fine, Overholser, and Berkoff, quoting. Brehm, call "an increased preference for threatened choices."[24] Usually they take fixed stands about something relatively unimportant, and fuss about whether or not a needed action is worthy and important enough to be either optional or actually mandated.

Withholding

The classic and most often-mentioned OCPD passive-aggressive anger style involves withholding behaviors like chronic lateness and/or promising others something in preparation for disappointing them. After committing to mutually acceptable goals, passive-aggressives refuse to live up to their part of the bargain. They even train themselves to be sensitive to what other people want and need—just so that they can avoid giving it to them.

A man is never ready on time for a date. He puts eager potential partners on hold by making tentative arrangements, only to cancel them at the last minute, leaving the other person with nothing to do. A surgeon's secretary, he delays telling his boss' patients that their biopsy reports are negative. For days he leaves them hanging because he was "just too busy" to pick up the phone before going on vacation—forcing patients to wait for his return to obtain the favorable results he knows they would long to hear. He reasons, speciously, "It's good news, nothing needs to be done, so what is the rush?"

A medical administrator does not mollify criticisms given for jobs poorly done by offering his staff complements when they do a good job. He writes letters of complaint to his congressman when something goes wrong in his district, while withholding letters of congratulations when something goes right. He asks doctors he likes, "Is there anything I can do for you?" but when they answer, "Yes, you can send my boss a positive testimonial about me," he laughs at what he perceives to be their having told a little joke, and then takes no action whatsoever.

A man describes how once he watched in mixed awe and surprise from the riverbank as another neighbor and her husband abandoned their boat, stuck in the mud, and, without an operative boat, had to crawl to shore. Instead he stands idly by as the two, slowly sinking in the mire, make their way through muddy reeds scratching their bodies. When they finally arrive on shore safely, a half hour later, at last seeming to wake up, he rushes over to ask, "Is there anything I can do for you?" In like manner, according to his wife, once he watched his own child climb 10 feet to the top of a ladder in a hardware store, without saying a word or moving a finger to stop her, until a few terrified witnesses insisted that he do something and do it right now.

Often what OCPD passive-aggressives withhold from others is emotional support, as they express their hostility by not recognizing when, and that, others need comfort. Instead they disagree with everything others think, say, and do, doing so even when others' notions are entirely valid. When others are being reasonable, they refuse to accept how reasonable they are being, and instead act dense, refusing to acknowledge that they understand what others with reason want, need, and are saying. Sometimes they defend the indefensible just to be difficult. Often they excuse what is their own cruel neutrality or lack of empathy in a number of creative ways. They might say, "It is better if I don't get involved," or "It is in your ultimate best interests for me to leave you, and you will understand my actions more fully when you get older." According to Mahrer, these are the individuals who are "passively complicit in the delivery, or neglect of stopping the delivery, of interference, damage, harm, hurt and violence."[25] They take sides not to support what is right but to be antagonistic via supporting others who are simply wrong.

A spouse infuriated her husband by withholding emotional support when he needed it. When her husband, looking for consensual validation, complained that the man who lived across the way had torn up his property three years ago and then never finished the building project, creating a neighborhood eyesore, in reply she said, hostilely, "I prefer to look upon it not as an unfinished project, but as a work in progress."

When her husband complained that his boss herself often came in late while holding him to a different, stricter standard, his wife responded by defending the boss, saying, "She is just doing her thing," and "If you have to be the one who works a little harder, well then, so what?" When her husband said, "What a cheap gift your sister gave us last year, and did it again this year," the wife replied, "But the last one was nice," and reminded her husband in a cautionary tone that, "blood is thicker than water" and "it is we who likely did something to offend her."

When a couple told a mutual friend that the cooperative board in their building responded to one of their legitimate requests by voting it down and writing them a curt letter in explanation, instead of being sympathetic, the mutual friend condemned the couple for expecting too much and being too demanding, especially of a management not set up to resolve such minor disputes.

Excessive Frugality

Excessive frugality combines elements of stubbornness and withholding in a single act, often directly related to money—one of the passive-aggressive's favored vehicles for expressing hostility to others (as well as to oneself).

A man's wife wanted to hire a contractor to do repairs around the house. The contractor's estimate was $5,000. The husband, in effect telling his wife that *she* isn't worth much, said, "Too expensive," and found another, "cheaper," contractor, one who "only" charged $4,950. To save the $50, the wife had to drive the contractor, who had neither truck nor driver's license, around town so that he could pick up the tools and materials he needed to do his job

Ambivalence/Doing and Undoing/Compromise Formation

Millon and Davis note that patients with a negativistic personality disorder are characterized by a "deeply rooted ambivalence about themselves and others. . . . intrud[ing] constantly into their everyday life, resulting in indecisiveness, fluctuating attitudes. . . . and a general erraticism and unpredictability."[26] Ambivalence is the product of instinct alternating with guilt creating conflict next harnessed as a vehicle to torture others by "keeping them guessing," and guessing in anticipation of a resolution that they know will never take place.

Each July 4, a patient invited people over for a barbecue and then canceled, often at the last minute, if there were merely a mention of rain in the weather forecast. With one eye always open to the effect her vacillation was having on others, she acted in an unreliable fashion because she wanted to convey to them her mixed feelings about seeing them. She was expressing her negative feelings to others by leaving her victims uncertain about their holiday plans and ultimately disappointed due to those (very frequent) instances when she told them that the party was off. (Her non-passive-aggressive obsessive-compulsive counterpart canceled engagements on the basis of weather forecasts too, but mostly she did so because, suffering from OCPD, she feared that it would be ruinous to have guests inside her house, as she would have to do if it rained. The obsessional woman did not want to hurt others so much as she feared that they might hurt her—by hurting her home by ruining her furniture and Oriental carpets.)

OCPD passive-aggressives often do and undo by first acting admirably and then, resenting being suckers, making the recipient of their charity pay. Thus a woman told her son-in-law that her daughter could have done better in marriage, and with almost anyone else. She related how she demanded recompense from him for her own prior acts of largess to him by asking for his help with the menial tasks around her rental properties—trimming the trees and mowing the lawn to pay her back for everything she had done for him. In response to his refusing to help her put up some curtains, she invited the whole family to a Holiday Show and paid for everyone else's ticket—while making her son-in-law pay for his own.

For OCPD passive-aggressives, compromise formations are a way to do and undo by "hold[ing] two positions at the same time synthesizing both." Here being angry indirectly is accomplished by simultaneously expressing and undoing that anger. Often the expression of the anger, the doing, is merely implied in the very act of denying it, for example by saying "No, I am not that mad at you." In a compromise formation typical for passive-aggressives, OCPD passives-aggressives corrupt by undoing valid goals via using them as the vehicle for aggressive purposes, as when they unleash a cat from the home ostensibly to give it its freedom, but actually to chance that the cat might run away, or get run over.

In a common form of compromise formation, a negative remark is (supposedly) detoxified by a question mark to become "the innocent question," however much it is really a planned attack that one should in actuality feel guilty for having even considered such a thing. A son, a well-known surgeon, gave his father some surgical advice, to which the father replied, "How would you know?" A reasonable question is asked in a way that makes it possible to interpret it in one of two ways, one of which is as an attack. Thus a job interviewer asks the interviewee, "What makes you think you make a good candidate for this job?" in a tone implying not so much a desire to hear the man's qualifications as the man himself sees them, but a need to put the man down as unqualified for the position.

Retaliation

While for OCPD passive-aggressives retaliatory, eye-for-an-eye thoughts and actions are meant to achieve balance, for non-OCPD passive-aggressives retaliatory, eye-for-an-eye thoughts and actions are more likely meant to exact a degree of revenge. Little pleased a patient so much as the discovery that someone who had once bad-mouthed him had had a stroke and now, unable to speak at all, was unable to bad-mouth him, or anyone else, anymore.

Screwups

Screwups annoy by creating controlled havoc. The term "screwups" expresses the hostility of an otherwise competent or well-coordinated person via acts of carelessness or inefficiency. Some authors refer to people who screw up as bumblers. Berne refers to them as players in the game of Schlemiel, and refers to their victims as "Schlemazels."[27]

Passive-aggressive individuals might screw up by having frequent accidents, including the making of Freudian slips that involve forgetting an anniversary or a date, or saying the consciously unwanted thing because they fail to perceive their motivating attitude, perceive it too late, or mistakenly believe that their attitude is being concealable. Lapses of memory whose intent is to annoy and frustrate occur too, as when 100 miles into a family outing someone in the family begins to worry whether the oven, or the space heater, was left on. Pretty much knowing it is off, he or she still continues to worry to the point that everyone has to turn around and drive back, to see what, if anything, needs to be done to prevent some (likely imaginary) calamity.

Bad timing is a common form of screwup. A patient, a downstairs tenant, had a leak coming from the apartment above. The caulking on the shower above was defective, so that every time someone upstairs took a shower the water came through the ceiling and down into her apartment below. Her call to ask the upstairs tenants to repair the tub was legitimate.

The passive-aggressive part was that, although the problem had been there for weeks, she did not call to complain about it until New Year's Eve—right after all the plumbers had shut for a long holiday weekend. True to form, some months later, when there was another, similar leak, she contacted her upstairs neighbors once again—this time at 6:00 a.m., on Easter Sunday morning.

Sloppiness is a type of screwup particularly favored by passive-aggressives as a way to annoy others, doing so even more effectively because the sloppy person can easily counter that others are overreacting. For example, teenagers can, when a parent gets angry about their not straightening up their room, point to the trivial nature of the issue and, claiming that, "You are getting excited over nothing," never address the problem at hand. A spot on the tie of the man of a couple at an important event both he and his wife are attending is often part of the man's plan to make the woman writhe, in preparation for blaming her for being a too finicky hypersensitive elitist, and, if she attempts to self-defend against him, a hypercritical person to boot.

Repetitiousness

True obsessive-compulsive rituals relieve anxiety and guilt. However, the relief is incomplete, making repetition necessary. Obsessive-compulsive passive-aggressives also repeat themselves ritualistically, but a primary motive here is not so much to ultimately achieve closure as it is to make others uncomfortable, even to the point of feeling tortured. Thus OCPD passive-aggressives tell the same story, or joke, or advance the same idea, over and over again, motivated to make others cringe and, begging for mercy, yell "stop."

A patient reported that a passive-aggressive salesperson kept turning her back on her customers. Then she apologized for turning her back on them making them wonder why she kept referring to a problem that did not bother them in the first place. Ultimately, the patient, the salesperson's victim, in a response that reflected the salesperson's true intent, felt pummeled by all the repetition, frustrated by his own inability to discuss the purchase he wanted to make, and angered because he was forced to stand by helplessly while she wore herself and him down "with all this back-turning stuff." Yet he was cautious about keeping her focused on the matter at hand—the purchase—because he feared provoking her to "turn her back" on him even more.

Also, this salesperson could do no better than complain about how busy she was and how she had not had lunch or even time to go to the bathroom, then say "I'm sorry for complaining," only to then return to her complaints about being overworked. Her weaving between anger and regret changed nothing. It just added another dimension to an already difficult situation. While she did intend her comments to reduce *her* personal anxiety, she also, as a passive-aggressive individual, intended them to create personal angst in her customers for making her work too hard.

Being Hypermoral and Judgmental

While obsessive-compulsives are hypermoral and judgmental out of a sense of guilt, one they wish to spread around, OCPD passive-aggressives are hypermoral and judgmental as a way to be angrily nosy, intrusive, bossy, and condemnatory. These individuals are familiarly known as the sex police, or condominium commandos—people who righteously and intrusively insert themselves into others' lives to condemn these others for their thoughts and actions, while simultaneously justifying similar aspects of their own behavior on transcendental moral/religious grounds. Condominium *renegades* also exist and operate in the passive-aggressive mode— by behaving badly then coming up with excuses for continuing to do so thusly, and for not stopping what they are doing, as did the man with a barking dog who announced that since "we live in a multiple unit, some noise is necessary, and I have done all I could about it."

In summary, many passive-aggressives express their anger, often anger triggered by matters implying criticism of their behavior for being less than perfect, indirectly, in true OCPD style, by torturing others by vacillating, withholding, bumbling, the paralytic uncertainty of doing and undoing, and by the sticky sweetness of what Fenichel calls "reaction formations against affects."[28]

Histrionic Passive-Aggressives

Histrionic passive-aggressives are noted for their teasing; envying; invalidating, and demeaning of their rivals; as well as for somatizing—all ways they have of expressing anger indirectly.

Some histrionic passive-aggressives *tease* (using coquetry), as Wetzler suggests, primarily as a "way of dealing with insecurity."[29] These histrionics tease by pulling back just before they consummate things, for them a (compounded) way of avoiding the possibility both of full success and of abject failure, seducing then abandoning their victims, first promising a lot then not delivering anything at all. Teasing was a special forte of one head of a department of medicine who repeatedly asked his staff, "Who should be the leader of the team?" without ever answering his own question. His staff suffered, thinking, "It might be me, and I cannot handle the job," or "It might not be me, and I might have to work for someone less knowledgeable than I," or "It might not be me, because he is planning to fire me."

Teasing has passive-aggressives impact because where there is a tease there is both a promise (to deliver) and a threat (to refuse to come across). Because of the promise the victim comes back, looking for more, expecting delivery; only to experience a renewal of the threat that nothing will, after all, be forthcoming.

Many histrionic passive-aggressive are envious individuals as are those described in the *DSM-IV* research criterion number (5) for Passive-Aggressive Personality Disorder: those who "expresses envy and resentment toward those apparently more fortunate."[30] Envious passive-aggressive individuals express their anger in the form of seeking and expecting personal triumph in situations that are, or that they only imagine to be, competitive. Most such passive-aggressives go for the symbolic victory over the kill. For example, a man nourished a half-century-old grudge against a high school classmate for being smarter and handsomer than he. The fiftieth class reunion presented this man with an opportunity for the revenge he had long sought. To get back, he sent his newly refound classmate, whom he knew at the time to be struggling financially, a catch-up Holiday card that read "from our house to yours," picturing an aerial view of a country mansion with a swimming pool, tennis courts, and acres of land abutting on a natural lake, all proudly displayed in effectively poor-shaming detail.

Invalidating/demeaning histrionic passive-aggressives feeling enviously competitive might express their competitive anger by knocking the competition not directly by damning (Berne's game of "Blemish"[31]), but indirectly—by damning with faint praise. Knowing that a friend lived in a studio apartment with no bright light, a patient sent her the following letter: "My Christmas Cactus (a light-dependent plant) has very many buds." This patient remembers that when his big brother said to him when they were children, "If I do that I'll get 5 stars," he shot back, "And then what happens?" As an adult he received a copy of a new book from an author he knew personally. After he received it he did not bother telling the author it arrived, forcing the author to call him to inquire if it came. He said it did, made a weak excuse for not saying he got it, and then, in response to being asked how he liked it, said, unconvincingly, "My wife thought it sensible." As a music critic, in his daily columns he invalidated others' talent and years of sincere effort and hard work as his way of affirming his own (superior) identity, the one who was the most highly sophisticated, knowl-edgeable, and important individual of the two. His goal was to enhance his own brittle, low self-esteem and his method was to damage the self-esteem of another of his rivals.

A patient, a nurse, asked a lab technician, with an emphasis on the word "you"—"Is it true that *you* are going to be given the responsibility of being on call by yourself?" Then she invalidated her husband's years of work on an opera by telling him that, as she saw it, "There is no sense continuing to write something that will never be performed."

A patient, a literary agent, invalidated a fiction writer's attempt to write a nonfiction book about old people by telling her, without any statistics to back her up, "Old people don't buy books, they read them in the library." She criticized as "clients from hell" fiction writers who tried their hand at nonfiction books by saying that they were all "ruining a perfectly good career." She told a writer of relational self-help nonfiction that "this stuff doesn't sell in this town because the place is full of middle-aged men and, having already arrived in their personal, relational, lives, they don't buy books purportedly helping them develop something that they already have."

Semantics form the basis of many passive-aggressive's competitive/invalidating attacks on others. At the hardware store, a patient, a hard-ware salesperson, became angry with a customer for asking him for "the kind of picture hooks that don't make holes." He knew that the customer meant "the kind of picture hooks that leave only small holes, so small that you can hardly see them." But he flared, thinking her "too stupid to make the distinction," then put her down by giving her, instead of the hooks she wanted, a long condescending lecture on how "by definition all nails leave holes; it depends on what you are calling a hole. So get over it."

The more theatrical histrionic passive-aggressives tend to *somatize*, that is, to favor nonverbal, e.g., bodily, forms of communication of hostility. Their anger is expressed in the form of distancing bodily symptoms: gas-trointestinal disturbances/hostile headaches that stop sexual activity cold; vaginismus that makes sexual penetration difficult; impotence that makes insertion impossible; or premature ejaculation that makes insertion hardly worth the effort. Also favored are nonverbal gestures like eye-rolling to express disbelief; finger-tapping to protest the presumed burdensomeness of others' being boring; cuticle-picking to indicate impatience; audible sighs to express exasperation; and message-sending via symptomatic acts like carrying around to display a highly impressive book one never intends to read.

Histrionic passive-aggressives express their anger indirectly in two main ways. One is by first seducing and then hostilely abandoning others rankling them by leading them on and then withdrawing at the last minute. The other is by more overtly destructive competing where they "knock the competition." After identifying with the aggressor they imitatively turn the tables on them, but they do so less to win themselves than to defeat or destroy an actual or perceived rival—and to do so in kind, exactly.

Sadomasochistic Passive-Aggressives

Sadomasochistic passive-aggressives may be either predominantly sadistic or prevailingly masochistic. Sadistic passive-aggressives often express their anger passively in the form of death wishes couched as *schadenfreude*. Here they don't induce, but "merely" quietly enjoy, the suffering of others, who, as they see it, deserve comeuppance. After a little boy riding a bike almost ran into his car and fell from the bike just short of making contact with the driver's wheels (he was not badly hurt), the sadist driving said to a passenger with him in the car, "Good, I hope the kid broke his neck, that little rat. Where are his parents, anyway, and why aren't they supervising him?"

Masochistic passive-aggressives express their anger by cutting off their noses to spite others' faces. One man sold a valuable apartment for less than its true value just to tell his obnoxious neighbors that he never wanted to see them again. Then he quit a perfectly good job to make (hostile) coworkers feel guilty over the possibility that he had left just because they mistreated him. A woman moved far away from a hometown she liked just to get revenge on her critical parents. Part of her plan was to say to a potential partner who lived in the town she left, "I will never see you again because I love you, and I don't want to inflict myself on you anymore. No matter how much this hurts me, I am, after all, only doing this for your own good."

Other (Nonsyndromal) Anger Styles: Tactical, Cognitive-Behavioral, Interpersonal, and Biological Features

Tactical

Passive-aggressive tactics consist of interpersonal maneuvers designed specifically to get under others' skin and to do so secretly/sneakily, that is, so that all concerned don't recognize what they are doing and assume guilt for having done it.

Murphy and Oberlin list (eight) passive-aggressive tactics they specifically delineate as occurring in the workplace (and so presumably in other realms), as follows. Backstabbing, avenging, controlling, being cynical, whimpering and moaning, blaming, remaining mute (ignoring, avoiding, denying, e.g., by using silence), and being the star (using star power).[1]

My (supplementary) list consists of the following:

Relentlessness

Partly sadists, passive-aggressives enhance the impact of their passive-aggressive tactics by employing passive-aggressive methods continuously, although still with a degree of restraint. Nagging is a familiar example of passive-aggressive relentlessness meant to be (subtly) annoying. A man's sister hounded him to adopt homeless cats. He responded repeatedly that if he were to get a cat at all it would be the kind of cat that he particularly liked; and also he wanted a kitten because his last cat had recently died and he preferred to have a pet that would last a long time. The sister, however, repetitively countered, "But you would be doing an older cat a favor—at least it would have a few years of a good life instead of dying out on the streets, or in a pound." Then she called him each time she found a stray "just" to ask if he happened to be interested, and the sort of person who was and willing to help out "in my admirable causes."

Additive Behaviors

Passive-aggressives, as the expression goes, "pile it on" along the lines of "it's bad enough that . . . you make it even worse by. . . ." They do this in at least three important ways, which may be simultaneous or sequential: taking others by surprise; adding insult to injury; and double binding.

Taking Others by Surprise

Often passive-aggressive hostility is expressed not so much by what is said but in the way that what is said is presented: sprung on an unsuspecting victim—colloquially "coming out of left field" where the element of surprise gives a bland remark, or a seemingly innocent act, an intensified hostile touch, with enhancement of the hostility now more easily denied by simply overlooking the timing of the thing.

On a clear, warm summer's day, a patient and his partner are sitting in an outdoor café with their dog when a superficially pleasant elderly woman approaches and remarks that there is something wrong with their dog's eye. They strike up a conversation about dogs' eyes. The stranger confides in the men that her dog also has trouble with his eyes, and she is afraid to take him out of the house because he cannot see well, and he does not even want to go out now because of his compromised vision. The two men are enjoying this pleasant conversation with this seemingly friendly person—until, without warning, her eyes narrow and she suddenly changes the subject. "By the way," she says, reaching into her pocket, "You might be interested in this" as she pulls out a tract explaining why the Bible disapproves of homosexuality. The same two men while traveling enter a hotel to check in. A superficially pleasant clerk hands the men the necessary sign-in forms; only in this case the paperwork is topped off by a tract from the Bible that seems to tell of the Book's clearly stated disapproval of same-sex marriage.

A wealthy patient, for many years eagerly anticipating his children's pain, employing the passive-aggressive technique of using an inheritance to be hurtful after the fact, left everything to charity without telling his children in advance of his intentions—his (final) revenge for the way he believed they, his children, had mistreated him when he was still alive. He knew that they would be shocked when after he died they discovered that he had left them nothing. Now they would not only be unpleasantly surprised by the revelation itself, they would also suffer all the more because it came at the worst possible time—when supposedly they were just beginning to grieve over his loss.

Four children discovered when their mother died that she was trying to control them from her grave by leaving all her money to them in such complex trusts that instead of being able to use and enjoy their inheritance they had to spend anxious months trying to clear up her mess.

Adding Insult to Injury

Passive-aggressives enhance impact by harnessing the power of the cumulative effect of simultaneous/sequential minor insults, counting on their additive nature to create a whole that is greater than the sum of its individual parts. There is often another identifiable planned effect here too—one that takes into account that victims are likely to be more vulnerable on some days than on others. For example, passive-aggressives know that, other things being equal, indirect hostility on a holiday can have more impact than indirect hostility on an ordinary day. Christmas and Easter depressions in victims are often the result of the victims' heightened vulnerability to another's modest year-round passive-aggression, this time intensified by being issued forth on these holidays, giving the passive-aggression more impact due to its having been unleashed at such special times of the year.

Double Binding

As Bateson[2] suggested in a personal communication, passive-aggressives not only express but intensify their hostility by putting their victims in uncomfortable no-win situations while simultaneously rendering them helpless when it comes to extricating themselves. They do so by both issuing two contrary marching orders *and* by simultaneously cutting off all reasonably acceptable and productive avenues of escape—from each. (In the cases below all the victims' realities were such that the victims were in some ways highly dependent on the very same people who were victimizing them.)

A patient left her child with her mother five days a week, only to then complain that her mother was trying to take over, citing as evidence that the child had now started calling the grandmother "mommy." If the child's grandmother complained—about the five days being too many to easily fit in with her schedule, or about being unfairly accused of trying to take over as a substitute parent—her daughter countered by threatening to move out of state, taking the grandchild with her.

A patient disliked her son-in-law for being underemployed and without sufficient funds to properly care for his family. So she insisted he go to school, at her expense, to learn a profession by which he could earn enough to enable him to support his daughter. He became (surprisingly) happily involved in school only to have her next complain that he was spending too much time with his books and not enough time with his wife. Her exact words were, "He goes upstairs to his study and leaves my daughter downstairs, all alone with the kids." So, the mother-in-law, out of spite, threatened to make sure he didn't graduate by cutting off the tuition payments she was making for him if he did not pay more attention to his family.

A patient, a literary agent, sadistically enjoyed making her clients feel that they could do nothing to satisfy her completely. For example, she complained—unfairly, as the author's subsequent success seemed to suggest, that what this author wrote was not "specific enough for a niche audience." Then, after the author made the revisions the agent herself had requested, she complained, "Now that is too specific to reach a broad audience." She told another author that her writing was too simple, even for the children she was trying to reach. When the author changed her style to make it more complex, the agent complained that her work was now too difficult for a young audience. Each criticism hurt by itself. When taken together, as intended, a helpless feeling was imparted, deliberately, to further intensify the victim's pain.

This agent's husband contributed a double bind of his own, this time directed towards his wife. Retired from his work, he wanted his wife to join him in such daily activities as going to the movies—although those activities took her away from what work she had left. Then, when as a consequence of keeping him company all day, she made fewer and fewer sales, he complained that now they did not have enough money to do the recreational things he liked to do, such as going to the movies.

A man asked one of his sons, "What kind of coffee maker can I get you for the holidays?" Then when the son expressed his preference for a particular one, he got him another, the kind the father felt the son should have. Then the father complained to his wife that the son got angry with him, although he got him such a nice gift. Next holiday the father retaliated by getting his son nothing. The wife, adding an insult of her own—criticized the son for cavalierly mistreating his father by complaining that the father's gifting had dried up, and for no reason at all.

Passive-aggressives double bind by setting up "you-can't win with me, for with me no matter what you do is wrong" emotional traps. For example, they might condemn self-assured people as grandiose and less self-assured people as "wimps." Some aver that those who like sports are jocks, and those who do not like sports are elitist intellectuals. As far as too many passive-aggressives are concerned, most men are to be condemned for being insufficiently in touch with their feminine side, yet most men in touch with their feminine side are to be condemned for being feminized, and so to be regarded as sissies. They are condemned for criticizing women they view as too feminine for their own taste as people who are excessively passive and dependent, while they are being condemned for calling women whom they view as being too assertive for their own taste as "hostile (bitches)." Women with a strong personality have attitude, and those without one are wishy-washy. Men as well as women who can be easily understood are called simplistic, while people who cannot be easily understood are purportedly obscure. All religious people are fanatics, and those who are not religiously fanatical are heathens. Calm people are clueless, while nervously active people are excessively driven. Those who try to get ahead are pushy, and those who are content with their lot are inadequate.

Guilt Induction

One way to be passive-aggressive is to constantly implore (pressure) others to "do the right thing" by fiat, even when that "right thing" is already generally agreed upon, according to widely accepted but by no means universally accepted social standards, as entirely the wrong thing to do.

Setting People Up (Passively Promoting Others' Failure Behaviors)

Setting people up, according to Wetzler "lays traps" and gets others to "take the fall."[3] Setting people up allows passive-aggressives to be hostile to others and then afterward feel and act innocent ("I am guilt free because I didn't do anything wrong, only you did)." For example, passive-aggressives make open-ended remarks that invite misinterpretation in ways that make a victim, the-fall-guy, look foolish, and even paranoid. A wife says, "What a wonderful Christmas we are having." Her (passive-aggressive) husband, setting her up, replies, "But it's not over yet," leaving her to wonder, "What does that mean?" Does it mean, "More wonderful things are still to come?"

Or, does it mean, "Give it time, something bad can still happen?" The husband is now in a position to fault his wife no matter which way she subsequently responds.

Passive-aggressives often withhold the information others need just so that they can lead others astray and then complain afterwards about how these others responded "cluelessly." The typical victim, when brought up short, protests, "But you never told me . . ." only to be told, "It's so obvious; did I have to spell it out for you?" or "I did say something, but you didn't listen."

Overpermissive passive-aggressives, whether their overpermissiveness is accomplished passively by not intervening when indicated, or actively by actually giving others an inappropriate go-ahead signal, encourage victims to hurt themselves by "giving them enough rope" and "egging them on." When brought up short, the typical passive-aggressive comeback is to blame the victim, e.g., "You are just imagining things," or "you are simply being too sensitive for your own good."

Actively Undercutting Others

Competitive passive-aggressives, hating to be one down, are playahataz who in some specific way undercut people they see as being more successful than they are, especially those people they perceive to be obstructing their own paths to glory. A medical student announced to everyone in the dormitory that he did not study for exams. He wanted others to emulate him, relax, and not study, as he didn't, so that he could get better grades and a higher class ranking then everyone else. What he did was study at night, by flashlight, with the shades drawn so that others could not see through his windows and realize he was burning the midnight oil—to light his way to the top.

Elusiveness

Elusiveness, which some passive-aggressives refer to as "keeping them guessing," is partly a function of ambivalence in the relational sphere. It is intended to sustain a relationship without ever having to fully consummate it in some important regard. For example, when it comes to commitment, a man feels, and acts, now interested in, and now remote from his girlfriend. It's his way to torture a potential partner, one who hangs on his every word—spending days and nights agonizing about their future together, wondering what fate will bring, and (correctly) feeling hopeless as if she has no control over the outcome (as very well might be true here).

His girlfriend writes to columnists all over the country. All of them end up equally ambivalent in their advisory responses. For what else can these columnists say and do, but to hedge when they get a letter like the one that follows:

My date said he was eager to get to know me, before he admitted he was definitely anxious and had OCD to the point of letting me know that my coffee cup holder should be placed on my coffee cup (I had taken it off so I could grip the cup better), telling me that he would never move in with anyone because he had to have everything in order, would never date anyone who was against his going to Mass because Mass would always come first, and that before he would consider marrying me I should go to the gym because he only likes petite women, those who weigh less than 100 pounds.

Identification with the Aggressor

Passive-aggressives like to turn tables, exactly to give others a taste of their own medicine. A dependent man stifles an independent woman with jealousy and possessiveness until she yields and agrees to be his alone. Then, to express his resentment about how she held him off for so long, and to get back at her for having done so, he becomes as independent now as she was then. He waits for the day she finally says she wants him and then backs off, refusing to commit to her, instead now threatening to leave her. He justifies his behavior as, "You did it to me, so of course now I am going to do that very same thing to you."

Intrusiveness

Hostility can take the indirect form of minding others' business, invading others' space, or deliberately interrupting others' serenity. For example, a passive-aggressive talks at the back of the room at conferences—intentionally annoying the speaker and distracting him as the speaker wonders, "Just what are you saying; is it about me, and is it negative?" Passive-aggressives disrupt others' peace and quiet when, as if they are alone, they play iPods without using earphones, take and make long cell phone calls in restaurants and on trains, loudly talk at the gym to each other on two adjacent treadmills—disturbing everyone else as they yell to get over the background noise—or, worse, talk to each other on two treadmills separated from each other by one or more machines, so talking across (a) hapless victim(s) in the middle, one(s) who for them are people who do not even exist. At home, they install wind chimes they love—however much they disturb their neighbors, people who already told them that they hate that pinging sound. Then they continue to do such things seemingly oblivious to the effect they are having on others, neither responding to hints like hostile stares, nor yielding to direct requests to stop.

Passive-aggressives typically justify their intrusiveness by citing necessity. A boss cited necessity when he called his workers on weekends to ask them to solve a problem that could easily have waited for its solution until sometime during the workweek, or a problem that he could have with a little effort easily solved himself. A doctor's secretary, although asked not to, notified the doctor every time the next patient arrived in the waiting room for an appointment, disrupting the work the doctor was already doing with the last patient just to "give him notice" that his new patient was now waiting to be seen. Then, when brought up short, she excused herself by saying, "I was just trying to help you pace yourself."

Splitting

Passive-aggressives use two kinds of splitting. They split anger from its true object, and they split the ideational component of the anger from its potential/actual affect. In the realm of splitting the anger from its object, passive-aggressives criticize others in a general way without specifically mentioning anyone in particular. Others, although they have not been mentioned directly, quite naturally feel, "You are talking about me" and "I very much get that." The passive-aggressive can now respond by denying responsibility/complicity, needing only to cite lack of proof in self-defense. Splitting anger from the object additionally enhances anger's effect because victims feel triply wounded: first, because they have the sense that they have been attacked, however indirectly; second, because they cannot prove that, although they suspect it is going on, and so they question their own perceptions; and third, paradoxically because since they were not even mentioned by name, they feel "ignored" and "invisible."

Passive-aggressives, particularly OCPD passive-aggressives, also split their angry ideas from the anger affect itself. They do this by intellectualizing their anger, expressing it unemotionally (the defense of isolation of anger), e.g., by hiding their anger in long lists of grievances which they present as legitimate expectations that clearly have to date been completely ignored (the "anger report"). Then they can convince themselves: "I have thought this through, so it must be right" and "I was not angry; as you can see, I was just working hard simply trying to solve this specific problem."

Being Difficult to Impossible

Passive-aggressives typically express their anger, and achieve a measure of success at being hurtful, although with all the potential drawbacks, simply by being difficult. One way they do so is by taking unfair advantage of some position of their own strength. For example, they use their real, presumed, or unfairly/selfishly actively appropriated position of authority for such hurtful purposes as stifling argument, discouraging adequate self-defense on others' parts, and thwarting effective retaliation—by intimidating others and hoping to get away with it simply because of who they are, and some powerful position they hold. Almost daily we see examples of how difficult lovers misuse a dependent partner's trust to be hurtful to him or her; how difficult citizens misuse their legitimate civil rights to take unfair social advantage of others or of the society in which they live; and how difficult therapists misuse their position of trust to control and manipulate their patients. Here are eight categories of difficult people and a sampling of their passive-aggressive ways:

Difficult Business People

A realtor turned a business meeting with a psychologist into a discussion of the realtor's relationship problems. He secretly delighted in "making the psychologist sweat," knowing that the psychologist would be in conflict about helping him out (and keeping on his good side) versus keeping the focus on the main business at hand, the psychologist's real estate purchases.

Difficult Neighbors

A neighbor sends her neighbor, an emergency room doctor, an e-mail to his home inbox: "I just fell and hurt my knees; take over please and tell me what to do now." Another neighbor power washes his deck for days on end, making the apartments around him unusable. The deck-washer responds to his neighbors' complaints by saying, "I am trying to find a way to do this without bothering people around me," only to continue as before, apparently confounding good intentions with desirable results.

Difficult Patients

As Gunderson says, many patients with personality disorders come to "have a poor relationship with their doctors because they refuse to take responsibility for their behavior or feel overly distrustful [paranoid], deserving [narcissistic], or needy [depressed]. The doctor may then become blaming, distrusting, and ultimately rejecting of the person."[4]

Also, a few patients present themselves as individuals who cannot get help with their problems because of their problems. For example, a patient says, "I can't get help by reading a text or anything else about curing OCD because my problem is constantly thinking about OCD."

Difficult Psychotherapists

The counterpart of the difficult patient is the difficult, passive-aggressive psychotherapist. Such therapists might use diagnostic terminology as a vehicle for criticism of their patients—that is, pejoratively, as if referring not to a disorder but to a flaw, using medical diagnosis to overdiagnose healthy patients—to sadistically call them disturbed, medicalizing normality, as when these therapists diagnose individuals as paranoid for not being foolishly trusting; as dependent for being excessively, but still appropriately, loving and close; as depressed for recognizing life's truly overwhelming problems, ones that currently plague them, then responding accordingly; as hypomanic for wanting, and proceeding, to enjoy life in a carefree way; as obsessive-compulsive for being reasonably cautious, careful, and precise; as histrionic for being healthfully competitive; as phobic for appropriately avoiding dangerous situations; as passive-aggressive for being discreet about their anger even though it's appropriate to do so; as psychopathic for considering mainly their own needs and setting out to gratify them appropriately, me first before you; as addicted for liking, wanting, or needing something they should reasonably have (such as an appropriate amount of sex) and becoming anxious (feeling deprived) without it; and, if children, as hyperactive or obstructionistic even when provoked to the point of agitation by difficult others, including, or especially, their parents. With these practitioners, as the joke goes, if you come on time for your session you are compulsive; if you are late you are hostile; and if you are early you are dependent.

Some therapists (and physicians) are not merely unknowledgeable or careless. They are deliberately, purposeful bumblers, screwing up in order to be hostile, however much their carelessness/hostility is unconscious. Their unconscious goal can be to hurt the patient (and get away with it) either directly by their actions, or indirectly through neglect.

Such therapists/doctors not uncommonly make the serious mistake of criticizing their patients not to their faces but behind their backs. These doctors sometimes discuss patients as if they are inanimate objects.

Difficult therapists may condemn their patients for having the problem they consulted them for in the first place. Failing to realize, or too quickly forgetting, that, at least in the beginning, most patients do not know how to be patients, they identify all resistances as deliberate and purposeful acts when there is only inexperience, lack of knowledge, or cultural difference. Finding it too difficult or time-consuming to individualize a treatment plan and make it fit a patient's specific needs, they express their disdain for the patient's individuality by making a plan that is not based on a personal diagnostic assessment, but is instead part of a one-size-fits-all remedy that forces the patient into a procrustean bed of the therapist's devising. For example, a psychotherapist advocates that all patients get their anger out, regardless of individual diagnosis; the nature, intensity, and circumstances of that anger; and/or the level of tolerance of the victims of the patient for the abusive anger.

While some therapists do not give advice to patients because they believe it is always ineffective or risky to do so, other therapists, using various rationalizations to explain such action, withhold advice not because of the difficulties involved in, or problems associated with, advising, but sadistically.

Still other therapists use pharmacotherapy not therapeutically but punitively, and some use reparative therapy (curing homosexuals of their supposed emotional disorder) as a vehicle for antigay hostility rationalized on the supposedly "safely acceptable" ground of being "medically indicated."

Difficult therapists are also discussed in Chapter 15, more specifically with respect to their passive-aggressive countertransference (the therapists' response to the patient).

Difficult Teachers

Ideally, teaching consists of imparting information to a student working with the teacher in a mutually cooperative effort to learn, one "clearly" uncontaminated by transference (student-teacher) and countertransference (teacher-pupil) distortions. With some teachers the actual process is often quite different:

A patient remembers that when he was a boy one of his teachers made fun of him for mouth breathing, virtually ordering him to close his mouth and breathe through his nose. Then he called the small boy a "big cosmopolite." As a youth, the boy could not understand the term but he sensed it was something bad. Later he understood that the teacher was saying that the boy's worldliness and sophistication put him out of step with his peer group. He thought his teacher, sensing that the boy was gay, was indirectly criticizing him for being "a sissy."

A student using a published translation of the original presented the translation as his own work. After catching on and humiliating him for his actions, to make matters worse, the teacher involved did so not privately, after class, but publically, during class, in the form of a pointed upbraiding lecture on the virtues of honesty and the sins of plagiarism "directed to no one in particular." She made no attempt to understand how it was the student's motivation vis-á-vis their relationship that was the thing that led her student on to become dishonest. He did not primarily intend to cheat. Rather he had hoped to impress her with how smart he was—to bring her around so that she would stop criticizing him so much, and pay him at least one little compliment.

Difficult Parents

Passive-aggressive parents disguise their hostility by agreeing with each other as their way to more effectively deprive, criticize, harshly discipline, be unsupportive of, make too many demands on, and overwhelm their children by harnessing the power of two ("because mom and dad agree it means that they are in this together versus you") in order to make it an unbeatable two against one combo. A mother frequently aligned herself with her husband to make it a powerful two against one oppositional force where both parents worked together to stifle the healthy rebellion that was part of the son's growing up creatively on his way to developing an identity of his own. Also, when mother and father had a fight, they first asked the son to take sides and then, when he did, united, turned against him and savaged him for being so critical of his parent(s). To be particularly hurtful, they often did this when the family was on a trip together and the son was riding in the back seat of the car, effectively and helplessly trapped.

On those few occasions when another mother expressed pride in her son, it was for doing what she demanded of him—which involved his fulfilling *her*, not *his*, agenda. When he did something he wanted to do for himself, and did it successfully, she said nothing. For example, she admitted being proud of him when he excelled at the Little League sports she wanted him to play and win at, but not when he composed and performed an exceptionally good percussive piano piece, when she could do no better than retort, "I hope you got that out of your system."

Half jokingly, but half seriously, she frequently upbraided him for being simply human. She told him, in so many words, that he was born in slime; was indistinguishable from the baby in the next bassinet; and that, when he was very young, he cried too much for too little reason, keeping her awake at night, and as a consequence during the day interfering with her concentration to the point that she was unable to work at home. She harped on how he developed unpleasant-looking and annoying tics; carelessly broke her favorite gewgaws; ate too much junk food, not the food that she wanted him to eat and that was good for him; refused to mind her; only wanted to watch TV, never to read; and foolishly cringed in fear in the presence of strangers who in her opinion were a lot friendlier than he gave them credit for.

She saw him not as a normal child with problems due to his biological immaturity but as a backward adult. As if all his accidents were intentional (which could only be true if he were much older) she responded with corporal punishment in retaliation for his making a minor mistake. Worse, she regularly put the blame on him in situations where he was the real victim. For example, she called him hyperactive and oppositional in school, although he was merely responding with restlessness to teachers who ranged from exceptionally dull to actually brutalizing.

Throughout his life she expected him to delay gratification at a time when doing so was beyond both his grasp and his psychological/neurological capacity. She expected him to always think of others first, although he was too young to be so empathic. For example, starting when he was only four, she constantly nagged him to write thank-you notes for even the most trivial of birthday handouts. And if he failed to do so immediately, she made him return the gift, along with a letter of abject apology.

Difficult Children

Even very young children can be passive-aggressive, and especially so to their parents. Children can act like infant kings, as did a boy who had quiet temper tantrums in the form of not getting into the car when his mother wanted to take him shopping. Later he led a gang of peers that walked up and down the street scratching cars as well as stealing merchandise from the five-and-dimes in the area.

When he was six, his grandmother moved in to live with the family. He hated her because he was ashamed of her inability to speak English and because her Parkinson's disease kept the family from traveling. Knowing how dependent she was, and how afraid she was that they would go away on a trip and leave her behind, just to rile her he would "playfully" take a valise down from the upper shelf in the closet and start packing. As a teenager, he made it clear that he saw his parents' admirable sacrifices only as signs that they were suckers; their altruism as a sign of weakness; and any self-interest on their part as a manifestation of disinterest in him.

Difficult Bosses

Difficult passive-aggressive bosses rule through microaggressions. These involve being unsympathetic and unsupportive. As bosses they mishandle their employees by being confrontational. Instead of asking, they order. Instead of assisting, they criticize. They imply that there is a fault just because there is a problem. They take sides, for example, with other doctors to embarrass the nurses. They keep their employees in a state of fear that they will be fired, and they mainly do this in a tight job market.

Instead of acknowledging a legitimate complaint with a simple, "I see why you are upset," such bosses hide behind their authority and either say nothing at all or blame the victim for overreacting. After hurting their employees' (legitimate) feelings, they accuse them of being hypersensitive. They withhold deserved compliments no matter how much these are indicated, saying, "Bad job" when their workers make a minor mistake, while rarely saying, "Good job" when their workers have done well. And instead of setting a good example, they have double standards—one for themselves, another for their workers, suggesting that, although everyone in the office is on the same time clock, workers who come in late should be fired, even when the bosses themselves have the most unacceptable attendance record.

A boss' employee evaluations were really criticisms—demoralizing missiles that made his workers feel as if they did not belong and were completely unloved. That prompted the employees to retaliate in kind by taking sick leave although they were well, or by developing somatic symptoms such as carpal tunnel syndrome, chronic fatigue, occipital headaches, or eczema that made it difficult or impossible for them to do their job adequately. Some workers even quit without giving notice, leaving the corporation with the considerable expense of training one substitute after another, and under emergency conditions.

Kernberg, in effect describing difficult passive-aggressive bosses, calls them "paranoiagenic" to emphasize how they make their victims feel. For example, some leaders "agree with everybody . . . unconsciously . . . intensifying the competition among them." Others create "contention among subordinates" because they "cannot say no." For some "control becomes an objective for its own purpose" as "reflected in micromanagement." "Narcissistic leader[s] . . . unconsciously devalu[e] those who work with [them]"; and "absentee leader[s] lack . . . availability."[5]

Biological Aspects

Paris, deemphasizing the role played by the child's upbringing by the child's parents in the development of personality disorder, instead emphasizes "gene-environment interactions" suggesting that "personality disorders would be shaped by both diatheses (temperamental variations) and psychosocial stressors (life events)" including those that come from outside the family (in experiences with peers and community). Paris feels that biological factors determine a sensitivity to stress that in turn determines whether the stressful situation will be meaningful, and the likelihood that one will be exposed to actual stress "i.e., how likely it is that stressful events (such as marital difficulties) will occur [and be seen as such]."[6] As mentioned in Chapter 3, in the context of describing the biological origins of anger, Millon has noted that identification or modeling occurs not only as the product of shared experience and learning, but also as the product of a "biophysical substrate for affective irritability . . . transmitted by genetic mechanisms"[7] that contribute to a child's being (biologically) like his or her passive-aggressive parents.

Important physiological sources of anger/indirect expression of anger are excess ingestion of alcohol, and improper usage of antianxiety agents or other tranquillizing substances that sedate individuals to the point that they find it difficult to express their anger directly. As a result, anger builds, flares, and can finally spill over. Therapists must spot these influences so that they can suggest the appropriate therapy.

Healthily Passive-Aggressive

The indirect anger of passive-aggression is a natural and healthy force in children, partly because it is suited to and appropriate for individuals who are too small, weak, and dependent to effectively and safely express their anger in any other way. In addition, many healthy children are too loving to feel comfortable with their anger, but, unable to do away with it entirely, compromise by limiting the scope of its expression. They use bad words or simply act mildly oppositional to avoid having severe temper tantrums or actually becoming assaultive.

These healthy passive-aggressive children have as their counterpart healthy passive-aggressive adults whose reasons for deflecting anger are equally sensible. They hold their anger in to spare and protect a victim whom they also, or mostly, love. At work they get ahead by not flaring up at the boss, but instead by calling in sick or otherwise doing something that, not being a direct attack, is difficult to criticize them for having done.

Socially, they get ahead by reaching the pinnacle and staying on top via restraining their anger. These individuals are especially welcome in those social circles that value indirect over direct expression of anger, circles that sensibly believe that anger expressed indirectly regularly and predictably provides adults with a healthy, convenient, socially acceptable way out when faced with demands they choose not to meet, thus allowing them to accomplish their angry (obstructionistic) ends inoffensively, say, by merely stalling. For example, a woman, asked to give to a charity she was not interested in, instead of insulting a neighbor with an outright refusal, said, "Sure" and then did nothing, not responding at all until the neighbor finally gave up and, noting who she was dealing with, stopped asking.

CHAPTER EIGHT

Pseudopassive-Aggressives

Under a number of circumstances, individuals are designated as being passive-aggressive when they are not, as when they have some other emotional problem, such as OCPD. In this Chapter, I turn to a discussion of those mislabeled individuals, people I call "pseudopassive-aggressives."

Pseudopassive-aggressives are not passive-aggressive at first strike. If they seem passive-aggressive at all it is because others have provoked a retaliatory passive-aggressive response in them, to the extent that they themselves feel that both their anger and its indirect expression, which they see as merely a push-back along appropriately vengeful, retaliatory lines, is justified.

Pseudopassive-aggressives feel desperate because they have been faced with real interpersonal stress and have been unable to find any good way to cope/easy way out. They feel that they have simultaneously been provoked into getting angry and encouraged not to show how angry they feel. Their hostility to other people has in good measure been aroused by other people's hostility to them. And their inability to express their anger directly has been reinforced by other people's subsequent (negative) response to their initial passive-aggressive response to another person in the dyad.

For example, opening a drawer he has been forbidden to explore, by accident, a child discovers his father's will and that he has been left off it. This forces him to think of ways to subtly retaliate while the father is still alive and can feel the intended vengeance.

A patient was upset that a neighbor would cross the street each time the neighbor saw the patient coming. The patient wrote to a newspaper-based advice columnist asking him what to do? Should he, the patient-neighbor, also cross the street in an obvious way to avoid/get back at the

street-crosser? "I don't understand why he is doing this," the truly innocent patient/neighbor opined. "I never did anything to offend him." Alas,
the columnist wrote back, "Probably you did do something to provoke
him; only you then forgot what it was." And the columnist's solution was,
according to the "victim," equally off-the-mark: to apologize for something
he had presumably done. For clearly, according to the columnist, "You
should love your enemy and turn him into a friend via kindnesses to
him—with your heartfelt positive response to him now becoming the foun-
dation for an ongoing increasingly improving loving relationship between
him and you."

A patient annoyed his veterinarian by pushing him relentlessly to give
him a definitive answer to his question, "What can I do to keep my dog
from barking?"—as if there were some real solution to the problem. The
patient could neither use a bark collar because it would deprive the dog of
her only emotional outlet, nor snap a rolled newspaper before the dog's
nose because it would scare her beyond what all concerned would find tol-
erable. When the vet in his turn proposed a set of reasonable solutions,
one after the other, the owner negated all of them by saying that nothing
but continuing close contact would work, and that that was only possible
for a limited period of time and on very few occasions because, "I can't
stay home all day to be with him." In fact, no proposed solution seemed
adequate, since nothing the dog-owner tried, other than constant contact,
solved the problem. So the vet, whose advice was being routinely turned
from helpful suggestion into new quandary, finally gave up and, unable to
remain patient any longer, passives-aggressively complained that his
patient, the dog's owner, was annoying him by playing a passive-aggressive
game with him, the game of "Why Don't You—Yes But," raising questions
then dismissing all possible answers just to torture him. But the dog owner
did not intend to torture his vet. He was truly desperate. Feeling he was
in a no-win situation with his dog, and knowing of the futility involved in
coming up with a workable solution, the dog-owner was not being truly
passive-aggressive so much as he was using the vet as a sounding board,
abreacting, and angling less for a solution to a problem than for a sympathetic ear to listen to, and a little handholding to give comfort to, him.

Without first stopping to inquire why he was delayed, an aunt snapped
at her nephew for showing up too late to be in the family album's pictures
being taken at her grandson's wedding. What actually happened was that
the nephew's car had broken down the day before and he could do no better than take the first (too late) morning train to the ceremony. Besides, he
had acted responsibly, having called her daughter, the groom's mother, the
day before to ask, "Is eleven a.m. early enough?"—and had been told that

it was (the daughter having "forgotten" to remind him that the picture-taking was to start at 10:30 a.m., which was a time before any trains were scheduled to arrive.)

A patient was diagnosed as passive-aggressive after writing to his congressman to complain about a doctor at a Veterans Administration clinic. The patient, however, believed that his criticism of the doctor was fully justified. He felt that the doctor should not have put inflammatory critical statements about him in the chart—a record which the patient read when a clinic secretary, actually following protocol, asked the patient to himself carry the chart back to the central office to be refiled. The patient was insulted, and rightly so, that the doctor had, in writing, suggested the patient was an "addict faking pain just to get pills," when in fact the patient's pain was excruciatingly real, not something that he was falsely reporting to foster his addiction.

This VA patient had first been diagnosed as passive-aggressive in the military many years ago. According to him, he did resist authority, as the record said, but he felt that he resisted authority not because of a personality problem that he had, but because of a personality problem that authority collectively had. He felt that the diagnosis "passive-aggressive personality disorder" did not apply to him because, as he put it, "After all, doc, everyone knows what horrors some of those sergeants were," and that his refusal to follow their orders was due to a justified reluctance to "do something stupid," and that that didn't even remotely qualify him as being passive-aggressive.

Many veterans who are criticized as whining about the treatment they are getting in the VA are in fact justified in complaining about their mistreatment. Only instead they get themselves condemned as being crybabies, and this in spite of how realistic their complaints happen to be. Next, they remain silent because they know that if they take their complaints too far it would likely make matters worse for them, e.g., they might annoy the doctor and he might retaliate by having their disability stipends reduced. Certainly, the veteran with a brain-tumor whose appointment with a neurologist was six months later had a beef with the VA system, and that had nothing to do with the veteran's personality makeup!

Overall, special care should be taken to distinguish inherently non-passive-aggressive behavior, such as constructive criticism offered lovingly (however negative in some aspects), from truly passive-aggressive behavior, such as unconstructive sniping, criticism, nagging, covert backbiting and undercutting when these are all behaviors that dynamically represent indirect anger aroused in someone who was actually being provoked.

At home, interspousal relational spats are often not passive-aggressive but a response to (disavowed) reality. A patient was not, as accused, being passive-aggressive when he left cat food envelopes open after using them, even though his wife begged him not to. He did not do this just to annoy his wife. He did not do it because he was being stubborn, or careless, or deaf to her pleas. He did it because he had learned by experience that their cat actually preferred her food dried out. Too, he sometimes went through the express checkout line with more than the allotted items; but he did so only when he was just following directions given to him by the checkout clerk who, for the moment having no customers, had beckoned him to go through her line even though he was over the maximum number of allowed items in his cart. Also, he was not being passive-aggressive when he called work to say, "I am taking the day off, my dog is sick." The boss, thinking otherwise, replied, in a snippy fashion, and very hurtfully, "Guess you are out of dead grandmothers." (Then he added in an aside, "That is how you get back at me for imaginary insults you think came from me? Never mind passive-aggressive; you are paranoid.") In fact, the dog was ill, and subsequently took weeks to recover.

Some patients who look passive-aggressive are nevertheless still pseudopassive-aggressive because although they are difficult, covertly hostile people, they are this way not because they are passive-aggressive but because they are suffering from another, related, clinically overlapping, emotional disorder also involving the tendency to be subtly microaggressive. That is, they have another disorder marked by excessive anger which they hold back to be polite, or cautious, expressing it not so much indirectly (qualitatively) but in a reduced way (quantitatively) because, as detailed throughout, considering the possibility that different motivations exist, their covert anger expressed indirectly happens to be the emblem of a disorder other than passive-aggression, and in particular OCPD, paranoia, and depression. For example, individuals with an obsessive-compulsive personality disorder often refuse to grant requested help not primarily because they are hostile people withholding anger and expressing it indirectly by foot-dragging but because they have an exaggerated sense of responsibility, and with it deep uncontrollable fears about doing harm to others, thus making things worse for themselves and others in the very act of attempting to make things better. Telling little white lies can be either passive-aggressive or appropriately self-protective and/or protective of others, that is, defensive, depending on internal motivation and external circumstances. A doctor of my acquaintance told every neighbor who called him for emergency care that he couldn't be of help because he had just taken a pill for pain. He wasn't being sneakily angry—that was his personal (rational) way to avoid being sued for refusing to be a good Samaritan willing to help out a sufferer in a medical emergency, only to be held accountable for any bad results if his (admittedly untraditional remedies) didn't actually work.

An OCPD man feared giving people any advice because if it soured he would incur their wrath, and he too quite possibly would be sued. For example, he would not say either "yes" or "no" when questioned by neighbors about the most trivial of matters, such as, "Do you think it will rain today?" He felt that if he were wrong about that, someone might go out without an umbrella, have the rain ruin his suit, and hold him accountable. When someone he met by chance in the lobby of his apartment building asked him (when he was coming in and they were going out) such a question, if he answered it at all (mostly he acted as if he didn't hear the question) it would be only with a deliberately noncommittal, "I think it will be nice, but who can know if the weather is going to change and become nasty?" Once, when the driver of a car he was riding in asked him, "Which way should we go?" even though he knew the best route, he refused to give a specific answer to the question because he was afraid of being held accountable if the driver should get into an accident on a route that the patient had personally recommended. By being vague and noncommittal he felt that he, like the ancient oracles, had done what he could, and so he would be able, if circumstances worked against him, to deny responsibility for any adverse consequences of what he said.

There is an important distinction to be made between being passive-aggressive (being sneaky in an irritable way) and being fearful ("the potential consequences truly alarm me"). Shyness and fear, sometimes of *phobic* proportions, are typical alternative explanations for motivation that at first might appear to be microaggressive thinking and behavior with the anger airbrushed for all the reasons described herein:

A practical nurse had a sore throat and wanted to see a doctor that very night. So she approached one of the doctors she worked for and pestered him to treat her—in the hallway, outside his regular office hours. "Either you see me now," she threatened, "or I will show up at your office as an emergency and keep you from going home early." She did this less because she was hostile, and more because she was terrified that she had a strep throat and would pass it on to her child.

Pseudopassive-aggressives have as their counterparts pseudovictims of passive-aggression, people who think (typically in a paranoid way) that they are being the object of (passive-aggressive) hostility when in fact they are just overreacting, e.g., reacting extensively to nothing much. These pseudovictims, along with participating victims who bring a measure of others' passive-aggression down upon themselves, are discussed in Chapter 9. The patient, asked about "his nice shoes," should not automatically think he is being seduced by a foot fetishist; nor should a patient asked, "Where are you from?" automatically think that they are the target of a hostile speaker attempting to condemn them for coming from out of an impoverished background, when that sort of thinking is more likely to be of a paranoid than a passive-aggressive nature.

PART 2

Victims of Passive-Aggressives

CHAPTER NINE

Pseudovictims

Pseudovictims

Pseudovictims of passive-aggression are those who believe that when it comes to passive-aggression they themselves are true victims of this behavior—when in fact that is not at all the case. For they wrongly believe that they are being treated in a subtly hostile fashion by sneakily abusive individuals when these other individuals are just being neutral toward, or in fact actually feeling positively about, them. According to Burns and Epstein, such pseudovictims are "so intent on being judgmental and blaming that they [become] excessively defensive and closed to information which in any way contradicts their own perceptions."[1] And so they go too far in overinterpreting and pathologizing everyday normative behavior, doing so to the point that they see others' reasonably healthy/normative behavior as in fact abnormally passive-aggressive. Such individuals have recently been called snowflakes to emphasize their paranoid sensitivity and suspiciousness where they overreact to minor insults and overinterpret others' benign behaviors as personal attacks, and in fact they may be the likes of depressive individuals who overinterpret others' neutral comments as criticisms; phobic individuals who fear that they will be completely devastated in return for their speaking up; dependent individuals who are in the process of being rejected; or masochistic individuals who have provoked hostility because of their need to be mistreated. Such individuals create mistaken notions in their own minds about others' intentions as they craft adversarial out of nonadversarial (cooperative) relationships, and falsely spot what they believe to be sneaky challenges to their integrity and status. Thus they see every question however innocently intended as information-seeking as in fact containing a hidden attack.

They see "where are you from?" as a sly way of implying a sort of geograph-ical impurity ("no doubt you were born in a slum"). They overlook the possibility that somebody might ask, "How old are you?" not as a sly way to criticize someone for being "over the hill," but as simply a query looking for a real answer about how the questioned person so cleverly manages to hold off the ravages of age. Need-to-know queries become accusations, so that if people ask, "Where is that project you promised me for yester-day?" they see that as their being subtly accused of being slow to act even though others are simply asking them what they can count on in a given situation. As pseudovictims, they see microaggression in innocently or positively intended communications such as "I like your coat," which they misinterpret not as complimentary but as a sexist statement, or even as a sexual come-on; or they see the question "do you play golf?" as elitist due to being potentially exclusionary of the true sportsmanship of those who "ride the lowly skateboard."

Cognitive errors rule the way they think. Thinking that similar things=the same thing, or thinking according to exclusive causes, they fail to make a distinction between people who are hostile to them in small and people who are hostile to them in big ways, when covert anger directed and meant personally is a part, but a very small, part, of the issue, with no rejection, control, or humbling implied or meant personally. Pseudovic-tims may even view their pets in a negative light. For example, they might condemn a dog that chews up a carpet as hostile, although the dog chews not out of hostility, but out of understandable situational loneliness or boredom.

Perhaps the so-called passive-aggressive individual just made a simple mistake, like calling a doctor "Mr." not out of covert hostility but out of a lack of knowledge and/or experience in a particular arena. A patient, a doc-tor, was cavalier about the plight of his obese patients because, not having weight difficulties himself, he did not fully understand how hard it was for some people to control their food intake. A patient who lived in a met-ropolitan area simply did not recognize how much hostility and bigotry existed in the small town where a friend, a member of a minority group, lived. As a result, he was unintentionally unsupportive of the friend when that friend complained about all the prejudice that existed where he (the friend) lived, and said he wanted to move out of there just to get back to the big anonymous city, and to do so as soon as possible.

Perhaps what someone intended to say just came out wrong. When a handsome famous heartthrob died, a patient said to his partner that "My secretary was still mourning his death—for she, like everyone else, wanted to sleep with him." The partner claimed the patient was inadvertently revealing his own unconscious wishes. The patient denied it and said, truthfully, that what happened was that his tongue slipped, and he expressed himself badly (in a too-general way).

Perhaps there has simply been an accident. At night, on his way down the driveway of his house, a patient inadvertently hit the garbage bag he had put out the evening before for next morning's collection. A neighbor, believing himself the intended personal target of the misfortune, complained that the man had deliberately and carelessly put the garbage out where the animals could get at it, primarily to flout the condominium rules, and that not to rile just everybody, but to get at him personally.

Perhaps a situation is one anyone would find difficult to handle, or have/ get under control. Does a partner insist that a lover wear a condom, taking the risk of sending him or her a message that "I believe you are being unfaithful to me and I don't want to get sick from you?" Or does he or she accept another risk—the risk of getting a disease, in order to minimize the risk of getting a divorce?

These are generally thin-skinned individuals whose reality is in fact the product of sensitivity; one likely to stain their present adult interpersonal transactions with too many unresolved childhood conflicts.

However, as the following case illustrates, it is not always easy to determine whether one is a pseudovictim or a true victim. This is often because ultimately an observer has to base his or her evaluation on "nonscientific" mind-reading where others' true motives can at best be only inferred.

When a patient "victim" told his partner's mother that he intended to lose weight, she replied, "But why, you already have no rear end?" His partner interpreted her remark as a compliment, her way of saying, humorously, "Don't worry about losing weight—after all, you are thin enough already." The "victim" thought otherwise. He thought she was calling him misshapen, believed she had no right to criticize him that way, and hoped to never see her again.

Practically speaking, those who get a reputation for being passive-aggressive need to attend to how they phrase things, and when they speak to clarify what they mean exactly, so that they can avoid making statements that, being inherently equivocal, can be interpreted in two or more ways, at least one of which is damningly negative.

Participating (Contributory) Victims (Passive-Aggressive Enablers)

Participating, or contributory victims, are bear-baiters, e.g., they *actively* cause, enable, or perpetuate the passive-aggression that seemingly comes their way, at least at first truly unprovoked.

Participating victims may be passive-aggressive individuals themselves, or perhaps individuals with another, related emotional problem (such as a masochistic or paranoid personality disorder). These victims encourage, enable, and perpetuate others' passive-aggression toward them because they actually welcome being treated passive-aggressively—because the mistreatment makes them feel wanted, or real, and/or as if they belong. A few deliberately annoy their partners to provoke their own being nagged. Nagging is a passive-aggressive, low-key, but still unpleasant assault for most people; but participating victims welcome and even encourage being nagged, e.g., they get their way by doing the same annoying thing over and over and refusing to stop. For example, in those familiar cases where one individual nags a partner with a scraggily beard to shave, the partner might be getting gratification from all the attention (=caring). In addition, annoying behavior has a meaningful biological and perhaps evolutionary quality—for it is also found in pets that deliberately provoke their owners (in spite of knowing the consequences) to punish them.

Nonparticipating (Innocent) Victims

These are truly "innocent victims," but passively caught up in interrelationships (with sadomasochistic qualities) not of their own making. It follows that their plight can often be best relieved by their focusing on what they can do in reality to improve their lot—practical ways they might deal with the real passive-aggressives in their lives and the problems these passive-aggressives in actuality create for them. One of the best ways is, of course, getting out from under relationships with potential to invite sadomasochistic relationships as soon as one detects such a problem exists. Such victims often find it helpful to first think of difficult situations and salutary resolutions on their own, then second to invite their therapists in to give them input about how they can arrive at such a "preferred" outcome in real life.

As a victim, a wife, at least in the beginning, had little to no hand in creating her difficult circumstances. Only then, being human, she would lose patience and retaliate, by herself becoming relationally passive-aggressive. She and her husband attended a gathering of the wife's friends. She was having a good time until her husband, without provocation from her, told his wife that he found her friends so old and unattractive that he had no choice but to leave the gathering early and go to a strip joint down the block, just to see something good. When he returned, she was gone, sensibly, and left no note, provocatively but with the desired effect.

Nonparticipating, innocent victims are neither excessively hypersensitive nor unduly provocative. Some do not recognize that they are victims at all. Many feel overwhelmed, lost, and depressed. Some can develop psychosomatic ailments like insomnia, stomach pains, or hypertension, which they often fail to attribute to the interpersonal abuse they are receiving. Like the birds on a remote island that have not yet learned to fear humans, they relax when they should be tense, and although in danger, they continue as before, blindly, without protecting themselves from threats—instead carelessly continuing to expose their vulnerable underbellies to truly threatening enemies.

There are no true victims involved when the object of passive-aggression is the target of passive-aggressive techniques used in a healthy way, one that is more indicative of good, productive, interpersonal technique than it is the existence of a bad (personality) disorder. Examples include children who are rebelling passive-aggressively as a way to fight their parents as safely as possible (not wanting to antagonize someone they have to live with for a long time); the insult comic humorously sassing a member of the audience at a comedy show, e.g., a roast; an advice columnist using a "zinger" to make a valid, often humorous, point; or a debater refusing to capitulate, not out of blind stubbornness, but out of a legitimate desire (why he entered the contest in the first place) to win a round or two.

CHAPTER TEN

More Interactions Between Passive-Aggressives and Their Victims

As Mahrer describes them, passive-aggressives are "accomplished crafts[men] at forcing individuals into . . . roles"[1]

Passive-aggressives often intend, and know how to make, their victims *depressed*. For that reason they are what might be called (in line with Kernberg's 1994 term "paranoiagenesis")[2] "depressogenics," individuals who either deliberately and/or unconsciously, generate depression in others. These depressogenics might deliberately, if unconsciously, set out to target their victim's self-esteem, lowering it, crafting self-blame and self-criticism in others by not taking their side in such a way that their victims are led to think, "If you don't side with me it must be because you are against me, and if you are against me it must be because I deserve it."

Generally, the nature of the victims' discomfort and resentment ranges from mild to resounding, and depends to a great extent on the specific anger style(s) used by the individual passive-aggressive in question. Moreover, the *effects* of passive-aggression on the second party (the victim) are *diagnostic of passive aggression in the first party*. And that is because if victims' responses are carefully orchestrated by the passive-aggressive him- or herself, it follows that when these responses are detected, and they are generally detectible, one can walk them back to infer (diagnose) passive-aggression in the person to whom the victim is responding.

What follows is a detailed discussion of the different responses passive-aggressives elicit in those they victimize. This victim response to passive-aggressives consists of six phases, which can either develop rapidly, even within a few seconds, or take days, months, or even years to completely ripen.

Phase 1: Denial

Victims going into denial often first become dismissive of a passive-aggressive's assault upon them. Either they completely fail to recognize that it has taken place, or they view it as being of minor importance. Typically we hear, "So he uses me for a punching bag; I'll put up with that for the sake of the relationship" or "for the sake of mom's last will and testament." (When desensitized, as in a long-term ongoing relationship with a passive-aggressive relative, e.g., a spouse, many victims bypass this phase entirely.)

Phase 2: Becoming Emotionally Ill

As noted throughout, victims of passive-aggression often get depressed or paranoid, develop psychosomatic symptoms like headaches and gastro-intestinal disturbances, or, if children, become hyperactive as a way of literally and figuratively shaking off the incoming hostility.

Reactive Depression

Those victims who get depressed as a consequence of others' passive-aggressive behavior soon come to recognize the assault but blame themselves for having provoked it, and think they deserved being thusly abused. They ask themselves, "What did I do wrong?"—that is, "What is wrong with me?" as in, "Would she be more prompt if I were more interesting?" or "would my mother-in-law be more kindly disposed to me if I were more her type?" or "am I really a plagiarist or did I just forget to put quotes around that sentence?" Then they do nothing to resist because of their failure to ask themselves, "What is wrong not with me but with this (passive-aggressive) person?" Often we even see apologies offered in an attempt to make amends (for how the victim presumably created the problem in the first place, and/or mishandled the situation afterwards).

Passive-aggressives will have their greatest depression-inducing effect on victims primed to accept blame, that is, on victims who are already somewhat self-critical, who already think across many situations, "What did I do to deserve this; what did I do to bring this down on my own head; and what didn't I do to prevent this person from being abusive to me?" Thinking they deserve the snide remarks being hurled at them, they might get even more depressed than they already are, as they too readily condemn themselves for not accepting a relationship as it is even though the acceptance could only possibly come with serious reservations along the lines of, "You have few enough friends and hardly any family. Do you want to destroy this relationship, your last, too?" (It's similar to what happens to people with a sexually transmitted disease who, already depressed because they are ill, tend to buy 100 percent into the suggestion that their illness is not vitally caused, e.g., by a virus, but is self-induced, e.g., as punishment for something they presumably did wrong).

Depressive self-blame, often paramount and problematical, is routinely associated with passivity ("kissing-up") characterized by a reluctance to protest one's fate. A conviction that protesting at the very least will do no good generally exists as does a fear of the consequences of complaining ("doing that will only make things worse.").

Many abused wives, taking things out on themselves—thinking that complaining risks more intense emotional or even physical abuse than does just keeping quiet, prefer to continue depressed and full of self-blame just so they don't have to expose themselves to the consequences of having to complain about how they are being treated.

Depression here is often dynamically speaking an emotional compromise between tolerating abuse and doing something about it, an alternative to getting angry accomplished by retroflexing anger self-protectively, a way of asking others to please not "hit someone who is already down." This compromise, however, comes at a price. For targeting oneself to avoid troubling others, and changing for others when one should instead be changing for oneself, leads victims to stay in an abrasive relationship with a passive-aggressive individual.

Here are some examples of specific passive-aggressive assaults that produced reactive depressions in their victims:

The president of a patient's co-op board put up a notice: "We are looking for members to serve on the board, since some of the board members want to retire." The patient replied, "I would be glad to help out," and volunteered. The next day, by chance, he ran across the president of the board in the courtyard. She said, "We have had so many volunteers that we will have to cross straws." Her remark upset him. He had intended to volunteer, not to compete, and he understood, all too well, the implication of her words. She had contaminated the expression, "draw straws" with the expression "cross swords," and he thought he knew what that meant. As a result, he got anxious, feeling, "I may be wrong, but there is a good possibility that she is planning to throw me to the wolves."

At first he tried to deny the implication of her words. He began to think, "Aren't you being hypersensitive, even paranoid?" Then, almost in spite of himself, he got depressed. And his depression worsened when subsequent events proved him more prophetic than paranoid. For, a few days later she suggested he withdraw from the running because she had more volunteers than she could use. But he was the only one she asked to withdraw. He was not surprised, given the prevailing atmosphere, to discover that something even worse had happened to another man, one already on the board. When the latter was in the hospital with pneumonia during the weeks preceding the board election, he too got a message from this board president. At first he was delighted to receive what he thought were get-well wishes—that is, until he opened her card. It said, "I suggest that, considering your heightening age and your deteriorating physical health, you resign from the board, and you do so before the next meeting."

A patient noted that a woman he had not seen for six months had lost a great deal of weight. Truly amazed, he asked her outright, "How much weight have you lost?" Instead of just answering the question, she replied, "You don't ask a woman how much weight she has lost any more than you ask a woman her age!" In his typical response to his having his knuckles rapped he felt stupidly ashamed of himself, and blamed himself for misspeaking.

Clearly, therapists treating depression should look for causal interpersonal passive-aggressive skirmishes with important passive-aggressives in the patient's life and, when indicated and possible, involve these passive-aggressive people on some level in the treatment process.

Blaming the victim is a common, sneaky, often socioculturally manifest trick passive-aggressives use to defile and thus depress their rivals (or other class of those they see as adversaries). A particularly unfortunate but typical example of blaming the victim is blaming a woman for having been raped because she wore seductive clothing. Husbands who abuse their wives often seek reasons to convince themselves that their wives have provoked their own abuse, e.g., "you know I don't like my hamburger well-done. How did you think I would react to your practically burning it?"

Schizophrenia

Some years ago (around 1960) as he revealed in a personal communication to me, Bateson advanced the theory that being double binded acts as a proximate or direct cause of schizophrenia.[3] By double binded he meant that the victim is ordered to do something, or to feel a certain way; then ordered to do the opposite, or to feel the opposite way; then prohibited from ignoring/getting out from under both marching orders, for emotional (the victim is too psychologically dependent to rebel) or for practical (the victim is too financially dependent to complain) reasons. Since double binding is a characteristic passive-aggressive way of expressing anger, schizophrenia, according to this theory, might be a characteristic way to react to the "ministrations" of certain passive-aggressives (particularly family members) who make inordinate use of this anger style to defeat their targets, e.g., by rendering them too depleted to fight back.

Paranoia

Paranoid reactions often occur in victims of passive-aggression. Paraphrasing Kernberg, speaking of the paranoiagenesis (paranoia-inducing behaviors) of bosses, in the workplace victims get paranoid/more paranoid when they feel their dependent needs frustrated and their privacy invaded; feel that others are silent, distant, and unavailable out of personal disdain for them; feel overcontrolled or micromanaged; feel undercontrolled, that is, completely ignored and left to wither on the vine; and/or feel humbled or even sadistically humiliated—for example, when they feel they are being unfairly accused of being incompetent, or falsely accused of cheating sexually.[4]

A neighbor of mine asked me to stay home to await her parcel post delivery. I graciously (I thought) said no because I didn't like having my movements curtailed. In reply to my balking, both she and her husband gave me a guilt-inducing lecture on how what I needed to do was to learn how to be a better neighbor, one who in an improved way fit into the mood and spirit of this, a cooperative, not only in name, but also in fact.

Somatic Effects

An example of the somatic effects passive-aggressives induce in their victims is the iatrogenic or white-coat hypertension some passive-aggressive doctors can create in their patients, e.g., by making them fear doctor's wrath for not having done enough to keep their blood pressure down. Too many physicians, in effect attacking their patients out of hostility and disdain for them, perhaps just for their having "allowed themselves to become patients," slap the cuff on their patients even before the patient has been able to calm down, e.g., right after beginning a visit, thus creating a falsely high BP reading that reflects how the patient, sensing a true assault was taking place, goes into the fight mode, doing so in spite of him- or herself.

Impotence is another possible outcome of negative interpersonal enmeshments with a passive-aggressive partner. Chronic fatigue (syndrome) can be a way both to react to abuse and to express, "How tired I am of being abused." Asthma can be a response to disguised hostility. For example, Berne, noting that asthma can be a response to the passive-aggression of others, describes a child's asthma as the product of a mother's double binding her child in a way that the child "is not equipped to handle"[5] leading the child to play "the Asthma Game." Taubman also notes that asthma itself "like the other forms of passive-aggressive [behavior can be] a silent and not very effective way of retaliating."[6] Insomnia, ulcers, and headaches are other possible somatic outcomes that can occur as a response to the passive-aggression of others. As with depression and paranoia, those treating patients with any of these or other, related, disorders should, walking them back, try to determine whether the disorder they are treating in any way represents a response to one or more passive-aggressive machinations now going down in the patient's relationships/life.

Hyperactivity in Children

In children, a pattern similar to Attention Deficit Hyperactive Disorder can sometimes be induced as the response to a passive-aggressive parent or teacher. In this category belongs the provocation of the boring passive-aggressive classroom professor who basically dislikes teaching, and it shows. Such a child might need a change of teacher or schools instead of, or in addition to, any indicated psychotherapy or pharmacotherapy for ADHD. The hyperactive student as victim needs to be distinguished from the oppositional, passive-aggressive student as agent who is restless and uninterested because he or she lacks motivation—and is understandably not eager to pay attention, listen, or learn—and to self-excuse, then eager to criticize the teacher for being boring and out of touch, although the problem is that the student is the one, who as a participating victim feeling actively bored, is deliberately staying out of touch as a way to retaliate.

Phase 3: Slow Burn/Mounting Anger

The slow-burn phase begins when victims begin to feel uncomfortable—feeling themselves turning angry. There is dawning recognition that "you" are the problem, not "I." In some of the above examples ultimately there was a (healthy) cognitive shift from "What did I do wrong?" to "Why are you being so rude (cruel, critical, persecutory) to me?" For example, the man who asked the woman how much weight she had lost at first got angry with himself for acting in a way that he believed provoked his being abused. But then he got angry at the woman for putting him down, his slow burn intensifying as he began to recognize the faulty rationale of her complaint about him. In reality, as he came to realize, "Asking a woman about weight loss is not nearly as problematical as asking a woman her age. In fact, most people are proud of how much weight they lost, while many people are ashamed of how old they are, so that asking someone who looks newly thin, 'How many pounds did you shed?' is the rough equivalent of asking a proud grandparent, 'How many grandchildren do you have?'"

Phase 4: Overt Anger

In this phase, which may not appear in all cases, the anger ball bursts and the "slow burn" erupts into overt anger, typically ineffective in part because it is so delayed that the blowup only appears, if it appears at all, when it is too late to have much impact/be of much productive value. Often with the anger comes insight into the abusive nature of the interaction and a strong desire for fight (revenge) or flight (removal). For example, the victim who contemplates fight thinks, "I'll get back at him; I'll make a date and stand him up." Or the victim who contemplates flight thinks, "I will never see that boyfriend of mine again—I am sick and tired of his always standing me up." Sometimes the victim actually takes revenge, as did a woman who got her revenge on a noisy neighbor by throwing a packet of seeds of a fast-growing invasive vine into the neighbor's yard. It is not unusual for actual/physical violence to erupt, e.g., road rage as a response to passive-aggressive provocation—an important reason why there are personal and sociocultural gains to be derived from understanding passive-aggression and handling passive-aggression and passive-aggressives correctly, therapeutically, before it is too late, and things escalate.

A victim's overt anger can often start a spiral of interpersonal psychopathology, where retaliation for the passive-aggressive attack leads to more passive-aggressive behavior in the form of counterattack. This is the sadomasochistic interaction discussed in Chapter 11.

Phase 5: Forbearance (Forgiving and Accommodating)

Passive-aggressives are particularly adept at blaming the victim while setting their victims up to blame themselves—for being hypersensitive, overly dependent, uncooperative, hypercritical, and/or jealous. Not surprisingly then, victims soon learn ways to get along as well as they can with the passive-aggressives in their lives. One way they adapt is by exonerating those who victimize them. They might think, "He really doesn't do anything bad; or, if he does, it's only because he had a bad day, anyone can have one; or if he had many bad days it is because he could not help himself; and besides no one is perfect." Victims who are therapists typically even make excuses for their patients, doing so by bringing masochistic acceptance to his or her relationships with difficult patients.

Self-blame can often shade into a depressive-like attitude consisting of forgiving and accommodating in order to forbear and so to "heal through love." Since passive-aggressives mostly select dependent victims to be their targets, many victims of passive-aggressives, taking their own dependency and neediness into account, think twice about removal and vengeance, and instead think only about being practical—so that for them it soon becomes all about keeping friends and family, and doing what everyone can to keep everyone close. Victims often forbear because their own emergent anger elicits guilt in the form of self-questioning/self-condemnation. At the very least this avoids if not a continuation/repeat of the original abuse, then the vicious cycling around the issue of who is doing what to whom.

The explanation for why the victim stays in an abusive relationship can lie as much in the nature of passive-aggression as it can originate with any personality issues/problems on the part of the victim. This is because passive-aggressives deliberately, if unconsciously, in their relational behavior follow the model not of the parasite that kills the host, but of the saprophyte that lives more or less comfortably with it. Passive-aggressives make certain that there is enough in a relationship for the victim to stay put, perhaps hoping for a change for the better. They do so by providing real rewards for their victims so that, despite all the relational problems in this phase, victims stay put/go back for more, sometimes even stalking their persecutors hoping to get closer after convincing themselves that the relationship is not really over, but is in fact actually working, at least as best as can be expected.

Victims may in this phase accommodate by thinking up specific strategies to use to bring the passive-aggressive more fully around. For example, a woman whose boyfriend always canceled dates at the last minute thought, "I bet if I get him an expensive gift, or wear sexy underwear, he will want to keep me as his girlfriend."

Phase 6: Repetition

In most cases the scene is now set (successful suicide on the part of either the passive-aggressive or his or her victim obviously excepted) for the passive-aggressive to continue "business as usual." Indeed, the victim, already bruised, is now, being even more helpless, an even better object for further, cautious-as-usual, battering.

Case Illustrations

In the case of the unreturned books discussed in Chapter 1, the victim, when in phase 1, denial, said to himself, "They are only books; I can afford the loss; no sense getting upset over such a minor matter." Then, going into phase 2, depression, he began to think, "Life is cruel; nobody treats me right," and to think "It's my fault, I shouldn't have lent him the books in the first place." Then, going into phase 3, slow burn and mounting anger, he began to seethe, thinking, "I resent the books not being returned," a resentment that colored the next few weeks of his life. Then, going into phase 4, overt anger, he began to think, "I am furious—I need those books and I need them now" and, blowing up, left a nasty message on the man's voicemail, accusing him of insensitivity and selfishness. Then, going into phase 5, forbearance, he got depressed again. Blaming himself for overreacting and, fearing the consequences of having done so, he called his passive-aggressive friend up to apologize for some snide remarks he himself had made a long time ago. Then he invited the other man over for drinks, and even offered to give the books back to him, but only when he himself had finished with them. The stage was now set for phase 6, a repeat of the entire process, starting with his listing some other books he would like to borrow, but this time he promised to give them back promptly.

A patient's mother-in-law promised to take care of the patient's dog so that the patient could speak at an important conference out of town. Two days before the conference was to begin, the mother-in-law announced, "I cannot take the dog because I have a sick cat." She really strapped her daughter-in-law because her daughter-in-law's dog was an old dog who had never previously been in a kennel, so that the daughter-in-law rightly feared the consequences if the dog were locked up in a cage for a week. The daughter-in-law's full response took a few days to ripen. At first she felt numb. As she reported it, "At the beginning I felt shell-shocked— uncomprehending and unfeeling." The slow burn came next. She began to wonder why having a sick cat necessarily meant not being able to take in a healthy dog. With dawning awareness came fury for having been mistreated, as she began to tell herself, "I do not deserve this." Like most victims, she brooded about the various advantages and disadvantages of fight, flight, and forbearing/adaptation—the latter by forgiveness. She thought, "I will get back at her by making plans with her for Thanksgiving then canceling them" (fight). Then she thought, "I'll never see her again" (flight). Then she thought, recanting, "Well, after all, she does have a sick cat, and perhaps the two pets together would be too much of a burden." And she began to feel, "Perhaps I was asking for too much" and decided "I'll tolerate her for the sake of my husband and try to stop making excessive demands on her" (adaptation by forgiveness and accommodation). Masochistic self-abuse was a major component in her final decision to adapt by accommodating/opting for forgiveness. She asked herself, "What did I do wrong?" not "What is wrong with this person?" and thought, "Mom would stick to her promises if I were nicer to her," and, "Perhaps she was just retaliating for the times when. . . ." Ultimately, she felt thankful just for having emerged relatively unscathed from the encounter (she put the dog in a kennel and it did okay), and looked to those future times when she would be spared abuse, as in, "My mother-in-law backed out with the dog, but I will still make plans with her for Thanksgiving because I know that that is too important a holiday for anyone to cancel me out on."

Some months later, the patient's sister asked her mother to look after her dog when she, the sister, went off with the family for a pleasure trip. The mother, without giving it a second thought, said, "Yes," adding insult to injury by announcing that she, the mother, just couldn't bear the thought of a daughter of her's dog having to be put in a kennel.

Some victims of chronic emotional abuse have become either so desensitized to it, or so insightful about it, or both, that they respond in atypical ways right from the start. Others, such as some women whose husbands regularly beat them emotionally and/or physically, often do not go through these phases at all, at least clinically. Instead, they have flattened their response to the point that from the start they just give up and suffer in silence. They deny their injuries, doing so to themselves and others because they feel that they need a relationship too much to threaten it in any way with complaints or rumblings about retaliation. In effect, they cover their faces with their hands and roll with the punches. They tell no one about the abuse. They become secretive even with their own family, fearing that if family members try to come to the rescue that will only sooner or later bring further trouble down upon their own heads by exposing their plight.

A woman blamed her black eye and torn skin on her hand on her having hit herself when she shut the door to the trunk of her car. Clearly she was hit, but just as clearly it was not by the car trunk door, but by her husband, a passive-aggressive man prone to becoming violent when under stress. She covered up her black eye with makeup as she covered up for her husband—out of fear that if she said anything to anyone about the incident he would find out, and would either beat her twice as hard, or simply abandon her completely.

Sadomasochism

In Chapters 1–8 I focused on passive-aggressive individuals themselves. In Chapters 9 and 10 I focused on the victims of passive-aggressives, in Chapter 10 focusing on the close/interlocking relationship between passive-aggressives and their victims. In this chapter, Chapter 11, I explore a specific kind of interlocking relationship between the two: the *sadomasochistic* relationship that routinely exists between passive-aggressives and their victims. For as Steckel might have observed in the context of describing passive-aggressives, "Masochistic and sadistic motives are frequently mixed—constituting not the whole, but a significant aspect of the whole picture."[1]

As many observers have noted, passive-aggression does not occur in a vacuum. Rather, as Stricker, quoting Small, suggests, its "primary area of disturbance [is] interpersonal"[2] According to Kaslow, passive-aggression is both an "intrapersonal" and an "interpersonal" phenomenon[3]; and, as Reich more specifically puts it, speaking of masochism, a term he often uses synonymously with passive-aggression to describe passive-aggressive-like behavior, masochism occurs both "in the inner life of the person" and in an "attitude [that] shows . . . in interpersonal relationships."[4] Many, if not all, passive-aggressives become sadomasochists in their interpersonal relationships because, as Rank suggests, "the individual . . . punishes . . . the other" and "the individual punishes himself."[5]

This sadomasochistic interaction is exemplified by those patients who can't say no even though saying yes inevitably starts a discernible passive-aggressive round robin interaction going.

Each year a passive-aggressive patient takes a vacation at the same time, and due to her being away, cannot attend one of the string quartet concerts on her subscription series. So each year she practically forces her ticket on an unwilling neighbor just because she fears wasting something she paid for. The neighbor, instead of telling her he does not like chamber music, in his turn masochistically accepts the ticket, offering not a polite refusal but profuse thanks. Then he, being sneakily defiant, throws it away. Next, when the neighbor returns from her vacation and (pointedly) asks him how he liked the performance, he lies and tells her he enjoyed himself immensely, and cannot wait to go again next season. She then, suspecting something is up, asks him about the specific works played. He clearly does not know what they were. She, just as clearly, realizes that he did not go to the concert, suspects he threw the ticket away, and brings him up short for what presumably was his bad behavior. He feels hurt and insulted. The two resentfully stop being so friendly to each other: until the matter of the ticket comes up again next year.

As for masochism, often both victim and victimizer are harsh and cruel to themselves out of an irrational sense of inner guilt about sins they feel they have committed. Some of these "sins" are strictly of a philosophical nature. Others, such as the "sin" of being successful, are not sins at all, only moral panics. Here it is really unnecessary to constantly brood about what preoccupies them, but they nevertheless can't stop their ruminating about such matters, even to the slightest degree.

When a masochistic passive-aggressive patient reached her fifties, she did a life-search primarily to be hostile to herself. She looked back, summing up her life less to seek final answers to important questions than as a way to devalue herself. She condemned herself by repeatedly asking herself self-accusatory questions such as, "Why did I miss all those great opportunities in life? What could I have been thinking at the time? Why did I take the low road but not the high other?" Also, with little justification, she continuously savaged herself for putting her mother in a nursing home. She had put her there for good reasons, as there were no better palliative/corrective measures she could have taken. She had acted when the mother set a small fire in her own apartment and flooded the apartment below by leaving the faucets on so that the management threatened to evict the mother and sue the mother and her daughter, my patient, for present and potential future damages. Although putting her mother in a nursing home was the right medical decision for the daughter to make, she punished herself for having made it. Soon the self-punishment became worse, first, when the mother, on the day of admission to the home, said the only few words she had spoken in months, and the last few she ever spoke to her daughter, or to anyone else: "I hate this place, and you for putting me in it." And second, the mother did poorly in the home, as she stopped eating, and went rapidly downhill, leaving the daughter to question her own actions even more. Her mother's illness clearly had worsened, but she only saw that as having happened not because her mother's illness had for endogenous reasons (on its own) taken a precipitous turn for the worse, but because of the mother's distress about having been institutionalized—because she was in the nursing home not in her own home, and because the nursing home, the very one she, the daughter, had selected, mistreated her (although in small ways). Painful self-questioning began. Should she, the daughter, have chosen a different nursing home? Should she not have authorized that feeding tube to be put in to keep her mother adequately hydrated? Her various cries of self-blame soon boiled down to one she constantly tortured herself with: "I wish I hadn't done this to her. If she had stayed at home she would have been okay. She did everything for me when she was alive. I did nothing for her when she needed me."

Masochistic passive-aggressives clearly can be as harsh with, and as cruel to, themselves as they are to others, and in much the same ways, and for the same reasons. Now, many years later, this daughter, passive-aggressive to herself, looked back on her life and judged herself, generally narrowly, as having or not having been a good or bad person. As she did so, the nursing home incident as well as other, generally minor incidents, regularly cropped up and her self-esteem once again deflated. And so she would get depressed, and especially over the equivalent of "what did I do to this really nice person who didn't deserve being treated as brutally as I treated her?"

As for sadism, the punishing of others, the more sadistic passive-aggressives torture others just for the fun of it, just to hurt them, just for what Steckel (1965) calls the "malicious pleasure . . . the genuine cruelty [of] joy in another's pain."[6] Passive-aggressive sadism is no less sadistic because the sadism is expressed subtly: in symbolic acts of defiance; through guilt-induction; through inaction; or by being hidden in the guise of the dictates of reality. Actually, it can be overall more sadistic that way, as it makes up in quiet intensity and faint persistence what it lacks in immediacy and power of acute impact.

From the cognitive perspective, sadomasochistic passive-aggression (both to others and to oneself) seems due to one's being unable to, as Beck (1999) puts it, make an analysis to include all the factors that contributed to the bad outcome, to dramatically "broaden . . . perspective."[7] As Beck might suggest, the daughter in the above case might have been thinking according to "exclusive causes."[8] She never asked herself, "How was I to know what exactly to do, and to know it in advance? Did I have any control over the progression of what was ultimately a fatal illness? Do I, in blaming myself and my past actions for everything, overlook the distortive effects of the emotions anyone would have had under such circumstances, such as those ranging about my mother's illness to those due to the real pressures on me from the management of the apartment in which my mother lived, considering the possibility that I could be held responsible for any harm/damage, emotional as well as physical, occurring both to my mother and to others? Also, couldn't social services even accuse me of having abandoned my mother?" And she, the daughter, overlooked the possibility that she had done a good thing by having put her mother in a place where in a sense she was fortunate to be: because there she and all her serious medical problems could be cared for adequately in her final days.

A patient, an owner of a cooperative apartment, hired a tree service on his own without first consulting the other people living in the building. He then had a large, valuable tree removed from the front of the multiple dwelling. It was bad enough that he removed the beloved tree just so that it would no longer block his view. Making things even uglier for his victims was that he vociferously bragged that he did what he did for the shock effect it would have on his neighbors. For him, the neighbors were the latter-day caterpillars that as a child he squished, or the camp director he defied when he and a camp counselor sneaked away from a camp on Cape Cod and traveled 27 miles, hitchhiking, to the tip of the Cape, without informing the director that they were leaving, panicking her when she found out they were gone and she suddenly recognized that she did not know where they went and what had happened to them.

Trends

Sadomasochistic interactions with passive-aggressives and their victims are overall characterized by the following trends:
One. Making oneself suffer as a way to make others suffer—that is, the masochism is indirectly sadistic.
A patient pulled out of her driveway almost into the path of an oncoming car. Instead of taking quick evasive action, she simply sat there angry with herself and depressed because she put herself in the position of being hit. In addition to the depression, there was also a certain amount of anticipatory glee as the thought flashed by: what being hit would do to her relationship with her husband, the co-owner of the car? He, she virtually gloated, would be furious at her for having yet another costly accident.
Two. Making others suffer, hoping others will "return the favor"—that is, the sadism is indirectly masochistic.

Passive-aggressives often seek punishment from others—for, as Rank notes in another context, for them "external punishment [is the] means for inner unburdening."[9] Passive-aggressives intentionally, if unconsciously, arrange to suffer at the hands of their victims by provoking these targets to outrage. Indeed, it is partly their need to suffer that motivates them to produce the characteristic retaliatory hostile reaction their victims classically end up having towards them. In this regard, Millon quotes Reich as having said that passive-aggressives suffer from "moral masochism"—as they "inflict pain upon and . . . debase [themselves passively]," that is, indirectly, through "provocative behaviors" that "torment. . . . others."[10] Reich discussing the masochistic character, emphasizes that the meaning of their masochistic behavior is "a grandiose *provocation of the adults*"[11] due to a "compulsion to *torture others* which makes the patient suffer no less than the object."[12] Along similar lines, Deutsch, "analyzing" the "personality problems" of Bizet's operatic heroine Carmen, notes that "active provocative coquetry is generally felt to be an aggression. . . . How is it possible that so much [of Carmen's] cruelty and heartlessness does not scandalize us? . . . We constantly feel that Carmen directs the weapon of her aggressions not only against other people, but also and principally against herself, to gratify her own cruel masochism."[13]

Three. Allowing others to sadistically make one suffer without setting limits on what is acceptable, setting the stage for passive-aggressive retaliation.

These three components of sadomasochism—*making oneself suffer* as a way to make others suffer; *making others suffer* hoping they will return the "favor"—provoking others to outrage and abusing them so that they hurt back in retaliation; and *allowing oneself to suffer* at the hands of others via enabling that consists of not doing much, or anything, to prevent/stop it, in order to set the stage for one's own later hoped-for retaliative passive-aggression—readily escalate into interpersonal vicious cycles of hurting and being hurt within which it becomes very difficult to know, "Who is the bully and who is the bullied? Who is the antagonist and who is the agonist? What is strike and what is counterstrike?"—all to the point that self-perpetuating spirals of hurt and retaliation develop where passive-aggression is both a favored shield and a welcome sword.

In such sadomasochistic interactions it is very difficult to know who started things and who is doing what to whom. Therefore, it is almost impossible to adequately and fairly apportion blame and responsibility, at least enough to be able to accurately and fairly apply a criterion like the *DSM-IV*'s "resist[s] demands to function at a level expected by others."[14]

Some extramarital affairs, some addictions, and most interactions involving road rage exemplify the relationship between passive-aggression and sadomasochism and illustrate how hard it is to determine "who started what?" Still, therapeutically speaking, it doesn't make too much difference; because attempting to break the cycle by stepping in trying to influence the one appropriate person here almost doesn't require knowing who went first.

A corollary from the cognitive viewpoint is that in situations in which sadomasochistic vicious cycling occurs it becomes difficult for the therapist to know what cognitive distortions are innate and which are provoked, and thus which are automatic thoughts and which are sophisticated perceptions of what was really meant/intended? For all conclusions must, in large measure, be based on reading other peoples' minds (a process akin to "intuition"). Is a man's belief that a woman is challenging his masculinity a personal fictive distortion on the man's part developed strictly out of allowing his own fantasies to go on to trigger a passive-aggressive response in him? Or is a fundamentally correct surmise based on an accumulation of evidence fed through the man's natively occurring sensitivity here being seen through a nondistortive lens?

In couple therapy, a husband became completely furious when his wife took unilateral action about minor things without first consulting with him. If she bought something without first asking for his approval, he felt that that meant that she did not care enough about him to have him join her in the decision-making process. In addition, he complained that she turned on a home and garden show on TV when he wanted to watch the football game, and that she disagreed with his religious and political views constantly and so, it would seem, primarily to frustrate and challenge him. As he saw it, she was "pushing my buttons, and in ways she had to know were meaningful—if only because they fought about the very same things time and time again." In her turn, his wife said she wanted her husband to get up earlier and earlier so that they could spend more awake time together, and complained that he refused what was a simple, easily gratified, request about their sleep time. He countered that he needed his rest, and anyway he felt that they did plenty of things together, if only later in the day. The wife in her turn countered that he was rejecting her by sleeping late instead of making love, and was out to control her by preempting their schedule. Then she added, for good measure, that he was humbling her by making her beg for physical contact.

A man asked his wife to stop by to pick up Chinese food on her way home from work when he could have just as easily picked it up or called for a delivery himself. She was tired after having worked all day, and fed up with what she felt was her husband's laziness, of which she believed this behavior was a prime example. She thought, "Just because he inherited all that money from his father doesn't give him the right to sit around all day, doing freelance work that doesn't sell, torturing me about his uncertain future, and refusing to clean up around the house, including not only doing the dishes but also taking the dishes out of the dishwasher when done; changing the kitty litter; and helping cook the dinner after I leave for work." The one time she did stop by the Chinese restaurant herself, she ordered the wrong items—to retaliate, in a way that she recognized was mean-spirited, but thought was not entirely unjustified.

Another time, her husband was rooting for his baseball team with the score tied and the winning run on third when his wife muttered something unimportant to him. He told her to be quiet unless she had something important to say. She got depressed and then got into the car and headed for the nearest bar, drinking then driving, as if to say, "If I crash it is because you made me do it." She blamed him for her drinking. He said, "You are responsible for yourself and your behavior" and threatened to leave her if she did not cut down on her alcohol consumption. He felt she did not respect his needs. She agreed that she did not respect *all* his needs, but added that he was too needy, as well as too sensitive and too easily angered, to see things as he should.

According to the husband, the "last straw" occurred one night when he bragged to his guests that he was too smart and sophisticated to fish, whereupon the wife delightedly brought out all his fishing equipment to show all the guests. She then excused her ratting on him not as contentiousness but as her way to, "Just tell the guests the truth." He felt she was threatening his masculinity. Next, to make repairs to his ego, he began to stare at other women whenever he and his wife were out together. She, feeling less feminine and alluring than before, attempted to repair her compromised self-image by getting a facelift and breast implants. He felt she was doing all this because she was developing an interest in other men. He reminded her how upset he had recently been about her suddenly buying fancy underwear when before plain would have been good enough. Then he began to take steps to consummate an affair of his own, one that he had already thought a lot about starting.

A patient complained that an eccentric lady next door constantly watched him for minor violations of the law and called the police whenever she thought she discovered him "committing a crime"—calling even when his "crime" was on his own property. For example, he groused that, even though his dog was still on his own property, she called the authorities to complain that his dog was unleashed and he was letting the dog roam about without any way to capture it. She felt that by letting the dog roam off leash, he was risking the dog's life, as well as virtually asking for it to scare her (it ran toward her growling when she first stepped outside into her own yard). As she saw it, it was much as if he were sending the dog forth to bite her. And to retaliate, she provoked her neighbor back by putting out an old toilet on the street near his house three weeks before scheduled pickup, and by calling in her cats at midnight, waking him up with her imitative piercing meow-like catcalls.

Clearly, ultimately, and often sooner rather than later, passive-aggressive behaviors can be as much exogenous, or reactive, as they are endogenous, or innate. Therefore, as we shall see in the section on therapy, an important implication for treatment is that personal or professional bias, especially when evaluation is based on homophobia, sexism, or any other preferential consideration arising in the countertransference, must not be allowed to blind therapists as to how many relationships with passive-aggressives are, sooner or later, most accurately characterized as a sequence of two-way responses and counter-responses where there are not one but two provocateurs and not one but two victims, which means that the therapist must not take sides with one participant in a situation where both participants have mostly had a hand in creating the final dyadic interaction.

Destructive effects on functionality both for the passive-aggressive and for those he or she victimizes occur in the corporate and in the artistic (creative) world as well.

In the corporate realm, somatization is a common passive-aggressive way to deny responsibility for laziness (it's my body speaking, not me, which is why I can't do my own work). Some cases of carpal tunnel (hand) syndromes are catalyzed or actually developed out of the wish to antagonize or gain revenge on a boss. Factitious disorders are common here too. Thus a once effective worker became partly crippled and unable to do her job properly after accidentally wounding her arm at work. She then mutilated her wound by manipulating it to keep it from healing, doing so to assume the sick role to avenge herself for her on-the-job injury by her becoming unable to work effectively. She also hoped to get a large insurance settlement. A depressive component of her disability existed too, for she had now found an excuse to feel sorry for herself, for to her being disabled meant her not being able to live the lifestyle that she felt she well deserved—as her reward for the sacrificial hard work she had done in her life to date.

In the artistic world, masochistically prone artists commonly, and even deliberately, (although often unconsciously) create professional problems for themselves. Some act hostile to their audience by writing complex music that is too audience unfriendly to satisfy many people (then they blame the audience for being unable to understand what is being communicated). Schumann may have mutilated his fourth finger in an autocastration and minisuicide combined.[15] Accidents with manuscripts abound in the annals of masochistic artists who perhaps to abuse themselves lose their writings either on their own or by sending them to someone unreliable to misplace them for them. Possibly Chadwick, who according to the album notes for his Fourth String Quartet, sitting in a beach chair on Martha's Vineyard, masochistically allowed the wind to take away all the pages of a just-completed movement of his Fourth String Quartet,[16] paralleling how Antheil masochistically after purchasing some valuable paintings in Europe sent them back to the United States for safekeeping, only to find later that he couldn't retrieve them because he couldn't remember who he sent them to.[17]

Passive-aggression to oneself often takes the form of artists ignoring available accolades. Rachmaninoff may have come to hate his *Prelude in C-Sharp Minor* because audiences continually demanded he play it.[18] His attitude seems to have amounted to no less than a paradoxically self-destructive response: avoiding trading on and up from an advantageous position. Some masochistic artists avoid available accolades by instead of pleasing those ready to be pleased, and accepting kudos from those ready, willing, and able to give them, frustrate themselves as they turn away from those who might like them, and toward those who are impossible to satisfy. They allow themselves to be shocked by rejections they should have expected, because they have indirectly asked for them; their vulnerability here ensured by the initial selection process, as they wish-fulfill by picking only those who were evaluating them negatively in the first place.

Some artists self-demean to be passive-aggressive to themselves. They become excessively modest and shy to masochistically discourage positive-feedback on others' parts. Often they consciously self-demean, hoping others will disagree with them and try to argue them out of that, while unconsciously knowing all along that others will instead buy into their self-assessment and agree with it—and their own excessively negative self-evaluation.

Some artists invite rejection by deliberately setting out to be what and who they are most likely not. An opera singer wants to be a popular tenor, and the other way around. Intellectual artists try to appeal by charm and seduction, and the other way around ("All I want to do is get away from writing popular songs and produce a symphony.") Some write books for a general audience even when remote academic tracts are their specialty and strong point, paralleling the mystery writer who stops writing mysteries and starts writing poetry just to get the romantic poetry prize in a contest that he shouldn't have entered in the first place.

Freud describes abdicating to rivals and critics in his "Case of Homosexuality in a Woman," He calls this specifically "retiring in favor of someone else."[19] Boito's partial musical block seems to have been at least in part an artistic abdication to his rival and sometime co-author Verdi.[20] Some artists as masochists constantly write and rewrite the same thing over and over again to torture and punish themselves by doing the most obeisance to those who are likely to torture and punish them.

Some creative artists figuratively set passive-aggression, others' or their own, to music. This is seen in Shostakovich's hostile anti-Stalinistic humor actually written into the orchestral score itself.[21] Also, Wagner's satirization of the critic Hanslick in Wagner's opera *Die Meistersinger*,[22] and Bartok's sour humiliating imitation of an opening fragment from Shostakovich's *7th Symphony*, can be found in the music itself, in the latter case in the last movement of Bartok's *Concerto for Orchestra*.[23]

PART 3

Treatment

CHAPTER TWELVE

Introduction to Treatment/ Psychoanalytically Oriented Psychotherapy

An Overview

Here in Part III, I discuss treatment, the ultimate goal of defining and understanding passive-aggressive personality disorder. To anticipate, I first discuss treatment of the passive-aggressive individual him/herself. I favor an eclectic form of therapy, one that will be most profitable due to being focused on both the "here-and-now" (e.g., interpersonal) and the "there and then" (e.g., psychoanalytic) manifestations of the disorder, thus employing psychodynamic, supportive, cognitive, behavioral, and interpersonal methods simultaneously

I explain how techniques useful for other patients may create problems for passive-aggressive patients who might, for example, respond angrily to an offer of *short-term therapy* because they view the therapist's setting time limits on treatment as an up-front rejection, then become less than fully responsive to what therapy they do get, perhaps doing so out of spite. Likely some passive-aggressive patients will view *cognitive-behavioral therapy* as argumentative and controlling, as they view a highly active/directive therapeutic intervention such as this as intrusive, e.g., as overwhelmingly meddlesome because they see the exercise of appropriate and necessary therapeutic authority such as that predictably involved in cognitive therapy as being inherently demeaning. And, paradoxically, it is equally likely that they will view forms of therapy that include support, e.g., *supportive advice-giving*, as presumptuous meddling—being put forth by some know-it-all stranger.

I then focus on therapeutic methods for handling the most neglected "patients" of them all—the victims of passive-aggression. In fact, passive-aggression almost by definition cannot occur in a vacuum. Its very existence virtually requires a victim, and so the victim's plight regularly needs to be paid attention to. But therapists, being naturally patient/client oriented, too often let the victims of this, as of any other emotional disorder, fend for themselves, resulting in a flourishing sadomasochistic interaction developing and coming dangerously close to one that cycles out of control leading to relational problems for all concerned, possibly in turn moving on to violence, even with fatalities.

A joint session between passive-aggressives and their victim(s) can often help diminish/avoid the spiral of sadomasochistic acting out that occurs between individuals one or both of whom are dealing with issues related to the passive-aggressive spectrum. One or more joint sessions can help concerned/involved friends and family of passive-aggressives assist rather than condemn the passive-aggressives in their lives. Condemning passive-aggressives enhances their passive-aggression; while helping them through understanding allows all concerned to have what Berne calls a "Jerk-free, game-free conversation between two autonomous individuals." Thus adults attempting to cooperate for the common good may find that what develops, according to Berne, is a true "intimacy . . . one that is not disturbed by the intervention of games."[1]

What form(s) of therapy are chosen depends in great measure on the individual patient's (s') goals. Passive-aggressive patients who recognize and want to *resolve* their characterological problems may require long-term insight therapy, while passive-aggressive patients who just want to *settle an acute relational crisis* may "only" need, and actually prefer, short-term treatment. Marital therapy might be indicated when a patient desires to cope with/rescue a difficult ongoing relationship involving passive-aggressive partners, while individual treatment might be preferred when the patient's goal is to walk away from that relationship/develop new healthier relationships. Of course, practical issues count too, such as the amount of time and money available for therapy.

When, as above, I suggest using several modalities together, I recognize that to some extent the specific treatment modality or modalities selected in any given case will depend not only on the patient's specific needs and goals, and what kind of approach the patient is comfortable with, but also in part be a product of the therapist's orientation and training.

Therapists who do not use one approach more or less exclusively with passive-aggressive patients but combine two or more approaches might employ what Pinsker refers to as "supportive-expressive psychotherapy." Here therapists specifically combine supportive and psychodynamic approaches thus providing the patient with "a comforting holding environment while resolving specific intrapsychic conflicts."[2]

These therapists tend to follow what Oldham and Morris call a form of psychodynamic psychotherapy, which they define as a method that "is based on many of the principles of psychoanalysis, but . . . offer[s] a variety of techniques from support to medication."[3]

Benjamin, speaking specifically of what she calls "reconstructive learning therapy," a method that works well for many passive-aggressive patients, says that a "reconstructive learning therapist draws from a wide range of available therapies. Techniques of psychoanalysis, experiential therapy, family therapy, group therapy, drama therapy, educational therapy, behavior therapy, gestalt therapy, and others are appropriate. *Anything* that leads to one of the five correct categories (enhances collaboration, facilitates learning about patterns, mobilizes the will, blocks maladaptive patterns, and/or teaches new patterns) is legitimate."[4] According to Benjamin, an important component of this form of therapy would involve establishing insight into "patterns" without "blaming."[5]

According to Murphy and Oberlin, reestablishing healthy patterns would involve passive- aggressives using an eclectic approach involving their having to:

1. "Recognize their hidden anger
2. Reconnecting their emotions to their thoughts
3. Listening to their body
4. Setting healthy boundaries
5. Communicating assertively
6. Reframing conflict
7. Interacting using mindfulness
8. Disabling the enabler."[6]

Is there a specific plan for determining the proper order of the various interventions? Often at the beginning, a patient is very anxious or in real difficulty. Support, including perhaps pharmacotherapy for anxiety, can be a good place to start. Uncovering might be reserved for later when the patient's problem is less urgent, and perhaps what suffering there is seems to be primarily of an existential nature.

Whatever modality(ies) therapists choose, they should consider modifying it to make it pertinent to, and suitable for, treating passive-aggressive patients' problems, as outlined throughout. The general rule is this: in these patients the focus should be on the anger itself; what arouses it, and how and why it can be expressed only indirectly. The therapist must also develop specific techniques geared to handling these patients' idiosyncratic resistances to therapy and the potentially destructive countertransference responses that patient resistances evoke in the therapist.

Passive-aggressives rarely voluntarily come for therapy complaining of their passive-aggression. If they come for therapy at all it is usually for another, concurrent or supervening, problem/disorder. Often they are depressed after having sustained a significant personal or professional loss. Often they are referred, typically in anger, by a less-than-neutral significant other, him or herself outlining what therapy the person being referred no doubt needs. This was the case where a parent referred her child to a child psychiatrist to be medicated: out of a hyperactivity that was little more than a manifestation of youthful high spirits, here including a passive-aggressive component that the child intended to employ to deliberately, and vengefully, annoy the mother. As happened with this patient, referrals are often made in a crisis atmosphere by one of the passive-aggressive's victims, here specifically the mother whom the child targeted as the primary victim. This was also the case when a patient's boss told him to get therapy or get fired. And the boss was so exasperated that he sent the patient this ultimatum, in the boss' own passive-aggressive mode—via an overnight delivery service.

Those referred for therapy by someone they irritate have the distinct potential for acting out in therapy passive-aggressively, and doing so right from the start, even in the initial selection of a therapist. For example, one patient told to go for treatment went, but did so against her will, that is, she went not for the treatment but just to comply, at least for now. Although she did agree to go, she rebelled by selecting the least competent therapist she could find, making as certain as she possibly could that the treatment she reluctantly agreed to accept would be a complete waste of time.

Psychoanalytically Oriented (Insight-Oriented) Psychotherapy

Developing Deep Understanding

According to Brandt, a main principle in treating passive-aggressives involves insightfully "identifying [their] anger and exploring the feeling [so that] you can hear the message it is sending and use it to improve [the] situation."[7]

As Pinsker describes it specifically, insight-oriented therapy refers to a form of treatment in which an attempt is made to "understand relationships or patterns of behavior and thinking."[8]

As Oldham and Morris suggest, an important goal of this form of therapy is "to help replace immature patterns with adaptive, fulfilling, mature styles of functioning that will enable [these patients] to get more out of their lives."[9] Healthy functioning comes about when individuals cease getting angry over something insubstantial in the first place; start holding much of their anger in; and begin expressing what anger is left over openly and honestly, instead of in a paranoid (blaming), narcissistic (self-oriented) and/or OCPD (torturing) fashion.

The authors of the Quality Assurance Project, which offers treatment outlines for Avoidant, Dependent, and Passive-Aggressive Personality Disorders, state that "individual psychoanalytically oriented psychotherapy (establishing insight) is the treatment of choice for these disorders." As this paper states, "a number of authors suggest . . . help[ing] patients become aware of the key roles they play in perpetuating their own difficulties."[10] For example, a mother who groused that her children never called her up benefited from learning how her own critical words, words like, "why don't you ever call me up?" were actually driving them away. When she became less openly critical of them, they becoming less passive-aggressively critical toward, and so, more accepting of, her, started calling her up on a regular basis.

Psychodynamically oriented psychotherapists can profitably use material from the transference to facilitate the development of insight in their patients. Transference material, consisting of passive-aggressive behavior manifest with the therapist, provides the therapist with some particularly good examples that bolster both the therapist's and the patient's understanding of the patient's problems, problems: with hair-trigger anger; inability to express the anger directly; and the need to express anger in specific "sneaky" ways (their characteristic "anger styles").

Passive-aggressive patients themselves learn from observing the transference to their therapists to see their passive-aggressive responses to others for the (transferential) distortions they happen to be, thereby learning to tease out the reality of who others are from the untruths about the people and the situations they currently find themselves in. As Oldham and Morris say, they "locate the inner sources of their anger and hurt" so that they can learn "inescapable truths"[11] that, as Millon suggests, will "set [them] straight."[12]

Here are some things passive-aggressives need to learn about themselves, others, and the situations they find themselves in:

Becoming Less Attentive to/Enmeshed in, and So Less Responsive to, Anger Triggers

Therapists should emphasize how learning about the origin of present-day angry responses involves recognizing that these are due to the persistence of core conflicts from the past. Additionally, learning about transference is a good, if roundabout, way to inform the patient that "such and such is of trivial import, not important for *itself*."

For example, a number of passive-aggressives suffer from traumatic-like neuroses—that is, their anger to an extent originates in early hurtful trauma, whose effects persist and lead to irrational responses when reactivated later in life. Passive-aggressive individuals can benefit from integrating and mastering present-day sequelae of hurtful early traumatic rejections, thus avoiding a rerun of the same disappointing (traumatically induced) outcomes.

Passive-aggressives can often reduce the anger itself to an absolute minimum by correcting the cognitive errors that trigger their anger. They may now be able to drop their rigid postures entirely and become more fluent in how they handle their anger, e.g., being more direct about what anger remains, expressing that less obliquely and less defensively, and instead dealing exclusively with any real problems that are there, and doing so in a more adult, game-free fashion

Particularly important is resolving the anger that arises in core conflicts about dependency, control, and competition. The goal is for the patient to identify and relinquish his or her knee-jerk angry responses involving *unhealthful* dependency; to be more cooperative instead of more rebellious, and to learn to stop competing with others in ways that are inappropriate and unconstructive.

In detail, as the Quality Assurance Project says, there are "special benefits that accrue from actually resolving extant core conflicts around dependency, control, and competition. A recurrent theme throughout [therapy with these patients is the] need for the patients to accept their dependency and find appropriate ways of expressing it."[13] Passive-aggressives who resolve dependency conflicts become more healthily dependent by diminishing their hostile dependency on others. In favorable cases they can develop what Wetzler calls "mutual dependency, which is a healthy dependency without panic in which they become appropriately dependent without feeling overwhelmed, and appropriately independent without feeling alone and rejected."[14] In other words, they can stop vacillating between the two extremes of becoming now excessively passive, needy, and extra sensitive to rejection, and now "commitment-phobic" in order to protect themselves from what they deem to be excessive closeness, as instead they develop Goldilocks relationships with others where the degrees to which they get close to and remove themselves from others are carefully measured and balanced to be neither too "here" nor too "there."

Passive-aggressives who resolve early struggles over control and submission will likely avoid having these early conflicts resurface in present-day interpersonal relationships. They will thus be better able to distinguish others' reasonable requests from others' unreasonable demands as they differentiate agreeing from submitting. They will seethe less because they will have less of a need to be alternately or simultaneously submissive (passive) and rebellious (aggressive). They will no longer accede to others' wishes without protest, to then protest their having acceded to others' wishes. They will stop saying yes and then foot-dragging because they really meant no. They will stop responding to sensible requests by either refusing to come across at all in a reasonable way, or by first actually coming across then second doing so in such a way that others cannot benefit from their generous gesture (Midas passive-aggression). They will be more assertive about getting their legitimate needs met and less assertive about satisfying needs that are inappropriate—especially needs based on their own inappropriate expectations of others. They will learn not to be like the uncompromising patient who expressed his dislike for his parents having forced him to go to college, by keeping his fingers crossed during the graduation ceremony, and to be less like the man who argued with his wife incessantly about the one and only right location in the living room for a new chair, one that he and his wife had in fact purchased jointly and in complete agreement about what they were buying, and where they were going to put it, before they bought it.

Passive-aggressives who understand and integrate their competitive struggles (struggles about status) will be less likely to become fixated on winning, which they too often attempt to do in arenas that do not really matter, as they become more likely to grow beyond old and new competitive hurts as they come to feel less resentful when they interact with others they envision as having become more successful than they. They will likely become less jealous of presumed interlopers based on irrational beliefs such as the one that all third parties are intruders who are likely to fully steal the affections of those they love. They will have fewer strong zero-sum beliefs that are products of the conviction that they live in a world where there is only enough for one, and so what others get they lose. They will become less wary of challenges from imagined competitors they believe to be around every corner; less elated by the vicarious pleasure they get from others' failures (e.g., less prone to *schadenfreude*);

less dependent for their gratification on subtly undermining others' efforts; and less prone to starting and maintaining unnecessary turf battles that no one really wins. They will become less driven feeling that they always have to struggle to position themselves on top in a world they falsely characterize as organized entirely according to the priorities of animals properly concerned with being eaten. And so, not surprisingly, they will become less alert to matters involving their position on the figurative food chains of life, and less fixated onto where exactly they stand in the pecking orders of today.

A patient, instead of reserving her competitiveness for professional situations in which rivalry was necessary, appropriate, and fulfilling, became much too readily angered over the mere thought that others had more than she had. For example, at Christmastime she became upset when she discovered that her sister-in-law had more Christmas gifts under the tree than she had. She became agitated to the point that she tortured her family by repetitively complaining about her clearly lowly status in life, and she could not even calm down when her husband reassured her that, "You can relax; they are mostly from flea markets, and some are even empty boxes placed there for show."

They will also stop acting out their me-versus-you competitive ideation self-destructively. For instance, the edge of a patient's property was on a busy highway. Pedestrians out walking or running typically stepped on the outer perimeter of her lawn to get out of the way of passing cars. Preoccupied with "keeping those interlopers off my soil," she put up a fence. Although it spoiled the look of her whole property, she still fenced her property in just to rescue her lawn from the occasional pedestrians who trampled a few blades of grass as they made their way across her turf to safety. One such pedestrian hurt himself by cutting himself on a loose wire that was part of that fence. He sued. The property owner said he shouldn't have been on her lawn; but the judge said that the property owner should not have set up a situation in which anyone could have been hurt so badly for what likely had been a trivial offense.

Developing New and Better Methods for the Indirect Expression of Anger

Paranoid, OCPD, narcissistic, and other anger styles can be reformulated via recognition/understanding to become more mature ways of expressing one's anger. This reformulation can provide the patient with new mechanisms for the healthier expression of anger while providing the therapist with valuable therapeutic footholds to help the patient revitalize (detoxify) his or her interpersonal relationships.

For example, narcissistic passive-aggressives, those who have a significant measure of what Beck calls the "self-centered perspective,"[15] can profitably learn to subdue their excessive self-orientation. They can learn to take others' impersonal remarks or actions less personally, and make fewer demands on others—as they stop constantly feeling unnecessarily disappointed in those around them, as if they are living in a world where all people refuse to give them what they need. And they can in the here and now stop sullying others who refuse to go along with them. They might think twice about what a narcissistic family did: while doing some repairs in their apartment they put some of their possessions in the common hall of the building, although some of these possessions having been out on their balcony for 40 years had all the while been accumulating dirt, and—especially disgusting—now harbored dead insects and a dangerous fungal growth.

Generally speaking, endless repetitive competitive feuds that no one wins; relationships lost by being unreliable, hypercritical, or remote; self-punishments inflicted just to spite others and to be able to later say "Look what you did to me," are all forms of self-destructive narcissistic acting out that create illusory temporary gains that but ultimately exact a heavy price not only on their victims but also on the passive-aggressives themselves.

Passive-aggressives do not need to suppress their anger entirely as much as they need to develop new and better ways of expressing what anger they choose to set loose. One way they can do this is to attend to the defenses they use. They can become generally less defensive, and they can also learn to use other, healthier defenses, projecting and retroflexing their anger less, healthfully sublimating it more (within limits), and talking out, rather than acting out, their angry feelings. Specifically, *paranoid* passive-aggressives can benefit from not projecting their anger to the point of creating adversaries in the form of people whom they irrationally come to believe are persecuting them (when in fact it is they who are persecuting others). Projection of anger onto others may be self-affirming, but blaming others projectively, that is, blaming them for one's own (miscreant) thoughts and behaviors, invalidates, hurts, insults, and antagonizes far too many people and for far too few reasons.

Obsessive-compulsive passive-aggressives in particular can benefit from not burying their anger in overconcern and other reaction formations, such as those in which anger, as Fenichel notes, becomes the character trait of pity, one that is "connected with an original sadism."[16] For while reaction formations like killing with kindness may temporarily spare others, including the passive-aggressive him- or herself, from a full awareness of the extent of his or her anger (and associated shame), ultimately the passive-aggressive fools few to nobody, and so in fact often wounds others more extensively by putting them to the proverbial "death by a thousand cuts."

In conclusion, increased self-awareness that is the benefit of reduced defensiveness, can in many cases lead to a personal program of psychological fence-mending that effectively holds off/repairs what interpersonal damage can be/has already been done. Thus, an important step in helping passive-aggressives improve their character involves lessening their passive-aggression by identifying and highlighting the passive-aggressive behavior of which they are presently unaware. That can help to promote understanding of Oldham and Morris' "inescapable truths," so that, as these authors write, "If the passive-aggressive person has the strength, courage, and faith to begin to see his or her behavior for what it's worth, there is great hope of change."[17] In favorable cases, those who develop deep insight will also relinquish the few (undeniable) benefits of feeling and expressing anger sneakily in favor of being less angry—thus contributing more positively to the lives of all concerned, their own as well as that of those others with whom they interact.

CHAPTER THIRTEEN

Cognitive Therapy

Cognitive therapists treating passive-aggressive patients focus on, in order to help revise, specific distortive cognitions. These are the ones that lead the patients on to feel excessively angry and to, getting angry, find themselves unable to express much of their anger healthily, so that they can do no better than use problematic anger styles to express themselves, all the while justifying their anger and its (modest) expressions by employing support- ive (il)logic—where they feel and act, as they see it, out of reasonableness and necessity, but where others, as others see it, respond inappropriately— usually, the patient believes, because these others are themselves problem- atic people who as such can do no better than be unreasonable and act in an unreasonable fashion.

While psychoanalytic and cognitive terminology superficially seem rad- ically different, psychoanalytic and cognitive theory overlap, especially when it comes to matters of assertiveness, its inhibition due to anxiety, and such fears as a fear of retaliation. There is a marked similarity, for exam- ple, between the persistent underlying schema that characterize the per- sistent unresolved childhood developmental conflicts that psychoanalysis tells us remain throughout life to affect adult functionality, and a passive- aggressive patient's logical distortions that according to Oldham and Mor- ris, result in how "what you think determines how you feel and act."[1]

In the realm of why passive-aggressives *feel excessively angry* (with their anger alit by specific triggers), cognitive therapists emphasize the role played by *automatic thoughts* (reflexively activated patterns of belief) in first, creating, and second, reinforcing angry *responses*. In the realm of *too-readily- triggered anger*, Beck discusses the "hostility complex" and focuses on its "crucial psychological and behavioral components." He studies how a "disturbing thought" can lead to "distressed feeling" when "exaggerated meanings" are attached to communications and evoke "inappropriate or excessive reactions"[2] in vulnerable individuals. For example, the cognitive error of "some=all" helps create and validate the troubling belief that if you criticize me a little you criticize me a lot—even, it would seem, completely; as, often simultaneously, the cognitive error of "thinking according to exclusive causes" contributes to feeling provoked when an individual, unable to think of any alternatives, views even another's neutrality as being deliberately, and so punitively, antagonistic.

A patient, wanting to know because she was thinking of purchasing a similar dwelling herself, asked a coworker, a woman who owned her house but not the land under it, "Since you don't own the land under you, do you have to clear the snow from the land yourself, or does the municipality do it for you?" In response, the individual so questioned lifted her eyebrows, rolled her eyes, shook her head, and then angrily snapped at her questioner. She responded this way (emotionally) because she had thought to misinterpret his question as a putdown, an accusation that what she owned was somehow inferior just because she did not own it all. Her misinterpretation hearkened back to her mother's complaints about her daughter's musicality, so that each time the daughter played an original piano composition of hers, the mother would treat it as excrement, by saying, "Well now, Doris, did you finally get that out of your system?"

Many of the central faulty beliefs that we might see taking hold involve:

- believing that risk being excessive means that harm and danger are predictably soon to occur;
- thinking strictly according to ideology—the virtual opposite of emotional reasoning;
- thinking magically (e.g., believing that thoughts being omnipotent, can actually kill). A patient's magical thinking involved thought-action fusion. This consisted of the idea, and its elaboration, that one can "murder with wishes." Unable to distinguish "thinking from doing," and (as is often the case in those who are inclined to be passive-aggressive), "thinking about from having done," a patient equated contemplation with implementation. This patient angered his wife by his being a sloppy dresser, the result in large part of his thinking magically, for he believed that his "elegant taste in clothes" actually assured his dressing himself well. He patronized the best clothing stores and had a superb clothing collection. But, afraid that his good clothes might get ruined, he preserved them in garment bags while wearing the same torn pants and worn dress shirt every day because "who cares if something happens to those?" His wife told him she was very disappointed that he was so mistreating her. He replied that she could leave if she didn't like it. On a number of occasions, his therapist, trying to be helpful, countered, "Why do

you accept, and almost tolerate/almost welcome, how a spot on your clothes means so little to you and yet bothers her so much?" But the patient, stubbornly rebelling, became agitated in the face of what he imagined to be his being ordered about by his therapist, somebody he presumably was paying to *help*, not *criticize,* him, and certainly not to push him around via:

- catastrophizing (e.g., "the making of mountains out of molehills").

- personalization, thinking that independent random events are initiated by the individual.

- emotional reasoning, where one's ideas do not participate much in determining one's beliefs.

- dichotomous, or absolutistic, thinking, which involves an ability to see only two polar opposite possibilities leading, among other things, to characteristic passive-aggressive pessimistic, and hostile emotional responses marked by an inability to accept that those individuals who are not all for us are not necessarily totally against us.

- magnification, where molehills become mountains as minor issues become major matters leading to unnecessary angry discomforting thoughts about others—and specifically those others who in their responses to us are in fact not somewhat off the mark but entirely imperfect in their reasoning.

- minimization, the reverse of magnification where minutiae are inflated to assume gigantic proportions as some trivial matter "takes over to run the whole show."

- omniscience, where my involvement and the rules I make therein are the one and only rules of the game.

In the *arena of expressing anger indirectly,* Burns and Epstein discuss the cognitive distortions responsible for patients being unable to express their anger directly, such as "confusion about the appropriateness of feeling the anger" and the belief that there are high costs to angry responses, e.g.; "I'll get fired."[3]

In the *arena of chosen anger styles,* these too can be partially the derivatives of cognitive errors. For example, there is a close relationship between some = all thinking and anger over oneself and others for being imperfect expressed in the anger style of "if you are not all good, e.g., if you are at all flawed, you are no good at all" (also expressed in the anger style of perfectionism).

Therapeutic Approaches

Beck designs specific cognitive interventions to deal with anger responses derived from the making of cognitive errors. According to Beck, therapists can, by taking the role of an "impartial observer," "refram[e] the meaning of a situation with objectivity."[4] A therapist might help a patient reframe "conclusion[s] about the supposedly noxious behavior of another person" by applying rules of evidence and considering alternative explanations based on a "history of [similar] noxious previous interactions" thus helping the patient to "[re]frame [any present negative] conclusions"[5] thus to meet, as Burns and Epstein say, the goal of rethinking "anxiety-inducing schemata."[6]

As an example of angry conclusions needing reframing, a man, believing that no neighbors are ever to be trusted, complained that one of his neighbors had deliberately and maliciously crossed the line onto his property and was trespassing on his turf.

In self-defense, the accused pleaded carelessness—for not having studied the site plan adequately, thus being unaware of the true boundary line. The neighbor, refusing to accept what he thought to be an obviously self-serving explanation, however plausible it at first seemed, continued to accuse the man of deliberately attempting a land grab, and threatened to take him to court to get his own rights restored—this in spite of the neighboring man's expressed willingness to stop crossing the property line and even to pay for a fence that would clearly and permanently separate the two lots.

Cognitive therapists often deal with interpersonal anger by focusing on an individual's underlying problematical temperament, especially that associated with his or her overall hypersensitivity. Therapists might do that by correcting cognitive errors that lead to hypersensitive "paranoid thinking" as the patient, projecting his or her own hostility onto others, sees nonexistent hostility as being there in the world, and/or rises to the bait of very modest hostile provocations that don't in fact amount to much, or, if they do exist, are likely to be somewhat trivial, if not entirely imagined.

To overcome resistances and transference distortions, cognitive therapists correct cognitive errors about therapy and the therapist. Beck mentions what is perhaps the most important of them all—the belief that cooperating, in this case with the therapist, is tantamount to "giving in."[7]

Millon speaks of a downside of cognitive therapy rarely mentioned: the patient becoming "unduly guilt ridden, depressed, and suicidal."[8] Passive-aggressives allow their hypersensitivity to cause them to misinterpret cognitive therapy itself as being overall too critical of, unsupportive of, or even assaultive toward, them as patients. They especially emphasize and complain that cognitive therapeutic interpretations seem to undercut their *protective*, particularly their protective *projective* ("it's not me, it's you") defenses. Cognitive therapy by definition assigns patients a measure of responsibility for what happens to them by focusing on the central role that patients' cognitive errors play in their presenting problem—the problem with passive-aggression. The more paranoid passive-aggressive patients, resenting being the figure in the spotlight, begin to feel negatively about the therapist for so saying, or implying, that the patient is central to creating his or her difficulties. Although they do not always admit it, patients often secretly feel, projecting self-blame outward, that their therapists are blaming them for everything. Then their projective defenses having been undercut, patients react accordingly by getting depressed, and/or by developing somatic symptoms like headaches. And so, in the transference, they become even angrier, and so all around, more passive-aggressive, than before.

This said, cognitive therapists too often do inadvertently, mistakenly, and hurtfully side with the enemy in struggles between the patient and another person. For example, the man who despite his track record of reliability was awakened at 8:00 a.m. on a Sunday morning to be reminded to do something he had already agreed to do that day, told his therapist that in his opinion the person who called him was a passive-aggressive individual in the process of being hostile to him, and went on to explain why he thought that way. His therapist disagreed. Instead she corrected his "thinking according to exclusive causes," saying that other possibilities existed. Perhaps, for example, this person had had a number of bad encounters with less than sanguine outcomes along parallel lines, and was, having been thereby traumatized, simply acting on the basis of past experience. The patient, thinking his therapist was as passive-aggressive as everyone else in his world, felt unsupported—and felt this way not completely without justification. Then he became depressed; and subsequently quit treatment to "go see someone who understands me, e.g., takes my side."

Even therapists who identify themselves as noncognitive therapists use, without necessarily acknowledging it as such, cognitive methods therapeutically—if not openly, then at least in various guises, such as the guise of "reality testing." For example, a classic Freudian analyst dealt with a patient's transferential fear of being "fired," that is, "thrown out of analysis," if he expressed any negative feelings at all about his analyst. The analyst dealt with these fears by "reality testing them." She asked him, "You feel that my basic feelings about you will change if you aren't careful about what you say to me?"—her way of correcting a flawed belief by asking the loaded question: "Would you think less of me just because I said something negative about you?" This was not so much a question as it was a practical hint as to how her patient ought to adjust his thinking about her, and so about some of the other important people in his life.

On their part, most cognitive therapists knowingly or unknowingly use ancillary methods as they combine cognitive approaches with noncognitive methods, especially those that are intended to be supportive. I believe that it is virtually impossible to do cognitive therapy effectively without simultaneously lending the patient a sympathetic ear, one cornerstone of *supportive* therapy. In fact, some believe that cognitive therapy should almost always blend with interpersonal therapy in the treatment of passive-aggressives since cognitive errors are invariably associated with, and lead to, destructive interpersonal interactions, and, in particular, to such passive-aggressive negativity as vengefulness.

In conclusion, the phenomenological (descriptive); psychodynamic; and cognitive views of the nature of passives-aggressive psychopathology are mostly compatible one with the other. This is especially evident in the area of the "stable underlying assumption[s]" that Burns and Epstein cite as the basis of "negative cognitions or automatic thoughts."[9] Therefore, the belief, cited by Burns and Epstein, "that the world is an unfair, unpredictable place in which one is likely to be disappointed and in which one must be prepared to shift one's approach to people at the first sign that they will fail to meet one's needs."[10] *phenomenologically* speaking has a paranoid cast; *psychodynamically* speaking can originate in past hurts such as oral disappointment; and *developmentally* speaking can be potentially explainable by psychodynamically-oriented/insight-oriented theory that establishes patterns that have started in childhood and can be retraced through to the here and now in somewhat of their original form. The therapeutic implications thereby become clear: developing insight into oneself and making cognitive correctives go together, so that as Benjamin says, patients can likely benefit from relinquishing their faulty forms of thinking and so giving up the passive-aggressive symptoms that are generated by these as they "give up self-criticism [and criticizing others in a way] that is global, absolutistic, moralistic, invariant, and irreversible [so to develop behavior that is] relativistic, nonjudgmental and reversible [thus developing] a better version of perfection."[11]

Behavioral Approaches

In the behavioral approaches that are almost always a handmaiden of cognitive therapy, the therapist directs his or her attention to modifying specific symptoms, focusing away from explanation and onto recommending *direct* corrective measures meant to help the patient alter his or her pathological behavior. A potentially useful behavioral approach involves suggesting that the patient minimize irrational fear by asking him or herself,

"What is the worst that can happen?" then comparing the "worst" of what he or she fears with the worst possible outcomes to see which is actually the least toxic..

Another useful behavioral technique involves, after identifying abnormality, approaching normalcy in stages. Here patients are advised to take small "baby" steps toward acting in a healthier, less passive-aggressive fashion. For example, a therapist might recommend graded therapeutic measures to deal with the anger style called "hoarding." He or she might attempt to reduce the anger style of hoarding gradually by having the patient (acting incrementally) throw away some, then some more, of what he or she has hoarded, for example, old nonworking stereo equipment and unplayable LP records. Rationalizations such as, "It takes time to declutter," are identified as such, and deemed impermissible at least for more than a very short time.

In this form of treatment, patients are asked to force themselves to face things they fear (e.g., fears associated with specific threatening interpersonal situations) bit by bit, in small measures. The belief is that this gradual approach (akin in some ways to the slow withdrawal of addicting substances), can help patients ultimately come to tolerate, or at least to accommodate to, their fears, by dealing with them in a measured incremental fashion. The first positive outcomes likely to be obtained reassure patients that they can succeed in at least one area of their lives. Patients can now see that success can be followed not by failure but by actual accomplishment, and that is likely to inspire them.

In some cases, behavioral therapy is combined with psychodynamic psychotherapy to actually meet the goal of *inducing* anxiety. Now the patient, impelled to talk about what makes him or her anxious, will thereby be more motivated to relieve painful anxiety and therefore be in a better position to be able to work things through.

In a related behavioral approach, the therapist can absolutely prohibit passive-aggression just in one arena, for example in the realm of distancing (e.g., the therapist says, "No more relational teasing is permissible"). Most patients can stop one of their passive-aggressive behaviors at least for a short period of time. Anxiety will build and so can be discussed and its reasons thereby determined. A patient who didn't change his underwear for days at a time believing, "I don't do anything to get it dirty, so why should I replace it?" was prevailed upon to do just that just once, the next day, then to analyze why he became angry at the therapist who in "making him do that" was only being reasonable. (The patient was helped to recognize how unreasonable *his* anger was, which turned out to be over "cleaning me up enough to open up the possibility that I might have a relationship with a woman.") He could then change his view, and in a way that his improvement would subsequently spread to many related areas of his life.

Where there is depressive cognition, this can be dealt with by being analyzed along conventional lines. Thus a patent's depressive feeling that "all will be lost if I go through with that" was analyzed as the product of internalization of anger at others who, as the patient saw it, were ordering him about, and so were by definition predictably, and inevitably, as he saw it, leading him astray.

For those suffering from OCPD spectrum issues, a passive-aggressive negative response to the giving of good, therapeutic, advice is often triggered by the revival of childhood core conflicts around problematic toilet training. This leads to the revival of presently (inapplicable) adult stubbornness that can lead to diminished overall functionality. A patient who was prevailed upon to simply replace his favorite outfit—one consisting of baggy pants and scuffed shoes—with a new, better-looking outfit—told his therapist that he was upset because his new pants bunched up when he sat down, making it look to others as if he were sexually aroused. Therapist and patient could now analyze, and thence dispel, the fearful erotophobic fantasies that had emerged just on account of his simply being asked to change his clothes.

Behavioral approaches can be used to help the worried passive-aggressive patient relax. Suggesting patients "stop overreacting and worrying about every little thing" can work—should the patient identify with the relaxed therapist instead of perceiving the advice as a command the patient can't or won't follow, and thus, inspired to dissent, as something he or she ought to rebel against.

Relaxation emerging from "mindfulness" ("so what") techniques can sometimes help passive-aggressives overcome their various anger responses. As Brandt says, "By teaching yourself to be mindful of emotions and your biological responses to them you give yourself the power to pause, to create space between your triggers and your response to them."[12]

When he went outside, a patient hid in the shadows because of his fear that he would meet someone who knew that he had anglicized his name and who would then expose him as a phony. The therapist reassured the patient that many others had anglicized their names, and that in this day, age, and city, no one cared. "Besides," the therapist added, "Does it make sense for you to give up your whole life in order to avoid your neighbors' finding out that your family had an ethnic name? The worst that can happen is that a neighbor will shun you. So what? Such neighbors are not worth trying to get to know, anyway." The patient ultimately saw the wisdom of responding as follows: "I used to become afraid when the possibility that my neighbors wouldn't love me came up; now I just pause and think 'good' because all I want is just for them to leave me alone."

Manipulation, a form of behavioral therapy, is a word that in the therapeutic lexicon refers not to something seditious but to "a strategy," or to a "maneuver." True, the therapist who manipulates is being exploitative, but he or she is doing so strictly to the patient's advantage—yes, as a contrivance, but yes, too, as one made in the service of helping a patient attain useful, satisfying, pleasurable change. In other words, the word "manipulation" when used to describe a form of therapy, doesn't imply that some nefarious action is being advocated/to be taken. All it is, is a way to bring about improved health directly, if somewhat seditiously.

An entirely ethical, and, in the context of treating passive-aggressiveness, an acceptable and simultaneously effective manipulation, involves suggesting escape hatches as a way out—those of the sort that, when they occur to the patient spontaneously, can result in the making of a functional out of a nonfunctional individual, especially in the realm of his or her relationships. In this realm, patients often come around to reassure themselves that all is okay by their saying to themselves, "so-what," a mindful-way of saying to themselves and others, "Who cares?" Many of my more flexible, more creative/less hidebound passive-aggressive patients have on their own found rational escapist thoughts such as "I can live without her" to be particularly helpful when one is stuck in place in an angry enmeshment that doesn't seem to resolve itself.

A common example of a masterful manipulation might be (manipulative) reverse psychology, such as the reverse psychology used by the boss who encouraged his tardy employees to come in on time not by harassing or criticizing them, but by giving them permission to come in late, but only if *pressing* personal problems arose at the last minute. Now feeling good about the boss, some employees, formerly antagonistic to him, but now no longer full of enmity arising out of his seeming to act as a martinet who threatened their freedom and intactness, came in on time just to please him, simply to give him their all, doing so out of a new, profound, sense of relief that he wasn't coming down hard on them for being difficult, and rather than meeting out punishment for their having been bad, was giving them a reward for their being good

Reverse psychology has the effect of undercutting/depressurizing a situation, thereby allowing forward motion via paradoxically recommending stasis/motionlessness.

Blame-shifting can be a temporary manipulative expedient for treating passive-aggressive anger and the troublesome symptoms that accrue from it. Here the therapist offers to take responsibility for any unfavorable outcome that might occur should the patient deal with his or her anger more healthfully, and especially not act it out. The therapist can say, "Let me worry about that," thereby shunting responsibility onto the therapist him or herself. By taking the responsibility on his or her shoulders such a therapist is now freeing the patient up by the expedient of allowing him or her to deny personal responsibility for any negative outcome of his or her thinking/behavior. The therapist is saying in effect, "Do what I suggest, and if it doesn't work, then I'll take the blame."

But, like any manipulation, the danger is that this approach may actually itself lead to a paradoxical response, and thus to a worsening of the problem. In some cases, the passive-aggressive, sensing the trickery/ coming to learn of its possible truly seditious intent, responds in a way that is a reverse of the (desirable) reverse response, constituting payback to the therapist for acting foolishly—the patient's way to say, "I am too smart to fall for something so inherently dishonest and dumb as what you just suggested."

CHAPTER FOURTEEN

Interpersonal Therapy

Interpersonal psychotherapists, a category that includes some group, marital, family, and individual therapists, view people, in Oldham and Morris's formulation, as belonging to "an interdependent system and [their] emotional problems [as] develop[ing] within the context of the whole family."[1] Accordingly, interpersonal psychotherapists doing individual therapy emphasize such issues as hostile dependency, fear of being controlled, and fear of loss of status and explain them as group-engineered phenomena taking shape in Oldham and Morris's "troubled . . . unit[s]" And they then treat these troubled units as a way to manage their "individual member[s]."[2] Wetzler and Jose, along similar lines, say that "interpersonal gambits" exist within "dyadic relationships" where issues of "power" and "punishment for anger" loom large. It is thus reasonable that "passive-aggression" is "best detected in our own feelings of anger at the frustration imposed by [the passive-aggressive person's] calculated incompetence."[3]

In *group therapy,* the therapist, again according to Oldham and Morris, facilitates the group members observing the patients' problems as "manifest . . . in the group." Also the group gives the individual members help through "feedback" and "mutual problem solving."[4] An advantage of treating a passive-aggressive individual in a group is that the patient's individual transference negativity is spread over the many members of the group. Thus it can provoke less discomfort per individual in multiple individual targets of PAPD than it might in any one individual in the room. A disadvantage is that most group members are characteristically neither trained nor inclined to deal with transference issues, especially of the negative kind. Instead, the individual group members tend to have kneejerk emotional responses that, being mostly retaliatory, are not especially helpful to a patient whose problem is making people angry and causing others to seethe. This, as emphasized throughout, is a patient difficulty that needs to be treated, not a patient misbehavior that, as can happen in a group setting, needs to be condemned.

Marital therapy can constitute a subtype of interpersonal therapy geared to helping two individuals who are committed to each other work out their mutual, interactive, problems. The basic principles of marital therapy, while generally mostly applicable in the home, are by extension also applicable in the workplace, where they might be adapted and followed in order to resolve occupational problems that arise between a boss and his or her employee(s).

A review of the literature and an informal sampling of therapists reveal that marital therapists do not always agree on exactly how to help "couples" work out problems when one or both members of the dyad are passive-aggressive. Various marital therapists advocate different methods for resolving the interpersonal difficulties that can appear under such circumstances. Possible (often, but not always, mutually exclusive) methods advocated are: forbearance and compromise in those relationships where change is unlikely; abreaction (talking things out to resolution); developing interpersonal understanding (attaining interpersonal insight); and ending a thwarting, oppressive, and punitive relationship. (Some of the following methods, being of a generalized nature, have also been discussed throughout this chapter in the context of therapy geared to helping passive-aggressives deal with their anger.)

Dealing with Troublesome Passive-Aggressive Individuals

Forbearance

Therapists who advocate forbearance on the part of the partners of those who are passive-aggressive may encourage such partners to say little to nothing even when they feel angrily retaliative.

A patient told his therapist, "My wife constantly wears my shirts, and gets stains on them, then I have nothing to wear. I am furious," then asked if "I and my wife should sit down and have a talk about what she is doing and why?" Then he himself suggested that in the meantime, "I should tell her to start wearing her own blouses, no?" The therapist disagreed. First he asked the patient how much money his wife contributed to the household, and whether or not she contributed enough to the household to cover the costs of dry cleaning or, if necessary, of replacing the shirts.

Receiving an affirmative reply, the therapist then advocated forbearance based on thinking, "That is just the way she is, and in the infinite scheme of things it clearly matters very little either in terms of cost or convenience."

For marital therapists who advocate forbearance, the viability of the marital relationship as a whole is more important than the sanctity of any one of its parts. Such therapists put relationships first and make maintaining/rescuing them their priority. They recommend overlooking a lot, and keeping many of one's opinions to oneself—holding one's tongue, not getting upset, not arguing, and not nursing grudges about issues that really overall do not matter so much. One therapist cited that her reason for suggesting this was that, in her experience, patients who were married more than once, when looking back on their lives, claim that their first partner had been the best of them all, and regretted ending that relationship for another one, incorrectly presumed to work out better.

A mother-in-law whose son-in-law would not put up her curtains for her in time for Christmas, three Christmases later was still speaking of how she resented his behavior, "and with all I did for him." Instead of trying to analyze her grudge, say, by going into at least part of its origin in early deprivation, or its in-part derivation from her making cognitive errors ("you feel that if he doesn't put up your curtains it means that he doesn't love you *at all*"), the therapist expressed her opinion that, overall, the relationship was too important to allow it to be destroyed over such a little matter, and suggested that the mother-in-law forget about the incident and forgive her son-in-law's failings, perhaps catalyzed by identifying and understanding the very personal problems her son-in-law had (in his case, with compliance). The therapist also reminded the mother-in-law that no one is perfect, and recommended that she not react anew each day with surprise at a selfishness she had already long ago identified as one of her son-in-law's characteristic personal difficulties. In this therapist's opinion, making the peace was worth losing this one particular battle.

A couple in couple therapy fought about a tenant who wanted to pay less rent because his disability check, the source of most of his income, did not cover the full amount of what he owed. The wife argued, "No, why should we take the loss?" The husband said, "Be compassionate." The wife then responded by escalating other, even unrelated, complaints about her husband, doing so directly to him. For example, she added, "And besides, you never do anything around our rental properties anymore." Her husband shot back, "You are too cheap to hire a contractor and I'm too old to do everything myself." The wife then decided that "forgoing a little rent, and hiring a contractor, is cheaper than hiring a divorce lawyer" and took an extra job, which parenthetically she actually enjoyed, to make up for the cost involved in hiring outside help.

Sometimes forbearance consists of being the big one in a relationship, and not allowing pride and hurt to interfere with the possibility of making healthy compromises. This involves looking at the interpersonal gestalt with a view to toning down all the negativity wherever it starts, and whatever it's about, rescuing a viable relationship by keeping it from becoming the casualty of petty squabbles, whoever started and was maintaining them. Importantly, participants thus shy away from microanalyzing and micromanaging interpersonal interactions with passive-aggressives. They often find that doing thus avoids assuming several risks including one big one: someone significant, like a therapist, taking sides in struggles between two people who are both in fact contributing equally to the problematic relationship, thus exonerating one by blaming everything on the other, offering unilateral support in a way that is too easily mistaken for validation because one partner has been cleverly set up by the other who has been able to lure a therapist into harshly criticizing the wrong person.

Abreaction/Talking Things Out

Therapists like Berzon feel that sometimes forbearance can be just another way to yield to abuse. Berzon suggests not "convinc[ing] yourself that you can live with this annoyance because there is so much in the relationship that is right and good." Instead, Berzon often advocates "taking the risk of antagonizing a partner in an effort to make the relationship work better for both of you."[5]

Developing Interpersonal Understanding (Interpersonal Insight)

Therapists who advocate developing interpersonal understanding (interpersonal insight) ask passive-aggressives to take responsibility, sometimes unilaterally, for how they contribute to their relational difficulties. The passive-aggressive patients in the following cases learned how they first unnecessarily brought their personal and professional relationships to the brink by their own words and deeds, and then compounded their errors thus escalating the potential for actual rifts.

One worker who complained that she was being mismanaged in fact suffered from a fear of success that caused her to bumble in a way that made it likely that her boss would frown upon her actions and even recommend her demotion, or her being fired.

At home, a patient, an older woman, complained that her husband was mean to her. She surmised that this was because she was too old to satisfy him sexually. The therapist wondered whether her husband was reacting less to her age than to the selfish demands she was making on him outside of the sexual sphere. Her first response to that formulation was that the therapist was blaming the victim. Later, however, the patient agreed that it might be helpful if she stopped pushing her husband to take vacations they couldn't afford; to buy new furniture they did not need; and to adopt yet another cat although they already had seven.

A patient constantly groused to everyone that he had no friends and no wife. Yet he still dismissed out of hand meeting women who were from out of town, even those who wanted very much to be his companion. He was dismissive of a potentially good matchup just because it was "geographically undesirable," e.g., it was necessary for him to travel a few miles to get together with this person. As a result, he continued to rule most people out even though the persons themselves were highly desirable in most, if not in all, other respects.

Because sometimes it is the so-called troublemaker who is not the one who is actually the most troublesome member of a dyad, cautious interpersonal therapists will not view passive-aggression as entirely the MO (responsibility) of one individual when it is in fact partially provoked and dictated by others/circumstances. Attuned therapists seek out possible contributions of various externals such as other people and events acting as provocateurs or enablers in a given situation so that they can make certain that, as Brandt says, "victims themselves are not unconsciously enforcing the very behaviors [they are] hoping to be rid of."[6]

A passive-aggressive patient left treatment because his therapist missed how the patient's partner and professed victim was contributing to the problem by downplaying his own contribution to the patient's passive-aggression by covering over his own antagonistic actions with a series of glib rationalizations based on the specious claim that "everyone does thus and so," e.g., cheats on a spouse, and "anyone who says otherwise is lying."

It is difficult to help couples develop interpersonal insight without seeming to be critical of, or biased against, one, if not both, of the two individuals in the dyad. Trying to break through this barrier, therapists like Beck have their patients *role-play*. In role playing each individual sees the other's position, and its associated difficulties, and "considers [and acts-out] alternative, more adaptive, responses, all without being critical to the point of leading one or both individuals in a given relationship to feel diminished."[7]

Other therapists try to avoid being critical/seeming to be biased toward one person by *treating passive-aggressives in group therapy* in the belief, not always justified, that patients accept criticism better from peers than they do from such authority as a therapist.

Some therapists suggest *reading assignments* in (self-help) books in the belief that self-help books are sufficiently impersonal and written for a large enough audience to avoid the fatal flaw of at least to seemingly be personally insulting, accusatory, and humiliating to one person in a dyad, while letting the other off the hook.

Recommending Ending the Relationship

Some therapists think that at times separation is a reasonable/admirable goal, while others routinely see separation as a failure both of a relationship and of therapy. With certain exceptions, as when there is strong evidence for severe physical or emotional abuse, therapists should think twice about advocating separation—and even hinting at that as a solution. To avoid being set up by passive-aggressive patients, who express their (transference) hostility by setting traps for an unwary therapist, therapists should leave the final decision to separate (or not) up to the people involved, and then go no further in intervening than offering to help the individual(s) involved implement whatever decisions they first make on their own. This way, a patient meets his or her own goal, not one determined primarily by someone else, in too many cases someone, perhaps even a therapist, who knows little to nothing about what the contributory factors in a given dyadic relationship in fact happen to be.

Problematic Negative Passive-Aggressive Fallout

Many people, including spouses, families, friends, peers, employers, and employees of passive-aggressive individuals routinely complain that the passive-aggressives they know and often love can be a challenge to get along with. Even some passive-aggressives themselves admit of the difficulties they are aware of causing for others, only they can't or won't stop doing that.

Passive-aggressives often appear indecisive; unable to be satisfied; rejecting; and hypercritical as they, as Fenichel says, "use objects for relief of inner conflicts [, and] that inevitably leads to impaired object relationships."[8] Their imperiled relationships are in particular characterized by the targets of passive-aggression blaming themselves for their own discomfort, inappropriately asking themselves, "Have I done something to cause him offense? to start an argument? to hurt her feelings?" and/or, "Have I said too much, and in some ways gone too far?" only to then routinely conclude that, although in reality it is the passive-aggressive who is the one being provocative, "It is I who, although in actuality the victim, feel inappropriately guilty about my having provoked that person to seemingly be victimizing me."

Fussy passive-aggressives catch others up in relational patterns where they think they are the only ones who can be completely good/right; *hypercritical* passive-aggressives annoy others by being accusative to them; *hypersensitive* passive-aggressives routinely act paranoid as they see others' neutral comments as deliberately intended criticisms; *defiant* passive-aggressive bumbling renders others helpless; calculated *shyness* (sometimes excused as relational anxiety they can't overcome) disrupts potentially workable relationships via causing distancing; assumptions and misimpressions they have of who others are and what others are thinking leads either to disengagement or to spousal abuse; and unnecessary *complaints* about lack of exclusivity on the part of partners of married passive-aggressives can foster paranoia whose content is excessive jealousy where the individuals imagine the possibility that a spouse is cheating on them.

As overly *orderly* individuals, some passive-aggressives become excessively prudent, conventional and tidy, e.g., in cleaning up they put things in places where nobody can find them.

Stubborn passive-aggressives tell us in essence, "Just see if you can get me to do or stop doing something" accompanied by various forms of rebelliousness that readily makes them off-putting, bossy and demanding, individuals.

A *reluctance to express positive feelings* often makes passive-aggressives seem aloof and uncommunicative to their spouses. At times as a result, sexual activity slows or stops.

Passive-aggressive *OCPD-like ritualism* generally cannot help but be annoying—by making others uncomfortable, restless, unable to any longer concentrate on what they should be thinking and doing, and/or bored to the point that they defensively become lost in their own diverting fantasies. Excessive *intellectualizing* on the part of OCPD passive-aggressives may culminate in their developing a thought-through interpersonal style where reason, not warm support, prevails.

As *perfectionists*, some passive-aggressives often go on to become personally/politically absolutely correct individuals who devalue others often around something minor to which they themselves assign major significance, too often as if trivialities are the one and only yardstick by which all concerned should, and do, measure their value and solidity. This can even culminate in their becoming tyrannical people who trend toward being overly scrupulous, arbitrary, critical, argumentative, and controlling, as they come to value principle over people, including over common sense and over their own and other people's humanity, disregarding their own and their victims' comfort, needs, well-being, and overall welfare.

When perfectionism turns passive-aggressives into sadistic individuals who ultimately embrace correctives first and only, making those a substitute for the humanity of all concerned, passive-aggressives tend to be seen as depriving others of what even they themselves feel others logically should have, doing so based on the use of jerrybuilt principles that they concoct for purposes of rationalization of their own inhumanity and inhumane views. As one result, they reject people who are imperfect as lovers because they themselves look not for Mr. Right, but for Mr. Impossibly Perfect, and they dismiss friends and coworkers as not good enough to survive their scrutiny because these others aren't as flawless as they would want them to be. In this overall perfectionism it is often the little (supposedly negative) things others say and do that come to count the most. In one case, it was, "I like this guy, but I can't get past brooding about his name being 'Peter.' How could I introduce him to my friends with his having a name like that?" The individual who said this also refused a perfectly good offer of marriage because the man himself "spoke crudely," by which she meant that he pronounced Russian composers' names incorrectly. She was always looking for that ideal partner, yet finding everyone who came her way to be wanting in some (often realistically unimportant but deal-breaking) respect, e.g. "he is too much the artisan, and too little the artist."

It is such perfectionism that makes these passive-aggressives into serial dating men or women—people who have become uncompromising in their negativity because they subject relationships, as they do all things, to an assessment based on fixed, absolute, dichotomies of their own devising, where, as far as they are concerned, as with all dichotomies, there is no viable middle ground, only two extremes, each unpalatable, and therefore on bipolar grounds, each unacceptable.

Needing to always be the one in control, some perfectionists proclaim themselves omniscient individuals who leave little or no room for the appreciation and acceptance of anyone else's legitimately formed rationally maintained points of view when these differ from their own. There is an intolerance of others that often takes the form of their advancing ad hominem putdowns, where they become somewhat, if not highly, contentious toward others' ideas and positions, often dubbing others "complete idiots," especially when it comes to matters of politics and religion. This is not always because of the principle they stand for; it is sometimes because of who they fundamentally believe themselves to be.

Perfectionistic passive-aggressives often become absolutistic individuals who leave no room for compromise as they hold others in low esteem—unless others meet some exacting, but trivial and arbitrary, standards, which they impose unilaterally. Mostly they use matters of correctness, honor, propriety, and etiquette as reasons to deselect, that is, to overlook, ignore, and remove themselves from, others who are in fact perfectly adequate, and are actually so in many, often overlooked but still significant respects.

As excessively competitive individuals, some passive-aggressives routinely involve others in their own personal need to assert superiority. As Fenichel suggests, in the context of describing OCPDs, these individuals are preoccupied with issues of "Which of us will win [and] which of us is the stronger?" At times, they can be passive toward others (at least at first), but they are that way only in anticipation of ultimately taking over and overthrowing others; e.g., "passive toward the master for the purpose of later becoming the master himself."[9]

As they are also competitive, many passive-aggressive individuals are motivated to refuse to compromise because to them compromise involves consideration for, and the acceptance of equality with, others, with equality as a position seeming to be inherently, no arguments accepted, disappointingly inferior to superiority.

Positive Aspects

Here I attempt to counterbalance the above partial listing of passive-aggressive's troublesome qualities vis-á-vis others with a partial list of their positives and so the positive effects they can have on others and on the world. My goal is to emphasize how passive-aggression isn't all bad because there are some good things associated with it. Their positive qualities include:

- Rigidity. Fastidious, e.g., overly neat and clean, passive-aggressives can provide a model for organization which although it has features of rigidity can in the long run facilitate rather than stifle creativity and progress. A too rigid morality can make passive-aggressives admirably highly principled, although admittedly it can be annoying to others due to sanctimoniousness and the refusal to compromise just in order to be able to say "I stick with my principles no matter what, and in particular so that I can be viewed as highly honorable, and admirably upright and trustworthy."

- Frugality and hoarding tendencies. This may involve saving for hard times. Hoarding only becomes negative when it is seriously at the expense of self and/or others, e.g., when a person fills up the house with things nobody really needs and puts persons out to make room for objects. But it can be positive when it involves the admirable trait of saving up now for hard times to come.

- Perfectionism. Perfectionistic passive-aggressives who manifest a rigid pre-occupation with details, and stiffness/formalism amounting to being overly disciplined and unbending, can be more productive than those who are too relaxed and are so in situations that fail because they don't require much in the way of flexibility.

- Omniscience. This can give passive-aggressives a know-it-all quality that can actually make them good scholars/leaders, particularly when they are leading those populations who respond positively to the organization and sense of certainty of the mind-made-up, even to the point of becoming in some ways unhealthily inflexible themselves. The passive-aggressive "I know better than you" view can lead to passive-aggressives being steadfast chiefs and good bosses who guide, and gurus to rally around who can protect/influence others when others do in fact get out of line. And when they are being arbitrary they can provide superficially good answers to tough questions, seeming platforms in space that help those of us who may be floundering, as they instead establish a sensible, doable, creative, and workable life plan. They make especially good leaders when they know when to retreat strategically after having gone too far arbitrarily.

- Controlling tendencies. Controlling passive-aggressives can set firm, if excessively arbitrary, limits on others. A controlling spouse who jumps in to disagree all the time can sometimes save the other spouse from doing things that he or she will later regret. The annoying passive-aggressive who always says "turn down the heat you are burning the onions" may save our breakfast (at the expense of cowing us into abject, unwelcome, submission).

- Workaholism. This can model a strong work ethic for others leading them on to become a strong, productive worker/employee.

- Withholding. This when in the form of indecisiveness can stave off the making of bad decisions in situations that others incorrectly/prematurely misidentify as being of an urgent nature.

- Vacillating. Passive-aggressives whose aggression is marked by hostile vacillation consisting of seeing all sides of an issue can be overall more perspicacious than paralytic as long as they contribute to the healthful "evolutionary growth" of the thinking of all concerned

- Doubting. Doubting passive-aggressives can, via delay, help themselves and others avoid making serious and sometimes fatal mistakes that are the product of impulsivity.

- Slowness and stickiness. This when not a passive-aggressive attack that can lead to a virtual paralysis of forward movement can result in a protective sensible cautiousness on those fronts where impulsivity is the enemy.

- Punctiliousness. This can account for being sensibly reliable and take the valuable form of being highly motivated.
- Stubbornness and argumentativeness. This can enhance functionality in those situations when others' opposition is powerful but misguided, accounting for sanguine obstinacy, sometimes cultivating useful social advocacy, where one resists pressures from, and refuses to succumb to those who in fact are, charlatans.
- Worrisomeness. When this doesn't amount to unproductive fretting about minor issues it can provide the basis for life-saving prompt/early interventions
- Sadistic tendencies. Empty torturing of others in the form of harsh rules and regulations rigidly enforced can on the bright side spin off regulations that encourage (force) others to get things done.

CHAPTER FIFTEEN

Transference and Countertransference Issues

Transference = the patient's feelings about his or her doctor/therapist based on the patient's characteristic (idiosyncratic) misinterpretations of the reality of who others, such as the therapist, are and what they say and do.

Negative transference in particular almost always appears to cloud and seriously compromise the treatment of passive-aggressives. And the exact complexion of this (negative) transference is determined by the same factors that determine the passive-aggressive pathology itself, including the patient's anger triggers, as well as his or her core conflicts, and the special defense mechanisms that the individual employs to deal with these and related matters.

Transference negativity (anger) making patients that much harder to treat originates in:

Comorbidity (Associated Disorders)

As Wetzler puts it, "passive-aggression [needs to be] studied in the context of other psychiatric problems [including] comorbidities."[1] Thus:

Paranoid passive-aggressives get angry at their therapists because they suspect their therapist's motives. Perhaps they believe that the therapist is siding with such of the enemy as a partner with whom the patient is fighting. And so they resist treatment for so-called "rational reasons"—as they come to believe their resistances to therapy are warranted due to being self-protective. Also, a given therapist's neutrality becomes instead a rejection of *the patient*; friendliness an invasion; attempts at doing cognitive work a being critical of how and what they as patients already think; behavioral interventions as annoyingly, even dangerously, meddlesome; and offers of support as babying, e.g., just another example of a typical therapist infantilizing his or her patients. In the double bind, which passive-aggressive patients almost always put their therapists in, when it comes down to the problems paranoid passive-aggressives have with taking offered advice, the therapist who gives even the best advice to such a patient is always in danger of being held responsible if things go wrong, while the therapist who doesn't offer specific suggestions is in danger of being thought of as deliberately neglectful.

Depressed passive-aggressives sulk because they feel too personally unworthy to be helped. Feeling as if all is lost from the start, patients respond to offers of help with, "Why bother; if you don't give up trying with me right now, you are just wasting time, mine and yours."

Narcissistic passive-aggressives, feeling entitled to direct and immediate satisfaction, when faced with the necessary frustrations of therapy (usually having to do with the patient being asked to curtail his or her acting out) grouse vocally that they are not being treated right, even humanely, which often means that they feel that they are being inadequately gratified on some important level. Feeling deserving of special (e.g., more permissive) handling, patients react negatively to having to follow the basic rules of therapy, instead expecting these to be bent to suit their tastes, and meet their special needs.

Liking themselves just the way they are, they resist change, and misinterpret being asked to alter their behavior, seeing this, like any demand made upon them, as a possible threat to who they are and what they stand for, including a threat to their preferred identity, e.g., "I am already perfect just the way I am" and so I am "reluctant to give up on being me."

Obsessive-compulsive passive-aggressives have control issues that lead them to stubbornly fight therapists' interventions by turning what should be a cooperative working venture into a mutually antagonistic struggle. So they come late to, or fail to keep, their appointments; do not pay the fee, or pay but not on time; and otherwise oppose, tease, and frustrate the therapist in response to perceived or actual therapist expectations of them— expectations that OCPD passive-aggressives deem unacceptable or inappropriate, however rational these expectations happen to be, or just because these are the way they are.

Histrionic passive-aggressives feeling competitive with the therapist, try to guide their own treatment instead of being guided by it. Aroused aggression comes from feeling angry that not they, but their therapists, are "the one in charge," and therefore they are not the ones "on top."

Sadistic passive-aggressives sense therapist vulnerability which leads them to become, in Millon and Davis's terms, more "abrasive" than "circuitous."[2] And *masochistic* passive-aggressives become angry partly tactically: because they sense that this is a good way for them to provoke the punishment (e.g., the rejection) they feel that they deserve (and so hope they will get).

Core Conflicts (Revived)

In this realm, conflicts around issues related to dependency, control, and competition almost always rule. Patients with problems related to *dependency* too readily feel rejected by something the therapist does or does not do for them meaning "you don't love me."

Patients with problems related to independence fearful of being *controlled* become annoyed due to feeling that all therapeutic suggestions made are being imposed upon them as commands from without. In response, the patients angrily take charge of the proceedings by figuratively assigning the therapist the patient role then evaluating the therapist—as their way to express their annoyance over being evaluated by him or her. Wishing to control the therapist, they do exactly the opposite of what they perceive the therapist expects of them. They stubbornly resist offered insight, or, if they think the therapist wants to curb insight, they demand it, announcing that their main if not only intention is to bare their soul in a deeply emotional learning experience. Or they absorb everything but refuse to apply it—as Millon (1981) puts it, "The patients . . . verbally appreciate the therapist's perceptiveness but [do] not alter their attitudes at all."[3] Some absorb everything but misuse what they learn. Instead of applying insight to improve, they use it to stay the same, employing self-knowledge to rationalize their behavior, thoroughly understanding themselves but using their developing insight as a substitute for change. For example, patients often (conveniently) cite early developmental conflicts as a reason for present-day hostility they have no real intention of relinquishing. Some patients quit therapy to show the therapist that they can do it alone. They then call to say that they got better without therapy—just to prove to the therapist that he or she is neither relevant nor needed, that is, "to show you how independence is one of my most admirable features."

A patient felt thrown out of therapy because his therapist recommended time-limited treatment ("short-term therapy" with a preset termination date incorporating 12 sessions exactly). So this patient sought the opinion of another therapist, who suggested long-term treatment (without a preset termination date). But then, when this new therapist told her that she actually needed to come three times a week indefinitely to undergo a full psychoanalysis, she complained that clearly her therapist only had his self-interest at heart; for he seemed to want not a patient but a lifetime annuity.

While *noncompetitive* passive-aggressive patients bask in the reflected glory of the "big doctor," *competitive* passive-aggressive patients actively seek out someone not well-trained and hardly experienced—because for them someone like that is far less intimidating.

Often competitive patients sneer at a therapist's presumed lack of training to humble him or her further, just the way they feel humbled by him or her. They ask for therapists' disclosures about professional qualifications, marital status, or sexual orientation less because they want to know about these things, and more to embarrass the therapist as being an amateur, e.g., an inadequate healer due to having compromised credentials. For every therapist who is uncertain whether to disclose he is gay or she is a lesbian, there is a passive-aggressive patient who knows that by simply asking these questions (without actually wanting to know the answers) he or she is putting the therapist in the hot seat, while enjoying every minute of it.

Another humbling behavior is devaluing therapy itself. Frequently heard is, "Pay for something that is all talk?" or "Isn't it true that you doctors are only interested in the money?"

Patients with problems related to competition often make therapy into a contest where they fear both winning and losing. When they do well, fearing winning, they have a negative response and quit treatment; when they do badly, fearing losing, they stay in treatment so that they can turn things around. Those who fear winning self-efface, becoming unduly, and hypocritically, deferential to the therapist, doing what they are told to do while resenting it to the point that they make certain that most or all therapeutic efforts are unproductive. Those who fear losing assume parity with the therapist in order to undermine therapeutic authority and expertise by turning the therapeutic relationship into an almost personal one where they go on to debate with the therapist as equals, thereby undermining therapeutic authority and so effectiveness. They sabotage their therapy by allowing their reluctance to pay for it to prevail because, as they see it, the therapist already has enough money—more than they have, and way over what he or she needs to earn a good living. A patient of mine stopped therapy because, as she said, she couldn't afford it. She then made a serious near-fatal suicide attempt as her way of attacking me, her therapist, for charging much and doing little. A social worker involved in the case discovered that in fact she was a multimillionaire. When confronted by her many millions she shot back, "Yes, that's true; but that's money I am saving for my old age."

Defenses Employed

Expectedly, passive-aggressives also draw upon their usual repertory of *defenses* to influence their therapy and the therapist. Using *reaction formation* they initially present themselves as sweet and cooperative patients, doing so all the better to set the stage for sabotaging treatment. Those who *do and undo* may in therapy take one step back for every step forward, seeming to get better just before seeming to get worse. Some *identify* with the therapist as aggressor and retaliate exactly in kind for what they feel has been, and is being, done to them.

As in life, where they follow the eye-for-an-eye code of Hammurabi, they slavishly submit to the talion principle: that in therapy patients who fear rejection of their dependency needs, identifying with the therapist-aggressor, readily threaten the therapist in his or her pocketbook by not paying on time, or at all; or, again identifying with the therapist-aggressor, readily agree to participate in treatment but strictly on their own terms, so that to be on top and have the upper hand they arrive in the office not when the hour is scheduled to start, but when it is convenient for them to come. Or, citing a spurious or modest emergency, without giving it a second thought, they cancel a session at the last minute. Patients deal with their various fears of being cooperative by undermining therapy by doing then undoing the good things they have done, having become alternatively (but unproductively) submissive then and excessively (but counterproductively) competitive, even rebellious, then submissive once again.

An OCPD passive-aggressive patient, angry with the therapist for setting all the rules, especially those related to time, routinely using the defense of doing and undoing, called the therapist before each appointment to double check on the hour of the session, although he already knew it perfectly well. Then he forgot to write the time down, so that he had to call to double-check again. Then he called to say that he was just leaving for the therapist's office—when he was supposed to be arriving. En route, he called once more to say that the traffic was bad and so he would be even later than anticipated. Then he called to say that he was down the block and would be there as soon as he could find a parking space. Ultimately he arrived too late for the start of his appointment; blamed his lateness on his obsessive-compulsiveness; and then, although he was told the therapist was completely booked for the rest of the day, asked for a full session, right then and there.

Using the Therapeutic Relationship (Transference) Therapeutically

The therapeutic process starts with outlining the basic rules of therapy—the facts of life for patients in psychotherapy with a particular therapist. Too many therapists forget to be clear about these rules and then blame, and get angry with, their patients for not following them. Perhaps the rules should be presented dispassionately and so in a nonthreatening manner right from the start, as therapists warn their patients that they will interrupt therapy if the patient does not follow the rules substantially. But according to other therapists, there is plenty of time for caveats, that is, to issue warnings, while issuing them in the beginning only gives passive-aggressive patients big ideas up front—on how to break them. In any event, therapists should not outline the basic rules of therapy as a vehicle for the (in advance) expression of hostility towards their patients. For example, they should not set forth the terms of a therapeutic contract as a way to sadistically (and suggestively) list possible transgressions before the patient has even had a chance to transgress. Limits on what resistance is acceptable might however be clearly delineated right from the start. Therapists might say to selected patients, "I need to be paid on time because that is how I make my living," or "Lateness is not acceptable because of the way I schedule my day."

Therapists should use the transference (1) diagnostically, to discover what the patient's real interpersonal problems are—as distinct from what all concerned might initially think that they happen to be, and (2) therapeutically, interpretively, to clarify the patient's negative (and sometimes even positive) repetitive behaviors and so to capture the essence of the patient's problem with passive-aggression here made even clearer as their specific relevant problems appear in the relationship with the therapist.

Involving the patient in a kind of role reversal can promote patient-therapist empathy and thus therapeutic accomplishment. When a patient came 30 minutes late, his therapist said, "I am uncertain as to whether to run overtime or stop on schedule, and if I stop on schedule whether or not to make up the time in a later session, and whether or not to charge you for lost minutes. What do you think?" The patient responded, "I deserve the extra time because it wasn't my fault that the train was late," so the therapist added some of the lost minutes back that day and some of them at a later time. Perhaps if the patient had responded, "Even though I knew she was making me late, I didn't think it kind to get rid of a chatty coworker who insisted on showing me her dog pictures," the therapist might have responded differently. She might have given the patient not a longer session but a different/deeper interpretation (this time, about masochism).

Therapists can resolve transference problems with patients not only by what the therapist says but also by what the therapist does. In particular, the therapist should him or herself be overtly non-passive-aggressive in order to make a healthy role model for the passive-aggressive patient. Therapists who do not respond to a patient's little provocations but are instead forgiving, and nonjudgmental under fire, are thereby as corrective as they possibly can be given the circumstances, and so will ultimately prevail therapeutically—not only by the cleverness of their formulations, but also by the sincerity and humanity of their overall attitudes regarding the possibly troubled therapeutic relationship.

Countertransference Issues

Countertransference may be of the nonparticipating or participating type, as follows:

Nonparticipating Countertransference

Nonparticipating countertransference is a countertransference-like response mainly or entirely provoked by the patient. This happens when the passive-aggressive patient interacting with a relatively healthy well-trained therapist causes the therapist to overreact in human fashion, that is, by feeling and manifesting a degree of anxiety and hostility that overflows into the therapeutic hour because the therapist is not fully able to control how he or she truly feels. In this form of countertransference, relatively healthy therapists, being human, feel and act almost exactly like all the other victims of passive-aggressives, precisely as described throughout.

The remedies for these "victim therapists" are basically the same as the remedies for any victim of passive-aggressives. Therapists as transference "victims" of passive-aggressives can choose between being unilaterally forbearing, remaining emotionally detached to avoid overt struggles, or (generally the most appropriate response for therapists) clarifying the patient's behavior by interpreting it psychodynamically, cognitively, and/or interpersonally.

A week before a psychiatrist was about to take over a large inpatient service, his mother, whose closest friend had a son hospitalized on the unit, visited her friend and the friend's son in that hospital, then introduced herself to all the doctor's patients-to-be as "the mother of your new doctor." The patients, using this as an opportunity to humble feared authority, attempted to humiliate the doctor when he arrived on the job by making him somehow responsible for, and in some ways a "chip off the old block of," what they thought to be his mother's infantilizing behavior. But instead of overreacting and getting defensive, the doctor simply recognized what the patients were trying to do and stepped aside. Instead of buying into his patients' hostility, and instead of feeling bad about and being embarrassed by it, he simply pointed out that he and his mother were two different people, that he should not be judged, either positively or negatively, according to her thoughts and actions, and that, anyway, it made no real sense for him to get caught up in something that was clearly not his problem or of his doing in any meaningful way.

It is not enough just to identify that the patient is provoking the therapist and to then react therapeutically. The therapist must also tell the patient the details about what has been learned, and so about what needs to be changed, and how to go about changing it. Here, as always, the therapist's "gut reaction" to a patient's passive-aggressive behavior helps identify problem interactions patients likely manifest *outside* of therapy. What emerges outside the therapy hour can be harnessed to become grist for the interpretative mill overall.

Participating Countertransference

I now discuss a topic not usually emphasized in the literature: how therapists, themselves passive-aggressive, can react, relatively unprovoked, to a patient in a way that mostly reflects the therapist's own primary passive-aggressive psychopathology. The therapist's response involves psychopathology brought to life in the therapist taking the form of the therapist's reaction to his or her patient.

Indirect Anger Aroused Via Touching Upon Specific Triggers

Masochistic passive-aggressive therapists can respond to provocations with indirect hostility consisting of being overly self-sacrificial. After fuming all the while about "how tough this patient is to treat," they strike out, or, as they come to see it, strike back, passive-aggressively. Too often the therapist, uncomfortable with a patient who runs up bills and keeps promising to pay but never does, or whose patient treats him or her emotionally like a punching bag in one realm or in several venues, instead of saying something about that, continues to work with the patient in therapy and then acts out his or her anger indirectly by hurting the patient in subtle ways, ways that are actually more harmful than open outbursts or clean termination would be. Not atypically, such therapists wind up avenging themselves on such patients by sedating them out of their "bad" behavior, e.g., using pharmacotherapy when psychotherapy alone is indicated, or is indicated not instead of, but in addition to, pharmacotherapy.

Sadistic passive-aggressive therapists often make scheduling issues a vehicle for their indirect hostility. For example, one such therapist insisted a patient attend sessions twice a week when the patient could afford, and needed to go, only once. Then instead of putting the patient on a fixed schedule, he assigned him different therapy hours every week. The therapist also would not let the patient take a vacation except when the therapist took one, even though the patient's boss would only allow the patient time off when he, the boss, closed down the shop for his own personal vacation. Finally, the therapist made the patient come during the day, although the patient had a full-time job that made it impossible for him to attend therapy sessions during business hours.

Also in the realm of unprovoked negative (passive-aggressive) countertransference is how a sadistic therapist talked about himself in a way that deprived his patients of the time they were paying for to talk about themselves. As a patient who went to a therapist to determine whether he needed psychotherapy commented after the doctor made idle talk about his own interest in sports, "I'm sick and I want to talk about me. I don't get better by hearing him talk about his kids playing volleyball."

In some cases, sadistic therapists devalue their patients subtly by giving them the advice that would be right for the therapist, as if the therapist, not the patient, were the one needing/in treatment. Some of these therapists make off-the-cuff recommendations that hurtfully undermine their patients' relationships outside of therapy. They might encourage patients to get their anger out regardless of the effect that that anger has on others. Excessive permissiveness, although in some cases useful, e.g., for guilty obsessive-compulsive patients, can be hostile and uncaring, as when OCPD passive-aggressives are being treated. Here what is intended to be affirming can in fact amount to supporting and condoning pathology that therapists should be attempting to relieve.

While some therapists sadistically take the patient's side when it is that side of the patient that needs challenging, others just as sadistically side not with the patient but with a patient's antagonists—as did the therapist who sided with parents who were calling a normal child oppositional when the child was in fact merely responding appropriately to his difficult parents. This same therapist once suggested to the wife of an actually very abusive husband, "He did nothing, you are imagining it all. Try being a little nicer to him and you will see how well that works."

Sadistic passive-aggressive therapists can make their patients feel bad or guilty by saying, in a very critical tone, "This is what you should not have done" rather than "This is what you might do."

Sadistic therapists hurt the patient in the guise of making unnecessary inappropriately harsh and/or wrong diagnoses, as did one therapist who called a patient paranoid although she had perfectly good reasons for being suspicious and for feeling persecuted. Some therapists, sadistically undermining, call paranoid patients depressed when the problem involves a more serious paranoid world view consisting of a need to see persecution everywhere in their lives.

Sadistic therapists may impart insight to in effect snipe at the patient in an apparently justified, they believe, civilized manner. A passive-aggressive man might need to know that he is too close to, or just like, his mother, but the patient cannot make use of what he learns if the information is conveyed to him in a critical manner so that he gets the impression that the therapist thinks that he is an infantile "momma's boy." Sadistic therapists hurtfully go deep in their interpretations less to reveal the unknown to the patient than to deliberately, if unconsciously, use an "aha moment" to make the patient squirm.

Sadistic passive-aggressive therapists not infrequently indulge in the passive-aggressive tactic of double binding their patients. For example, they ask patients to speak freely only to make it clear that they dislike what the patients have said thusly to criticize the patients for having said it, e.g., to use the patients' complaints about the treatment they are getting as evidence of negativism that necessitates either even more therapy, or an interruption of treatment.

Another tactic sadistic passive-aggressive therapists employ is using the patient as a pawn the therapist moves about to act out the therapist's own hostility to significant others in the therapist's own life. Unable to get angry with their own partners, they get their patients to live out their anger for them, now with the patient's own wife, husband, or family members. They typically do this by siding with a passive-aggressive patient in his or her passive-aggressive (and so un-called for) interpersonal struggles with a family member—identifying with the patient only to further provoke, and even enjoy, all the fireworks.

Sadistic passive-aggressive therapists often rationalize this (acting out of their own negativity) by claiming that what they do is helpful, not hurtful, and therapeutic, not antitherapeutic, for the patient. When a patient met her analyst at a professional meeting, the analyst looked away and refused to acknowledge the patient's presence in order not to "contaminate the transference."Another time the analyst said nothing when the patient wished him a happy holiday. The analyst believed that remaining silent was a good idea, for it avoided getting too close to, and so being too seductive toward, his patient.

Indirect Anger Reflective of Aroused Habitual Defensiveness

Hostile *dependent* therapists may, *in essence identifying with the aggressor-patient*, demand "an eye for an eye." A mother was late for her baby's appointment with a pediatric psychiatrist because she was delayed in traffic on her way to having her child evaluated. Thinking his patient had deliberately avoided him, and angry that his fee might not be paid because the time was not used, the therapist avoided his patient back, doing so by telling her, "I cannot see you today; make another appointment—only, the next one I have available is three months from now." His thinking was that anything the mother could do to him he could do to her back, and one better. Some therapists punitively terminate a patient who does not pay on time or comes late to sessions—just to do the rejecting actively, instead of being terminated by, that is rejected by, the patient, passively.

Indirect Anger Reflective of Aroused Core Conflicts

Dependent passive-aggressive therapists viewing all patients as a source of needed funds can antagonistically hang on to their patients in a way that is ultimately destructive to the doctor-patient relationship. A hostile-dependent therapist accepted a patient for short-term therapy and then at the end of the last scheduled session kept the patient coming, as the patient put it, "Kept me in his clutches" by strongly suggesting that the patient "continue anyway because not everything had yet been uncovered/resolved."

Controlling passive-aggressive therapists, thinking that they alone know what is good for the patient, care neither about what the patient nor about what his or her family really need or want. For example, one therapist asked a medical student he was treating, "What field do you want to go into?" "Dermatology" was his answer, to which the therapist replied, "That's crazy, you should go into anesthesia instead, that's where all the money is." The patient complied, resented it ever afterward, and did poorly professionally much of his career.

Controlling passive-aggressive therapists can become too easily exasperated with a patient reluctant to change and in a way that satisfies them. One therapist told such a patient, "I don't know if you can't, or you won't, but you have to change," seemingly meant as a valid therapeutic exhortation, when in fact it was just a crude substitute for understanding the problem at hand and attempting to resolve it using gentler methods.

Competitive passive-aggressive therapists may unconsciously try to humble their patients due to perceiving them as rivals. They may humble them by criticizing them for having the very symptoms for which they entered treatment in the first place. Some give interpretations not to impart insight but to impress their patients with how smart (and one up) they, the therapists, are. For example, one theorist, without confirming evidence, proudly told a patient, "You have five boxes of on-sale laundry detergent stored in your garage because you are an anal compulsive." Some devalue their patients by viewing them as being always and entirely responsible for their own (the patient's) fate, even when they are at least partly passive victims of their (medical) circumstances. Such therapists discount the impact of others on the patient's life and instead resolutely emphasize individual responsibility, no matter what. They identify and condemn the patient as the aggressor when he or she is in fact, partly or solely, the victim. This happened when a patient's Mother's Day flowers arrived on the Monday after the holiday. When the patient got mad and threatened to personally boycott the flower store, his analyst told him that he was overreacting, as usual, and should just let it go.

Still, other competitive therapists give psychoactive medication not to treat but to humiliate patients, in effect saying, "You don't have what it takes to work your problem out."

Therapists who envy their patients' success make jokes to other therapists like, "I hate to see my patients doing better than I." Such therapists may even do (big or little) things unconsciously to cause their patients to fail, ranging from giving advice that actually holds their patients back to suggesting that the patient take action that is almost predictably self- and other-destructive, often because the therapist gives the patient suggestions before all the facts are in. An older man just getting over a relationship with a young woman told his psychiatrist that he and another equally young woman, someone the patient had just met, were planning to get engaged/married. The therapist, before inquiring further, told him that women who were that young were just out for his money, and advised the patient against the match. If the therapist had bothered to ask, he would have learned that this particular young woman was an exceptional person truly in love with the older man. The patient quit therapy, went through with the "marriage," and at present writing is still with his wife after over 30 years. (Only later did the patient discover something about the therapist that made him realize that the therapist's judgment in matters of the heart was compromised, and even more questionable than anyone might have reasonably previously thought. For the therapist was in love with a patient of his own, and, not even trying to hide it, pursued her actively, without shame, and enthusiastically tried to marry her—doing so in full view of his own wife, as well as of the entire professional community.)

Competitive therapists humble their patients as much by what they leave unsaid as by what they actually do/say. They "forget" to assess what is healthy and right about a given patient and justify that omission by their own almost entirely "problem-oriented focus." They fail to offer congratulations when in order, and justify that as being in the service of therapeutic neutrality.

They may use silence not therapeutically, but in a disapproving way, deliberately, if unconsciously intending to lead the patient on to think, "My therapist is saying nothing to/about me because he/she has nothing good to say."

In conclusion, not infrequently, problematical countertransference characterized by dependent, controlling, and competitive core conflicts can cause therapy to deteriorate into a sadomasochistic relationship between the patient and the therapist, with the therapist acting in a less than professional passive-aggressive way—one that includes blaming the patient for everything that goes wrong.

Management

Two possibilities exist for resolving difficult transference-counter transference issues. These apply to problems that arise in a patient's daily life as well as to problems that arise in the course of therapy.

Resolution

Personal therapy, itself heavy on interpretation, may be indicated for therapists themselves manifesting difficult countertransference problems of their own.

Interrupting Therapy

Sometimes, in spite of the best intentions all around, therapy has to be interrupted, because it is not going well, or anywhere. If this is indicated, patients should be given the opportunity to return for more treatment, perhaps after a time for reflection. "Premature" termination is not always such a bad thing. Many passive-aggressive patients are too stubborn to learn much in the presence of the therapist. Their therapy seems to end with the therapist in despair and the patient furious about being thrown out. Follow-up, however, often tells quite another story. Some of these patients, especially those who have been in therapy for a substantial amount of time, come to best appreciate their therapist's endeavors after "therapy is over" and actually even do their best therapeutic work after termination of treatment. This is when they "no longer have the therapist to kick around"—when guilt about how shabbily the patient treated the therapist appears, and the patient decides to make amends by doing some real therapeutic work, however belatedly, on his or her own, as a tribute to his or her therapist. Perhaps as Reich says, "a definite dissolution of the masochistic character cannot take place until the patient has led an economic work and love life for a considerable period of time, that is, until long after the conclusion of the treatment."[4] If patients who have such a delayed positive therapeutic response return for treatment, they often do so as motivated and cooperative individuals—ready to resume therapy in a more productive frame of mind, and to produce better therapeutic results this time around.

CHAPTER SIXTEEN

Victims of Passive-Aggression

As Burns and Epstein suggest, "passive-aggression should be studied as a *dyadic* problem as well as an individual phenomenon."[1] That means in part that whenever possible, therapists should attend not only to passive-aggressive patients themselves but also to those they affect—their victims, who, as previously mentioned, may be nonparticipating (hapless) or enabling (part of the process).

Victims of passive-aggressives need to help create a better relationship with those who are being passive-aggressive to them. They can attempt to meet this goal by developing a specific action plan crafted to deal with the one or more passive-aggressives in their lives. But instead of taking corrective steps, many such victims do nothing. They think, "I can handle it on my own." True, it is difficult to deal with becoming a victim of passive-aggressives because passive-aggressives tend to create a honeymoon period during which time they entrap others into a relationship. At the beginning of a relationship, passive-aggressives are on their best behavior. For they hope to forge positive interpersonal bonds that will survive the abuse the passive-aggressive plans for later. Still their victims can theoretically at least find ways to survive the onslaught passive-aggressives plan for later, even ones consistent with individual preference, personal psychological comfort, and individual circumstances, such as the victim's age and financial wherewithal.

In particular, passive, nonparticipant, "innocent," or true victims of passive-aggressives need help with:

1. identifying others' passive-aggression;
2. understanding others' passive-aggression through and through;

3. identifying and understanding their own, often idiosyncratic, responses to passive-aggressives and refining/reconsidering this response, all in preparation for;

4. creating a sensible doable action plan for handling themselves better via listing steps that can be taken to more effectively manage the passive-aggressives in their lives.

One: Identifying Others' Passive-Aggression

Victims who recognize that passive-aggression is targeting them are in the best possible position to deal with it by acting correctively,

Identifying passive-aggression starts with emerging from denial, in which victims overlook assaults and their harmful personal effects. It means recognizing that some passive-aggressive behaviors that look superficially benign can in fact be deeply hostile. Recognizing hidden passive-aggression requires inferring, or mind-reading, the motives of another, and that usually requires becoming more, not less, paranoid, and often requires blaming loved ones most victims would prefer to spare. To develop recognition skills, victims need to become better (less trusting) consumers more familiar with, who come to believe in, the existence of, unconscious processes, and sincerely acknowledge the hidden agendas associated with these processes. They need to become more critical people, people who see not only the best in others but also the darker side of human nature that the brighter side of human nature is too often crafted to obscure. They have to renounce wanting to be loved so much that they suppress any thought of actually being unloved, if not hated; and they also need to suppress excessive empathy and altruism that might be good and valid in other circumstances, but are here ultimately not likely to be in the best interests of all concerned. They may have to admit that a colleague they like, or a friend or family member they truly love, has troublesome flaws. They certainly have to stop unnecessarily blaming themselves for being intolerant and unaccepting where passive-aggressive behavior is concerned, as was one patient who regularly encountered a new owner who every single day brought in digital photographs of her dog, pinning the patient, an unwilling (and busy) victim, "against the wall with no hope of escape from her endless picture shows." As the patient put it, "I know she was aware from clues I was sending her that she was being self-centered and intrusive, yet I grinned and bore it because I thought that how I felt was not important, and that I should not criticize a new dog owner because such a person has every right to be proud." Even when such behaviors at first appear to be innocuous and innocent, one may have to move toward viewing them with a jaundiced eye, as one would view the actions of the partner who "inno-cently" scooped his wife's expensive watch, on the dresser, into a drawer below and never told her he did that, leaving her to experience and accept the loss, and ultimately, never being able to find the watch again, having to buy a new timepiece.

Finally, victims have to think twice before misattributing what is truly passive-aggressive behavior to non-passive-aggressive forces, like inherent evil, or bad breeding. Instead victims who at first trust their own instincts and reactions may profit by moving on to be able to use the pathogno-monic, and so virtually diagnostic, uncomfortable response they as vic-tims have to passive-aggressives as a reliable way to spot passive-aggression in others. This (transference) response, as discussed in detail in Chapter 15 and throughout, may include physical components such as insomnia with nightmares (e.g., of being tortured); impotence; and headaches. It may also include emotional components, which typically consist of feeling depressed about not being able to get one's pleading message to others (to "please stop") across—an iteration of the helpless feeling that "enough is enough," and "so things must change."

For example, a victim felt "I am not getting through to you" when he complained to his partner that their four-year-old niece was remote, only to have the partner respond, "She is just like any other child." The victim's first thought was, "That isn't true because all the other children I know are not that way." Then he got depressed because now he had two prob-lems instead of one: a remote niece, and an unsupportive, uncomprehend-ing partner.

Two: Understanding Others' Passive-Aggression Through and Through

Victims can contribute to their own self-protection, functionality and even survival by asking themselves the question, "What exactly is going on with them?" in addition to, or instead of, the question, "What exactly is going on with me?" Full understanding of exactly how passive-aggressives think/work suggests specific countermeasures that can be taken to cope with them. There is an additional benefit of such understanding: it helps put the behavior in perspective as being less personally intended than it might initially seem to be. Victims feel less victimized when they realize that passive-aggressive behavior is a personality disorder and disorders are primarily due to emotional illness.

As suggested throughout, fully understanding passive-aggressives requires learning how to interpret innuendo. This means doing what Beck calls "reading other people's minds"[2]—that is, being able to look beyond the manifest content of what passive-aggressive people are saying and doing to glimpse (at least an *approximation* of) what they are really thinking. As also previously mentioned, understanding innuendo means suppressing one's natural tendencies to give others the benefit of the doubt, to think of oneself as very paranoid for seeing evil where it doesn't exist and to accept criticism for believing that you yourself always know it all, including knowing what others are secretly thinking.

A patient is attending an outdoor barbecue. The hostess is cooking chicken wings on the barbecue. There is a flare-up of the coals. The hostess' husband snaps, "I told you to buy ready-made wings, they would have been good enough." Is there a "for them" that he left out? Automatically thinking this man is, "Happy to see us but just a bit cranky because he is tired" would make it difficult for the patient, as victim, to know whether he should say nothing; put the husband in his place; refuse the next invitation as a warning; or, depending on other factors such as significant prior experiences along the same lines with this person, to decide then and there to forcefully defend one's integrity.

A special effort should be made to tune into the innuendo that characterizes nonverbal expressions of hostility, what Prout and Platt call "message transfer through nonverbal behavior."[3] Sophisticated interpreters of nonverbal hostility will not let raised eyebrows, eye rolls, and shoulder shrugs pass them by without notice and without the deep interpretation they require. For example, at a joint conference, a nurse visibly rubbed the arm of a colleague of a doctor she liked, then patted his back, and then looked up and around to make certain a second doctor, her primary target, was watching—her (indirect) way to tell the latter doctor how much she preferred his colleague over him.

Whenever possible, victims should try to identify/understand the unconscious reasons for why passive-aggressives get angry and why they deflect their anger instead of expressing it openly.

Why Do They Get Angry?

As noted throughout, victims of passive-aggression should consider following Keating's suggestion that "difficult feelings can . . . be somewhat lessened by understanding . . . the syndromes of difficult people [who] may be feeling depressed, guilty, fearful, etc., and refus[ing] to admit such feelings even to themselves."[4]

Victims can profitably learn to make a specific diagnosis in those they suspect of being passive-aggressive by identifying the *syndrome of origin* of passive-aggressive anger (especially paranoia), thereby better understanding the hidden agendas, secret motivations, and personal (unconscious) fantasies associated with the now newly more broadly understood abnormal psychopathology of those presumed to be passive-aggressive. For example, a patient was quietly listening to his mother-in-law talk about nothing much in particular, his eyes glazed over because she was lulling him to sleep, and in a not unpleasant way. The mother-in-law, misinterpreting his blank look as a hostile stare, shot back, "Why are you staring at me that way?" and then refused to accept his explanation—that he was just tired. At first, he got angry and wished he never had to see her again. Afterward, however, he said to himself, "Clearly, she has problems of her own, poor thing, and because she is probably paranoid, I should try to understand her and neither get upset about it nor try to retaliate. And, too, I should not expect myself to always avoid her wrath—you can never be careful enough with such hypersensitive, and possibly paranoid, people." The man who received a holiday card from a classmate he had not seen for 50 years, the card that showed an aerial view of the mansion this man lived in, recognized his classmate's need to show off how well he had made it in this world; so instead of taking it as a personal putdown he came to understand that the classmate's action was mainly a product of the classmate's own issues—involving fears about his (lowly, as he saw it) personal status in life. In similar fashion, married men who string single women along, promising to divorce their wives and marry them are sometimes correctly, and helpfully, understood (and handled) both as *commitment phobics* and as *narcissists* using people for personal gain. A friend who repeatedly says, "I must have you over to dinner sometime" and then comes up with one excuse after another to avoid making a definite appointment may be an *obsessional* passive-aggressive currently vacillating, or a *histrionic* passive-aggressive in the process of seducing and cruelly abandoning others, that is, he or she is a troubled individual, not just an ordinary (normal) person acting in a troublesome fashion, e.g., being slightly stubborn by refusing to follow through on a social promise.

Narcissistic passive-aggressives prejudge "what is good" using the extreme criterion of "what is good in others is what I assess as being good *for me*." Thus, a patient freely admitted that she would readily vote for someone running, not because the other person was a more competent administrator than his rival, but because this preferred person was promising not what was good for the country but what was good for the patient herself. Failing to make another important distinction, many narcissistic passive-aggressives view others who are in any way *different* from themselves as being *defective* (in comparison to them) in a major way.

Obsessive-compulsive passive-aggressives as perfectionists feel that anything less than 100 percent support from, is the same thing as zero backing by, others.

Depressive passive-aggressives often turn self-criticisms into criticisms by others. This process is explainable dynamically as consisting of a way to deal with one's own guilt about an issue by attacking others precisely for what one condemns in oneself, thus proving to oneself and others that, "I am completely against, not someone who embraces, that particular thing."

Awareness of the dynamics of passive-aggressive anger can help victims better cope with and manage their uncomfortable counterresponses. A son-in-law could manage his mother-in-law better when he came to understand the dependency, control, and competitive issues behind her constantly complaining about, and double binding, him. This is the mother-in-law who complained that her son-in-law was not making enough money to support her daughter properly, something he handled by going to school to learn a remunerative trade—only to have the mother-in-law complain that by studying all the time he was not spending enough time with her daughter—with the mother saying, "He comes home, goes up to his room to study, and then flops into bed, so that my daughter never sees him." First he thought, "What can I do to improve?" Later he accepted his fate without feeling compelled to change his behavior, doing thusly because he realized, "I am not the problem; she is. She is pushing me around this way because she is unable to forgive me for taking her daughter away from her."

Those who are targets of so-called professional rivalry will feel less personally defective if they recognize that sometimes what people tend to pass off as healthy one-upmanship is in fact punitive passive-aggressive hostility arising out of typical PAPD pathological competitiveness originating early on, in childhood. This recognition helped a patient who, returning to his 40th high school reunion, merely mentioned—and only because he was asked—that he was painting, and showing, but not making much money from, his art—only to be made to feel like a big nobody when a competitive classmate chimed in, "I have a son who is doing exactly the same thing you are, but he is making a fortune" and then added, "And I, his, proud father, am a full professor."

It can be very helpful to spot how passive-aggressive hostility originates in *developmental problems*, e.g., problems from childhood, as passive-aggressives abuse or traumatize others now just as they were themselves abused and/or traumatized when they were young. The history of one man, a competitive passive-aggressive, who satirized, and humiliated, anyone who dealt with balding by employing a comb-over, had a personal background notable for problems associated with his own parents, people who humiliated him in front of his peers by dressing him unstylishly and keeping his hair too long and curly for his gender and the times. A son bragged to his father that he just learned to drive, whereupon the father, resenting the son's youth, in tones of envy put his son down by responding, "And I just finished reading a difficult 800-page nonfiction work by a famous but extremely difficult to understand Russian novelist."

A woman had an apartment on the first floor of a cooperative apartment building. She also owned the basement storage area under her apartment. But she could not use it for living space because it had no window. Her solution was to make a window where none had previously existed. Without getting the building's approval, she took it upon herself to hire a construction crew to make a place for the window by tearing out a two-by-ten-foot section of the building's front wall, undermining the building's structural integrity in the process. Others complained to the board—to no avail, because she had a powerful board member on her side. He defended her by saying, in effect, that only those who had not sinned should cast the first stone. For example, as the board member pointed out, one man had put up a shelf, and another had replaced some floorboards, with both having done so illegally, that is, without getting written permission from the board of the building. Thus using the "logic" of "similar things are the same thing," (so that matters quantitative don't count) her advocate cowed impressionable others into withdrawing their objections. Only later did it dawn upon all concerned that not all similar transgressions are equal, and especially that personal minor sins do not necessarily disqualify one from being the first person to cast stones at major sinners.

Victims need to spot the defensive (pathological) aspects of passive-aggressive intrusions. Like the board member defending the woman who tore the hole in the wall of the cooperative building, many passive-aggressives favor the "tu quoque" defense, that is, instead of responding to the content of a justified criticism, they turn tables, shifting blame, excusing bad behavior on their part by citing equally bad (or worse) behavior on the part of others; e.g., by saying, "You are one too," that you also do what you accuse me (others) of having done—case closed. (The antithesis of this defense is to identify "what I do" and "what you do" as matters that, embraced by entirely different people, are themselves entirely different things, and therefore are matters that need be judged separately, each on its own in context.)

As mentioned throughout this text, passive-aggressives commonly hide their aggression using socially acceptable *rationalizations* such as minimization. They are "merely asking a question" or "just playing the devil's advocate." They may hide their hostility with the hedge word "but," as in "it's not significant, but"; or with the supposedly disqualifying words "simply," and "just," as in, "I was simply (just) asking you when you were finally going to get around to cleaning up your room." Destructive criticism is typically rationalized as a vehicle for helpful correction, as in, "I wouldn't criticize you so much if I didn't want you to be the best you can be." And passive-aggressives rationalize rejection of others as being fundamentally in the nature of "loving," as in, "I am only leaving you because I love you too much to hurt you." Playing Berne's game of "Wooden Leg,"[5] passive-aggressives frequently rationalize persistent annoying behaviors using justifying psychodynamic formulations, such as, "My nagging is not hostile, just part of OCD," or "I admit to brutalizing you, but it is because I have a childhood fixation, and as such I can't help treating you just like my mother treated me."

Victims also need to identify and correct for the passive-aggressive's cognitive distortions. Victims of passive-aggressives need to spot and correct for the cognitive errors passive-aggressives use to arouse their victims' guilt and shame and consequently to contribute to the victim's low self-esteem. Victims who recognize the *cognitive illogic* passive-aggressives employ to make their negative points can affirm themselves by invalidating the passive-aggressive's illogical, and thus unjustified, negativity towards them.

Three: Understanding One's Own Often Idiosyncratic, Responses to Passive-Aggressives

To be identified and understood are the cognitive errors victims make in their depressive self assessments as they come to view some of their negative past actions/less than stellar present performances as in fact constituting their entire inadequate, valueless, evil self. Victims of passive-aggression feel as if they are thoroughly bad if even one person (the passive-aggressive individual) reacts negatively to them; as they see any sign at all that they are not fully accepted by even one passive-aggressive individual as evidence that everyone has completely rejected them, meaning that they are totally unloved, and have been forever abandoned. Passive-aggressives subtly encourage their victims to overreact to their own minor peccadilloes as if they are major personal flaws, significant sins, and punishable crimes. For example, judging their own behavior in similar=the same thing terms, along the lines of assertion = aggression = murderous intent = homicidal action, victims are made to simply think bad thoughts in a way that encourages these bad thoughts to become bad things, things they have actually done.

Paranoid victims are most likely to exaggerate the importance/magnitude of any minor negative remarks they make in the course of interacting with passive-aggressives, deeming themselves bigoted and racist for little or no reason at all. They have a particular affinity for such looping cognitions as, "I did that because I am deficient, and I am deficient because I did that," or, "I can't socialize effectively because I don't feel worthy enough to attend social events, and I don't feel worthy enough to attend social events because I can't socialize effectively." Interrupting such vicious cycles allows victims to experience satisfyingly small breakthrough interpersonal successes that acting as exemplifying incremental accomplishments ultimately lead to less withdrawal and enhanced, more guilt-free, motivation to go forward.

Four: Creating a Sensible Action Plan for Handling the Passive-Aggressives in One's Life

Reduce Guilt

Victims of passive-aggressive individuals can profitably take responsibility for living as guilt-free a life as possible regardless of how other people look upon/treat them. What matters most is not that a passive-aggressive individual has victimized (stigmatized/marginalized) you, but how you have responded to the inevitable victimization that will occur in a world where passive-aggression is considered, at least in a limited way, the norm. Along such lines, victims should never join in with offensive passive-aggressives to make jokes at their own expense, victimizing themselves further because they feel that they are only getting what they deserve. Victims should rarely if ever tell self-demeaning jokes such as those which rely on *schadenfreude* for their effect. Such jokes are rarely if ever as funny as they are intended to be. And especially victims should not compromise their lives by becoming passive-aggressive to others as a way to retaliate against passive-aggression towards themselves.

Primary self-blame needs to be conquered as victims avoid blaming themselves for their own relational, and other, difficulties simply because they cannot always fully control their relational anxiety. While victims should try to avoid making as many relational mistakes as is humanely possible, if they do make some, they should recognize that we all make mistakes, and that mistakes do not make one a complete relational failure.

Indeed, victims should always keep in mind that there is a bright side to most or all personality problems. For example, when dealing with issues related to relational anxiety, always remember that many people like shy people. They find them appealing in part because they are less threatened than they are by those who are boldly, super-confidently, relationally asser-tive, competitive, and accomplished.

Use Defenses, e.g., Denial and Suppression

Denial—short of becoming shameless, puts a protective barrier between you and the unjustified negativity that comes your way from others around you, likely leading you to become depressed. Increasing suppression allows you as victim to engage and talk back to your guilty, critical, punitive con-science directly and demand that it be less critical of, and more positive toward, yourself.

Decrease Your Need for Impression Management

You, as a victim, should forcefully affirm your overall humanity to your-self and others, in spite of any minor imperfections passive-aggressives may identify as being yours. As a result, in spite of criticism from passive-aggressives you can accept yourself as you are, e.g., you love who you love; and accept your sexuality even if it in some respects falls short of what you think it *should* be. In general, not caring too much about what other people think about you is a good mindset to have and a healthy self-attitude to develop. Sometimes you don't need people to love you so much as you need people to leave you alone.

Decreasing your need for impression management involves as much as possible avoiding making your self-esteem entirely dependent on external sources of approval from a collective, and especially from a collective of passive-aggressives. No matter what you say or do there is always some passive-aggressive person to disagree with you or otherwise find you offensive—and imply, if not say, as much. Victims need to stop grading themselves based on what others might be thinking about, and how they are responding to, you. Instead they need to start developing internal strong, independent, unvarying, honestly promoted, personal self-standards and display those to themselves as well as to the world. Always view yourself as a basically viable individual, asking yourself not, "Do I have what he or she expects of me?" but "Do I think too little of myself?" Instead of calculating your self-worth entirely by what you assume your reputation with others to be, start finding strength and self-approval where it counts—from within. Never let the need for approval/congratulations from others trump your own self-standards and/or, on your own, lower these self-standards just to appeal to other people first, when that requires appealing to yourself second.

Seek Peer Support

Peer support will likely help you steel yourself against internal and external self-bashings that lead you to stigmatize and peripheralize yourself/allow others to stigmatize and peripheralize you, e.g., as immoral or disgusting. Because friends can be as unsupportive as enemies, pick your friends carefully, avoiding those who are passive-aggressive from the start and hard to change as time goes by. Don't feel you need to create a whole new loving family for yourself. Likely you will create a fictive family that is as dysfunctional as your family of origin. Many people do exactly this just to install some idealistic scenario into their lives. Don't depend on others who instead of giving you what you need and compensating you for anything missing in your life substitute exactly for those troublesome people you are, and should be, trying to avoid. The best peers/other associates for you are those who "sensibly" tell you, "In my eyes you are a worthy person." The most destructive are false friends—those who are supportive to your face, but undermining when you are out of their sight. As you try to recognize who the truly cruel people in this world are and dismiss them as having problems of their own, remain ever aware that people who criticize you are generally when speaking critically of you, in seeming to be talking about you, are in fact just talking about themselves.

Avoid Sadists

Especially avoid those passive-aggressives who as sadists enjoy deliberately setting out to make you feel guilty. Identify those "friends" who deliberately induce shame in you; and especially avoid going back for more to change their minds based on the false hope that they will somehow relent and come to like you better if you try hard to influence their opinion of you. In fact, consider at least temporarily protecting/enhancing your self-esteem by minimizing some, even considerable, aspects of negative social interactions with these people through protective withdrawal. Although what follows here is generally speaking a flawed and self-defeating method for managing a threatened self-image, there are times when it makes sense to *avoid* at least some passive-aggressives in your life, at least for now carefully steering clear of "accidentally" running into hateful others just to find out (again) what they think of you. Sometimes it is even a good idea to give up gain to avoid pain, as you diminish your functionality here, to enhance your functionality there, along the lines of "never reading your own reviews."

Understand Yourself

Understand how residua from your past still affect you. Understand how your past experiences determine much about your present, negative, relationships leading to the formation of stubbornly ingrained residuum that once formed continue to create a devalued self-view and via distortive thinking an equally devalued image of yourself. Parental deprivation of love and parental physical abuse meted out long ago (and now re-presented as if having been/currently being warranted/deserved) often lead sensitive individuals later in life to become overly attracted to similarly negative-thinking parental substitutes, trying to work things out with them only to find these people, and those like them, predictably perform as feared, which is in the same negative way that they once did. A patient would often compulsively engage others who were not in fact at all interested in engaging her—just to reverse the ravages of their coolness toward her, hoping that that way she could somehow be made whole again. Of course, others' devaluation of her continued anyway, and even intensified as a result of a vulnerability she was now making clearer to them. And naturally she viewed their continuing, even worsening, disdain as a further reason for self-disapproval because, as she concluded, it's not that she had picked people who for reasons of their own can't love her, or who can't and don't love anyone at all, it's that nobody can love her, and that is because of who and what she is—which is clearly "completely unlovable."

As one passive-aggressive victim put it, insightfully referring to the origins of her guilt and low self-esteem:

Everyone I meet now reminds me of my parents who kept the mood negative in my growing up years. All I got was deconstructive criticism, said in the most negative of spirits, telling me I was: embarrassing, dirty, had a bird brain, sported a big nose, was overall ugly, and was a tramp (that last name was for when an altar boy walked me home from church one Sunday in eighth grade and my parents accused us of having sex). Good thing at the time I thought a tramp was someone who had no home, so luckily I wasn't offended—until years later. You can see why my grandparents were my only refuge.

Permit Yourself to Be Successful

Allow yourself to be competitive without undue guilt over causing others their misfortunes. Especially avoid survivor guilt due to believing that the world is a zero-sum place where because there is a finite quantity of "X" anything you get by definition you got by taking it away from someone else. Instead of experiencing guilt over doing well because you believe that others are as a consequence (your fault!) doing poorly in comparison, and that somehow as a response to your success, start viewing yourself as a distinct entity entitled to fulfill your own destiny, regardless of whether or not others fulfill theirs.

Do Less of What Makes you Feel Bad

Do less of what makes you feel that you shouldn't have thought a certain way or done a certain thing.

Treat Others More Kindly and When Indicated with Greater Respect

Anticipate that if you love others, others very well might love you back. (As the expression goes, love that goes around will almost certainly come around.) Be secure in the knowledge that being a non-bully to others helps minimize the possibility that others will bully you in return.

Avoid Destructive Vicious Cycles

Especially avoid those starting with inept self-disclosure where you reveal yourself in a devalued way to certain others only to find that they are of the kind who use what little they learn about you against you, ultimately leading not to your taking more, but to you taking less, pride in yourself.

Develop Firm Meaningful Generative Goals

Remain positively goal-directed by avoiding impulsive behaviors that divert you from where you ultimately want, and ought, to be. Never let compulsively self-destructive behaviors become equally self-destructive substitutive goals.

Avoid compulsive/addictive behaviors that might include addictive shopping and hoarding, even if that only involves decorating and redecorating your apartment to loving perfection. Such things must not divert you from moving towards more significant life achievements, especially those char-acterized by loving relationships with others, and with one special per-son. It's highly misguided to do what one of my patients did: he moved to another state because there the bars stayed open later and so that suppos-edly enhanced the possibility that he could meet more people in such a place.

Minimize attempting to reverse the ravages wrought by low self-esteem through methods that either simply fail to work or are actually even more guilt-enhancing, like the following (some of which have been discussed elsewhere):

- Attempting to make up for your presumed flaws by devaluing other people (as being defective as compared to you).
- Redoing things previously found ineffective unless there is a real reason to repeat the attempt.
- Being flamboyant not because that is you, but to proudly, hypomanically, dis-play yourself to make up for your feeling ashamed of yourself.
- Becoming codependent in a way that involves hiding out with one to feel safe from all others because you believe the world to be a dangerous place for you, although the danger only exists in your own fiery imagination.
- Behaving excessively morally, for example, overindulging in abstinences, sex-ual and otherwise, whose main or only value is that they make you feel mor-ally superior and hence more substantively worthy.
- Trying to adjust your sexuality in all its aspects to placate and satisfy some-one or something else, such as your parents, or your Church.
- Seeking value for yourself by collecting trophy men/women. Notching your gun with sexual conquests—being promiscuous in order to make sex into some form of real accomplishment and meaningful triumph, an especially futile attempt to relieve feelings of inadequacy.
- Refusing to set limits on being you so that you can "be me all the way" even when being you entails a being "yourself" that you ought to stop fully admir-ing, and start relatively or completely disavowing.

Learn Empathic Skills

Victims who become more charitable by learning empathic skills find that they can better manage passive-aggressives by giving the identified passive-aggressives in their lives the benefit of various doubts. Espe-cially helpful is leaving room for considerations of "what trouble that person might be having in his or her life right now?" This involves the understanding of, and especially compassion toward, the other person and his or her present reality, which it is unlikely you know all about. Victims can profitably come to understand that a working mother who goes to school during the day and works for pay at night may have too many responsibilities to be able to always be on time to every social engagement. A father who does not listen to his son's medical advice, although the son is a doctor, may not be personally devaluing his son; he may just be a stubborn individual who takes no advice from anyone, or he may just be a frightened individual who is too scared to hear anything at all about his own medical condition, even, or especially, from his own son.

Of course, victims who are *too* altruistic and empathic should speak up and complain instead of making things worse by suffering about something, in silence. Giving others carte blanche and then a second and third chance sometimes amounts to condoning a behavior thus encouraging by allowing/enabling it.

Counter distortive empathy where you simply assume that others are judging you negatively because you, projecting, conclude, without evidence, that they are measuring you using rigid, unfair, and excessively self-punitive yardsticks you currently use to measure yourself. In fact, always distinguish perception from reality by distinguishing projecting from perceiving, and so "imagining" from "realistically determining."

When all else fails, try saying over and over again to yourself the two magic words of guilt reduction and self-esteem enhancement: "So what." Mean that, and add that all is not completely lost just because for the moment nirvana is not entirely found.

Set Appropriate Limits on Passive-Aggressives (Fight)

Some victims should try to reduce their distress by improving their circumstances. This can sometimes be done by fighting passive-aggressives back in a civilized way. One such method entails setting appropriate limits on passive-aggressives and their behaviors.

Certain rules apply: The decision to fight back by setting limits should not be an emotional one. It should be part of a plan the victim formulates after specifically considering his or her individual circumstances. For example, in the workplace, victims of passive-aggression who need the job and the money have fewer options and can take fewer risks than those who are independently wealthy or who have other potential employment opportunities.

This said, setting limits once is mature, and productive; while setting limits twice is likely to be the start of an unproductive sadomasochistic round robin.

Limit setting should be done in a nonhostile way. A victim simply explains his or her position and asks the PA person to go along. Maintaining his or her stance, the victim asks the passive-aggressive individual to "tone it down or cut it out," or, as Millon puts it, he or she "set[s him or her] straight."[6] As Kaslow (1983) says, "my experience with . . . students (and family members) has been that it may be best to answer the query, 'What happens if it isn't in or done on time?' with, 'Then it is not acceptable'—without further explanation."[7]

Nonverbal passive-aggressive counterattacks like yawning in a boring speaker's face can work, but too often they misfire and have the reverse effect as they make the passive-aggressive even angrier than before.

Victims can sometimes fight back by setting limits by restructuring and then reexploring a specific painful situation along newly desirable parameters. A man's sister-in-law often put him on hold, saying, "We have a tentative date for Saturday," only to cancel at the last minute after he had refused other invitations just in order to keep the date open for her. Then she excused herself for canceling by reminding him that she did, after all, hint that she might not be available. At first, although she had repeatedly inconvenienced him, he responded to being put on hold/cancelled, by saying, "Okay, no problem," only to have her do the same thing to him again—until it became a problem due to having become a pattern. Finally, he decided to only make arrangements to meet her someplace he wanted to be anyway, and where he was already part of a group of people he in any event wanted to be with—so that it would not matter so much, if at all, if she canceled him out at the last minute.

Some victims decide to try to set limits by teaching passive-aggressives a lesson. They do this by giving them a taste of their own medicine. For example, some guests never again come late if they find that should they not arrive on time the host is gone. Obstructionistic passive-aggressives asked to arrive for a dinner at 7:00 p.m., although the dinner actually starts at 8:00 p.m., may be thereby manipulated into actually arriving on time. Just as likely, however, victims eventually discover that there is ultimately a price to be paid for the dishonesty, as when their target, sensing the trick, still actually appears late—for an 8:00 dinner at 9:00 p.m. Or, resenting the deviousness of the countermeasure, he or she does not appear at all.

Therapists should determine whether people who continue to be victims of passive-aggressives have more widespread problems, consisting of a general difficulty setting limits all around due to some psychopathology of their own. If that turns out to be the case, the next salient question might be, "Do some victims, as is often the case, have difficulty setting limits because their self-esteem is low?" This was the case for a man who protested that his mother told him in the middle of a phone conversation, as if he did not exist, "I have to hang up now, your father is at the front door." Yet he was unable to put his foot down about being so sloughed off because he thought, erroneously, "If I do that, she won't love me so much anymore, and might never speak to me again."

Therapists should determine if victims like him being overly sensitive hesitate to say "no" for a specific reason, and if so, for what reason? Feeling that all asked questions have to be answered, and that all requests for information have to be processed and the information given, a woman regularly responded to people who asked her how old she was by telling them her real age, a figure she would have preferred not to divulge. A therapist regularly responded to people who asked him whether or not he was married by answering, truthfully, that he had remained single, although he would have preferred to hide his marital status so that he came across as a "regular guy without sexual orientation problems."

Overly compliant victims are sometimes too reluctant to challenge even those who do them serious harm. A patient, a doctor, hesitated to confront an intake nurse who was undermining him by saying bad things about him, prejudicing the patients even before they got to see him. The doctor hesitated to defend himself because he feared that if he complained she would both escalate her present behavior and find another, even more destructive, way to hurt him.

Therapists should also determine if victims have difficulty with being unable to distinguish setting limits from getting annoyed, and getting annoyed from becoming furious due to their making specific cognitive errors. It is these errors that cause them to develop a self-image that to remain positive requires their never feeling or getting angry. Characteristically, such victims first take a firm stand and then recoil because they feel that they have overstepped (some poorly identified, often pacifistic) bounds, doing so even when their own (initial) protest was a mild one. A patient merely asked his partner to let him be the only one to water the plants so as to avoid overwatering them, but then he worried that he had attacked and rejected his partner, and now, as his punishment, was for sure going to be abandoned.

A woman, in what a patient, her hostess, properly inferred was a carefully planned attack on her, dripped mustard more than once on an upholstered couch at a cocktail party, and then apologized, claiming ill health and poor eyesight. The hostess wanted to ask her to be more careful but had conflicting fearful thoughts that prevented her from doing so. First the hostess felt angry, but second she felt guilty. The hostess's first thoughts were, "She is destructive and is ruining my party and my house." Her second thoughts were, "After all, she is a nice person, and the poor thing has a tremor, and, anyway, no one is perfect. Besides, I do have more than she has, and so I should be more charitable, particularly since I can afford to have the furniture repaired afterward if it gets ruined."

People who are in committed relationships likely should, whenever possible, make limit setting on passive-aggressives outside the immediate relationship a joint affair. For example, it is often best if both spouses participate in resolving in-law conflicts, reaching a consensus before any words are spoken and action is taken, so that a firm conjoint comfortable closeness/distancing interpersonal decision can be made promptly and unambiguously, and not, as is often seen, "behind one person's back."

Because they are in some ways just like parents, professionals have a special responsibility to set limits on unruly passive-aggressive charges, whether adults or children. A doctor learned the consequences of not being firm the hard way. Trying to build up a therapeutic blood level of antidepressants slowly and safely, he started a patient up on low doses of antidepressants. Thinking that she was being deprived of the full dosage right now, and that it was being withheld for irrational reasons, and even spitefully, the patient complained to an administrator who held some sway in the clinic; and who promptly ordered the doctor to start the patient on a full dose of medication, and to do so immediately. The doctor reluctantly complied, and as a result the patient suffered adverse effects. Trying to determine if another patient being started up on antidepressants was pregnant, the doctor asked her right out, only to have her tell him, in no uncertain terms, that that was a stupid question because he was asking it of someone who was a lesbian. (But how was he to know?)

A child psychologist learned not to be so intimidated by parents after he reluctantly agreed to treat a child for obstructionism and hyperactivity, only to discover much later that the "child's problem" was little more than the product of youthful high spirits and the result of parental vacillating about enforcing any (even the good) rules of conduct.

Of course, victims' worst fears about setting limits are sometimes justified. In favorable situations, passive-aggressives respond to having limits set by backing off, and a relationship improves. However, sometimes, in unfavorable circumstances, things do end badly. A woman who for years lived solely on promises from a man who said he would divorce his wife and marry her, set a date beyond which she would refuse to continue in the relationship. The man went right down to the wire, still vacillating, then left her for someone else the day before the deadline, and, just to show her, subsequently married this other person—the very day after he left the first woman. And he even had the gall to invite her, the jilted one, to the wedding!

Also, limit-setting often works only imperfectly with passive-aggressives for they know how to foil the attempt, and to do so in their usual passive-aggressive fashion. For example, they respond by taking back what they said or reversing what they did without really basically intending to change in any significant way. Thus they apologize but it is only to make their victims feel guilty for having spoken up, and to set their victims up for a repeat performance, and more apologies to come. Sometimes passive-aggressives foil limits that have been set by escalating to violence. When the passive-aggressive's mechanism of deflection by expressing hostility indirectly is disabled by the victim's unaccommodating and sometimes threatening response, in such cases the victim can find that setting limits on a passive-aggressive is dangerous.

Victims of passive-aggressives can profitably use a number of *defense mechanisms* to fight back. Some therapists would not advocate their use directly.

Developing healthy, mature defenses (becoming a nondefensive adult without game-playing) is always a worthy goal. Always remember that when treating victims who have come up with and are practicing these methods on their own, therapists should generally take care not to undermine something that is working, and that can even have survival value.

Internalization of anger. Using this defense, the victim says "mea culpa" to disarm a passive-aggressive. The victim admits to guilt, however insincerely, to deflect criticism from passive-aggressive others via getting there first with a self-criticism, as in, "You are right, I don't dispute it, I know that that is the way I am, and I wish I could change." Productive discussion is, however, either partially dismantled or now entirely ended.

Identifying with the aggressor. Here victims turn the tables to "fight fire with fire." In the less favorable cases, identification with the aggressor is limited to revenge *fantasies* (including death-wishes) kept to oneself, an example of which is the revenge fantasies children routinely employ for psychological relief in burdensome relationships with passive-aggressive parents. This was the case with the child who, after retiring to bed and before going to sleep, fantasized getting away from his intrusive parents by running away from home—and running off with a comic book hero and his sidekick.

In favorable cases, victims can work things out with those victimizing them. Communicating clearly and keeping the expressions of anger to a minimum by focusing on reality, they can look for solutions to problems rather than for ways to avoid facing them or otherwise acting immaturely. But sometimes this approach does not work with passive-aggressive people. Sometimes victims just need to recognize that passive-aggressives often do not heed calls for discussions to clear the air and resolve a problem. Instead they respond by becoming even more sarcastic and humiliating. If a discussion actually occurs, it does not help if the passive-aggressive, as he or she generally does, views "the mere discussion" as a threat to his or her independence or as an attempt to control or humble the individual. Next the passive-aggressive proceeds to toughen his or her stand, e.g., to fight back with his or her usual weapons—like foot-dragging and "forgetting" what was just recently said, and meant.

Children often go on to become passive-aggressive themselves as their way of taking their revenge against a perceived victimizer. Some children become overtly obstructionistic to retaliate, as Millon (1981) says, "to spitefully 'get back' at and torture their [passive-aggressive] rejecting parents."[8] This was the case for a patient who remembered that when he was a child his mother would not let him watch any television at all. In reply to her saying to him, "Don't touch that set" he did her one better—by refusing to eat any food that was touching another food on his plate. The young child in love with a neighborhood little girl dealt with her mother's constantly telling the boy to "keep your hands off her, you are unclean," by achieving simple closure—involving throwing a pinch of dirt in her baby carriage.

Adult patients along similar lines sometimes speak of such thoughts as "healthy death wishes." Some public speakers who get anxious because they feel like fools standing before their audience feel better if they think of their audience along similarly foolish lines—shamed as fools for being out in their underwear, or, as even more foolish due to being there completely in the nude. A patient dealt with feeling humbled by a furniture salesperson by reminding herself of the time "another uppity artsy-fartsy salesperson humiliated himself when, thinking that all his customers were safely gone, he fell to his knees and searched beneath the sofa cushions for the loose change that might have dropped out of prior customers' pockets when they tried out the very expensive sofas on the display floor."

Adults have on their own discovered the usefulness of the childish "tu quoque" defense where identifying with the aggressor takes the form of telling one's accusers that, "You are one too" or "You did it first"—as a retort to a perceived, or actual, criticism, accusation, or other personal attack.

Use Flight (Removal)

Victims should consider staying out of predictably emotionally hazardous situations right from the start. Potential victims can at least try to recognize/anticipate warning signs before it is too late to avoid getting enmeshed in potentially or actually unpleasant situations as, for example, they conjure up in their minds what can happen if they go into business with some of their family members.

Victims should think twice before going back for more for what will amount to, if they return, a repeat of the same, as they go back just to see whether they can do something to lessen others' negativity toward them. Too many victims make the difficult passive-aggressive people in their lives the ones who count the most, often while simultaneously ignoring their most fervent admirers and their truest and most loving friends. Uninterested in the easy conquest, and blaming themselves for bringing all their interpersonal difficulties down on their own heads, they focus only on changing the minds of those whose minds are already the most set against them. Only desiring to win the hard games, they set out to meet only the most difficult challenges.

Some abused wives ultimately discover that walking out is the best—if not the only—method for handling an unstable passive-aggressive husband in danger of becoming potentially dangerous to her, e.g., should his passive-aggressive defenses (against his own anger) break down. (In many such cases it is best, and perhaps less dangerous, not to leave mad—that is, to not criticize the husband on the way out the door.) A driver might consider ignoring dangerous provocation on the road, and certainly should not pull up to institute eye contact with and/or make obscene gestures at someone who clearly is escalating, thus potentially becoming overly involved in a possible road rage type interaction where a physical fight is likely to ensue and people get hurt just to prove the point that "no one, not even some stranger, gets away with treating me like this."

However, it is not always clear whether someone should make a geographical move to get away from personal stress in the old environs or take a new job to get away from the occupational stress produced by a bad boss—at least without first seeking a consultation with a therapist. Some victims who move do well; but others take their problems with them when and where they go, sometimes even creating new, similar, abuses as part of their continuing attempt to master the old ones.

Many, following the whim or impulse of the moment, make the wrong move entirely. They leave a hostile anonymous city to go to a "friendly" small town. Then, to get away from the small-town mentality and its problems, they go back to a large anonymous city, only to reexperience the same hostile undercurrents they initially tried to get away from, as they once more feel isolated and lonely in the typical large city they flee to.

Of course, sometimes others' passive-aggression is so destructive that there is no real choice about whether to stay or go. When one cannot leave physically, on the spot emotional removal, e.g., stopping talking to someone, may be the best act of self-respect and affirmative self-preservation available to help one gain a measure of control over the situation, and to protect oneself from further abuse. Caution is indicated on the job for both quitting a job without notice and giving others the silent treatment, or finger, on the way out the door can jeopardize one's future job recommendations/ prospects, and almost certainly no really hurtful lasting damage will, as hoped, be done to on-the-job higher-ups by the act of quitting—because most workers, no matter how dramatic their departure, are forgotten the very day they leave.

A good solution for victims under temporary attack is to say to themselves, when applicable, something like: "That is not something for me to take personally—that is merely where she is coming from; he is doing his own thing; for that is just the way she is; and at any rate the immediate crisis, like most present crises, will likely soon be over and pass on its own."

An effective (intermediate) way of removal involves backing off by putting third parties between oneself and the passive-aggressives in one's life. Third parties can by providing a buffer between "natural enemies" offer a victim protection from passive-aggressives. This can often be done simply by the giving of good advice. So often marital partners battle it out endlessly over a particular point when an experienced consultant, really a referee, could keep the couple from squabbling or rapidly and effectively actually solve marital problems for them. Therapists can often by assuming the role of third-party buffers acting as go-betweens or referees, help resolve difficulties between victims and the passive-aggressives in their lives. But this only works if the therapist is sufficiently careful to avoid unfairly validating one member of a dyad over and in favor of the other, because almost always the validation of one requires the invalidation of another, and so often this validation turns out to be the product of personal bias on the therapist's part.

The following case illustrates the effectiveness of third-party interventions in squabbles involving multipartite passive-aggression:

Children often rely on third-party confidants like an honorary aunt to take their side in intra-familiar arguments and provide them with a comfortable, safe, haven; a retreat where they can run to in order for them to be reassured that they are not the losers that their parents say they are, and to be retold that their parents, not they, are the ones out of line.

When a patient was a boy, his father abused him by involving him in his (the father's) hypochondriacal worries about his own health and associated compulsive rituals. Twenty or more times a day the father demanded that the child "time me a minute." That involved the father making his son go over to the kitchen clock to act as a stopwatch so that the father could take and retake his own pulse to check and recheck his own cardiac status. This boy found solace in visiting an honorary aunt who listened to his complaints about his father. Her calm attitude and resolute rationality helped him develop a healthier outlook on life; her cheery attitude helped him with his sadness over his situation; and her good ideas about the right way that he should live (e.g., "live your own life your own way") helped him forge and keep a healthy identity—one that made him ultimately independent of his worry-prone father, ultimately saving the son from a personal neurosis.

Victims should make flight decisions (e.g., those related to staying in or to leaving a relationship) only after considering a number of practical and emotional factors—including their finances; whether they have a supportive family and friends to fall back on; their health and age; their personality type; any possibly intrusive personality problems they have; and their goals in life. They should not too readily take advice given by professionals who might not always know what is best for others in this, or in any other, arena. With very few exceptions, therapists treating victims of passive-aggressives can best do their job by encouraging the patient to make his or her own decisions about major life issues, then offering the patient guidance limited to helping the individual *implement* whatever decisions *the patient* makes on his or her own, independent of what advice he or she gets from anyone else.

Flight by Forbearance

Forbearance is a form of flight, although not a classic defense mechanism. Practically speaking, forbearance can, at least for some victims, be one of the best defenses against the passive-aggressives in one's life. It can even avoid serious victimization, sometimes with negative, irreversible, consequences. Of course, forbearance is only a viable option in situations where there is no important/deadly threat to one's major dependent needs; no real practical reason to have to be, and stay, in complete control of a situation; no significant rational for jealously guarding one's present status in life; and no looming serious physical/financial danger to oneself and one's family.

A woman who considered her relationship with a man on the whole worthwhile decided, "Maybe he is not the best one for me. He is lazy, cannot perform sexually, wants me to do all the work around the house, and sits in the bathroom half the day. But what is there better out there? I am 40, depend on him for income, and am lonely just having lost my mother. I think I will do what he wants, acceding to his demands just so that I can stay where I am in this, a minimally workable, barely satisfying, relationship, for that, however, is an improvement on having no relationship, and no one, at all."

When appropriate, therapists can advise their patients to not respond tit for tat, or even at all, to individuals who are passive-aggressive. They might suggest that patients avoid skirmishes by turning the other cheek, or by humoring or coddling the passive-aggressives in their lives, especially concerning such minor matters as conflicts about interior decorating.

Berne, in speaking of the antithesis to the passive-aggressive game of Corner—a marital game where the husband tempts the wife to provoke him and then becomes moody and goes "out with the boys . . . leaving [his wife] at home to nurse her injured feelings"—provides one example of another way to avoid perpetuating vicious cycles of sadomasochistic psychopathology. According to Berne, "All [Mrs. White] has to do is . . . take her husband by the arm, smile and go along with him (a shift from Child to Adult ego state)"[9] thus putting up with the bad for the good.

A patient asked a neighbor to "please keep your Chow Chow mix dog from running loose and into my yard," doing so in the main because his own little dog had a bad back and could be seriously hurt if jumped. The neighbor helpfully replied: "Sorry for any inconvenience. We're doing landscaping and the workers cut our invisible electric fence. It's been repaired and should be effective from now on." But just when the second man had developed a good feeling about the incident and its resolution, the first man added, "Incidentally, Christine, *my* little dog, is a pure breed and having had a self-esteem problem for years is at risk if she overhears the sort of derogatory assessment implied in your calling her 'a mix.'" The neighbor wrote, and was at first tempted to send, a note offering the following counterresponse: "If Christine is running on other people's property, her problems with self-esteem are amply justified." Then he reconsidered that approach, tore up the note, and put up an actual fence.

As previously mentioned, some therapists advise victims of passive-aggressives to sense where their passive-aggressive core sensitivities lie and quietly respect the passive-aggressive's adaptive defenses in order to avoid challenging them and otherwise asking for even more passive-aggressive trouble. They might learn to treat *paranoid* passive-aggressive people gently, explaining exactly what they mean as they speak, and clearly outlining what they are about to do before they actually do it. They should especially avoid humiliating paranoid individuals, in particular avoiding doing so in public. Knowing that paranoid passive-aggressives respond better to reassurances than to threats, to cooperation than to challenges, they might, instead of complaining, "You don't trust me," assure a paranoid spouse who thinks they are cheating on him or her that they love him or her and would never find it in their heart to do that. Whenever possible, they might interpret paranoid passive-aggressive behavior in a positive light, for example, "I know your jealousy is only a way to keep me on a short leash because you love me." They might try helping out paranoid individuals by reality testing their persecutory beliefs, but only in a way that doesn't challenge the paranoid person personally and directly. In tense situations with paranoid passive-aggressives, they might even consider taking some or all of the blame on themselves, for example, suggesting not, "You don't listen to me," but "Perhaps I didn't make myself clear."

To avoid body blows to a *narcissist's* positive sense of self, they might grant needs and flatter egos, giving credit where none is due, as when they give a spouse acting jealously points for being a good detective.

To avoid making *dependent* people anxious, they should not idly threaten to leave them. They should not let *passive* individuals who need direction flounder; and they should, as much as possible, avoid criticizing *depressed* individuals, knowing that depressives often rage when their self-criticisms seem validated. They should avoid nagging or trying to control stubborn *obsessive/compulsive* passive-aggressives, knowing that that only makes them more oppositional; and they should avoid inconsiderately smothering *avoidant* passive-aggressives relationally, knowing that many avoidant passive-aggressives tend to prefer to keep some regulatory distance. They should avoid challenging the status of, or otherwise emasculating, competitive *histrionic* individuals, for example, they should avoid bragging about how in comparison they themselves possess much, and "have accomplished much more in life, compared to you and a lot of others."

In professional (job) situations, they should wisely show forbearance toward difficult customers by putting their job requirements first, recognizing that they have a primary responsibility to their employers and that doing their job right means always taking the company's and its customers' needs into account, and before their own.

A patient, a director of residency teaching, was right that her boss's decision that the residents make unaccompanied home visits in the community put the residents in danger and might even wreck her teaching program (because few would apply to a training program where dangerous home visits were being required). But she soon realized that, "He is the boss; what he says goes; I am in no position to rewrite the residents' job description." She acted in an accommodating fashion to her boss for practical reasons. She knew that that way ultimately she would get much further professionally than others who spoke up in a way that antagonized him. As she put it, "My boss prefers not headstrong originals but those who do as they are told, people for whom the collective good comes before their individual wellbeing/identity."

On the negative side, forbearance can be overly humbling for the forbearer; for it can keep him or her emotionally fixed in a subservient position he or she might be better just walking away from.

CHAPTER SEVENTEEN

Helping Passive-Aggressives Become Less So

Those who relate to passive-aggressives might consider trying to deal with them in ways other than by flight or fight. Instead they might try to help them become less passive-aggressive, using health-giving therapeutic interpersonal interventions to assist them to replace pathological game playing with game-free adult enmeshments.

That goal generally requires striking a balance between setting harsh limits thereby risking a complete relational disintegration, and being overly permissive thereby risking intensifying their passive-aggression and being enveloped by it to the point that it becomes the entire purpose of a given relationship.

Being Sympathetic

Being helpful to, sympathetic with, and showing empathy toward a passive-aggressive individual is generally speaking a good way to mollify/diminish passive-aggressive activity on that individual's part.

Being sympathetic with a passive-aggressive individual starts with recognizing that some passive-aggression is not consciously driven but is rather something many passive-aggressive individuals can't help/change on their own. To this end, victims should try to avoid direct confrontation as a tool for change. They might, for example, instead respond to passive-aggressive provocation softly, by remaining noncommittal in its face. Even supposedly helpfully correcting a passive-aggressive's cognitive errors or reality testing his or her paranoid distortions can be inflammatory, as exemplified by answering a question with an (equally passive-aggressive) question in order to show the passive-aggressive individual exactly what he or she is doing.

As an example, a teacher accuses a student of being wrong when it is the teacher who is in error. A passive-aggressive response might be, "Why do you think that?" A non-passive-aggressive and therefore likely more helpful response might be a blander, "I'll research that further," as replying sympathetically that way both avoids succumbing and antagonistically counterattacking with hostile humor or irony calculated to cause embarrassment.

Setting Limits in a Healthful Way

Another good way to be sympathetic yet effective involves setting limits in a healthful way. This might consist of reality testing in an attempt to help replace a passive-aggressive's hostile (fantasy) distortions with new, undistorted, reality involving recommended increased flexibility in the hope that the passive-aggressive individual will consider alternative non-passive-aggressive responses, at least for the moment, and for starters.

One can also softly model desirable behavior, showing the passive-aggressive what might be a better way to think and behave. When it comes to empathy, a way to enhance empathy in the passive-aggressive might be, "How would you feel if I were to treat you the way you just treated me?"

Using Reverse Psychology

Reverse psychology works best for those passive-aggressives who are interpersonally highly attuned/sensitive people, and moreover stubbornly do the opposite of what they are asked to do even when others' requests are reasonable.

Here the victim expects less from passive-aggressives in the hope that they will give more. Stubborn passive-aggressives who use withholding in the service of being passive-aggressive deliberately structure interpersonal interactions to become: "Let me know what you want, that way I can know what not to give you." They won't do something because you want them to do it, even when they themselves also want to do that very thing. They withhold in the expectation that others will intensify their demands to which in reply they can intensify their resistances. It typically (but not predictably) follows, for example, that others who remain neutral or actually pull back from passive-aggressive stubbornness will likely discover that as one becomes less demanding of the passive-aggressive (the unacceptable, "Fork it over!" response) the passive-aggressive becomes more submissive/cooperative, at least in this one area/respect. Thus, with passive-aggressive collectors (short of being inveterate hoarders) many family and friends soon discover that they can more effectively get the collector to clean up the house if they don't push him or her too hard to do so, but instead take a nuanced, laissez-faire approach consisting of treating the passive-aggressive not like a child who needs to but won't clean up his or her room, but like an adult who responds better to gentle suggestions that they straighten up (as distinct from demanding that you "get rid of all that stuff"), all the while carefully explaining why all concerned will likely benefit if what is being suggested actually gets done.

Teaching Passive-Aggressives Healthier Interactive Thoughts/Actions

Passive-aggressives rarely fully know how negative the effects they are having on other people happens to be. As a result, they are unable to make a conscious choice to reconsider the unhelpful ways they might be managing their relationships. Passive-aggressives actually think they have bound their aggression by expressing it sneakily, but they don't realize that in fact they have actually become more aggressive merely by having flattened out the process.

Teaching respect might help the passive-aggressive directly enhance his or her empathy with others and hence his or her relationships with them. For example, one patient's family insightfully complained to a family member, "You are being disrespectful by washing that lettuce leaf over and over again." The patient sincerely on his part replied, "I don't see why you should be bothered by that; after all, how exactly am I hurting you?" In their reply, the family, not cruelly, but effectively, and helpfully, gave their passive-aggressive family member an actual answer to her question, and did so in such therapeutic, that is, usefully helpful, detail that they effectively drew a roadmap as to how the passive-aggressive family member might change around to handle this specific problem in a better way.

Also the passive-aggressive who is taught to respect differences may in turn come to feel more favorably toward a potential victim. Too often, others' differing points of view are what in the first place lead to tension that leads to arguments that don't solve anything. For example, partners often disagree about how much risk one should take. Of two partners in a couple, one wouldn't let the lawn be mowed except by landscapers who had adequate insurance, while the other was willing to take a chance on hiring uninsured workers just to not have to do the job himself. The other reasoned that because so few landscapers were adequately insured it came down to either taking a risk or doing the work oneself. Seeing each other's points of view went a long way in reducing friction between the two spouses, allowing at least this particular problem to be solved short of having an ongoing argument with escalating passive-aggressive features.

Avoiding Blaming Responses of Your Own

Passive-aggression often increases when the response to the passive-aggressive is one that leads him or her to feel scolded due to feeling corrected=being blamed. Passive-aggressives will not likely cave when they feel they are being given an argument. They will instead conclude that there is no real wish here to help them understand themselves, which even they might desire, and possibly accept. Instead, conversely, passive-aggressives, being made to feel guilty, will deal with their guilt feelings by going on a guilt-inducing counterattack of their own, further criticizing *others* to diminish the critical effect they believe others to be having on them. This is why talking things out, hopefully leading to a healthy level of consensual validation, can be helpful, but only if the prevailing wish isn't predominantly the wish to retaliate.

Letting Things Pass

Passive-aggressives know and appreciate it when things that are best to ignore are actually left alone to run their course. This is often the case when passive-aggressive intrusive worries that resemble OCPD-rituals virtually beg for a response/group participation to exist. An example here would be one patient's need to constantly complain that the house where they all lived wasn't neat enough, and demand that others straighten up their own bedrooms every morning before leaving for work, and even on weekends.

It follows that "talking things out" can make matter worse and only works selectively: with the right person and under the right circumstances. A wife's therapist told her to "talk things out" when it might have been better for her to keep some of her (negative) thoughts to herself. For example, she had dropped her husband off at his gym. The husband obsessed: "She won't remember to pick me up and that frightens me because I don't have enough money to pay for a cab home." The wife reminded him that he had an ATM card, and of the proximity to the gym of three ATM machines. But her reasoned approach was ineffective. For her attempt to even try to "talk sense" to him had no effect because when she tried to explain that his was not a reasonable concern she only intensified his worrying, as he replied, "Yes, but the ATMs can all be on the same circuit and so all out of order at once, leaving me stranded." It would have been best for the wife to just accept that her husband's passive-aggressive worrisomeness was not entirely rational, and so to not challenge her husband and his anxiety, but to rather just quietly accept that some passive-aggressive worry is neurotically driven, and so is too ingrained to change.

Giving Advice

Giving passive-aggressives advice involves advocating ways passive-aggressives can handle situations other than by getting angry and being sneaky about it. Such advice can be especially unhelpful for those passive-aggressives who feel as if advice is inherently all too abusive and awkward and especially harsh because it puts them in a double bind. An example of such a passive-aggressive is one man who if he takes advice and it works, then wishes he had thought of it himself; and if he takes advice and it does not work, then wishes it had not been offered to him in the first place. Too many passive-aggressives when given advice respond by playing the passive-aggressive game of, "Why Don't You—Yes But." Advised to leave an abusive relationship, they first respond with, "But I have nobody else," and then complain that "this person is unbearable," thus frustrating the advisor, who soon enough no longer knows what to say or how to help.

Too many passive-aggressives deal with confusion about what the right thing happens to be by being arbitrary about seeking a solution, even, or especially, in situations where there is more than one right good answer. Instead they persistently search for the one and only right solution to a problematic situation/dilemma. Continuing to ask the equivalent of, "Which is it? Tile or carpet in our shared hallway?" they brood: "Our hallway could use a new carpet, but maybe tile is better because it's easier to keep clean; but the super is a lazy man who doesn't clean anyway, so maybe we should go for looks and not worry about wear?" All one can do now is to sympathize with the plight of passive-aggressive individuals who cannot make up their minds about most things, while sticking to a plan of resolutely refusing to even begin to try to make up their minds for them. Once, I told a friend uncertain about a romantic relationship that I suspected that things would resolve, even improve, on their own, if given time. They didn't, so she avoided criticizing me directly for giving her bad advice by criticizing me for my excessively resolute hands-off approach—which according to her, did nothing to advance her cause.

Advisors should always keep in mind that almost all passive-aggressives see advice on how to do the right thing as a criticism for having done things wrong in the first place. This is even true for such seemingly innocuous advice as the mild suggestion to "go for help" advisory response, which the passive-aggressive still might distort as confrontational and controlling.

Therefore, any recommendations given are often best presented to the passive-aggressive not as a command or a demand but as one among many possibilities, with the decision as to which one will be implemented best decided by the patient.

Given at the right time and to selective individuals, the best-considered advice can come in the form of personal examples from the advisor's own life-experiences. Often it's profitable for advisors to set forth the parameters of how passive-aggressives might get help, by citing situations that parallel the advisor's own situational difficulties as he or she resolved them effectively.

Advocating Seeking Out Reassuring Supportive People

Many passive-aggressives, at home or at work, do well when the overall personal support that the advice giving process implies is there, doing so even when the advice itself is not particularly worthy. This is because passive-aggressives so treated, now view others' attempts as helpful because these others, however unknowledgeable, are treating them more like allies than as adversaries.

Recommending Behavioral Interventions

Those in the path of passive-aggressive fallout can recommend that their passive-aggressive friends, family and partners overcome their anger by the taking of small ("baby") steps in meeting something they fear head on. The hope here is that there will be progressively less and less in the way of immersion shock over change that the passive-aggressive perceives as being too radical.

Gradual, graded exposure can be implemented in vivo (in real life) or in vitro (through imaging), that is, by conjuring up images of a feared situations in one's mind, allowing one to think through and practice remedies without having to seek out actual (in vivo) difficult situations to use for practice.

In an opposite technique, called extinguishing, passive-aggressives deliberately flood themselves with a number of troublesome scenarios in order to ultimately cope with them better. The goal here is to help friends, family, , and patients turn flourishing anxiety into something so sufficiently known, repetitive, and hence tiresome that it virtually douses itself.

Being Good Humored

Humor when proffered without ridicule, can help the passive-aggressive reduce stress, and perhaps do so all around. Humor implies mindfulness that makes light of something that in actuality being of so little importance deserves to not be taken too seriously. Is your wife a controller to the point that you can't cook without her cleaning up after you before you are through, as you have to close the refrigerator door each time you take something out although you are just about to put this something back in again? Make light of this humorously and it may stop; get seriously mad and likely the cleaning-up/closing the door behavior will intensify. Caution is indicated here, however, because some passive-aggressive patients see the use of humor as teasing and that as telling the passive-aggressive insultingly, "You are acting like a clown."

Using Mindfulness Techniques

Mindfulness, an aspect of humor, involves according to the *Mindfulness Workbook*, "Relieving mental suffering by becoming a nonjudgmental observer of disturbing thoughts and feelings, rather than participating in them." It might involve nonparticipant nonjudgmental awareness "which exists for purposes of toning down emotional reactivity to the range of thoughts, feelings, and impulses that contribute to the emotional disturbances [of passive-aggressives]." Thus a concerned participant might tell himself or herself, "Don't try to meet your fears and worries head on; instead, just let them pass through you and your mind, along the lines of, 'So what if I feel this way? What's wrong anyway if I think in a worrisome fashion?'"[1]

Recommending Using Mindfulness Techniques

The use of these techniques does not require processes involving understanding and correcting false assumptions. It allows these false assumptions to remain and even participate in one's psychic life without allowing them to take over, and stick and be elaborated, e.g., by the making of cognitive errors based on feelings of excessive responsibility; what-if fearful thinking; and excessive regrets over past actions such as those based on the inability to recognize that foresight is routinely reliably less predictive than hindsight.

Friends and family can be advocates for mindfulness by recommending passive-aggressives choose to be less worrisome by saying to themselves, "I will no longer concern myself with all worrisome matters at hand. Rather I will come to care less. I will do so by asking myself, "What is the worst that can happen?" thus reassuring myself that any potential consequences of an event are likely to be either intrinsically trivial or entirely imaginary. Thus, passive-aggressives when angry can tell themselves, "You are not being careless or too unconcerned; you are in fact just being realistic. But still none of this matters much or at all anyway."

Mindfulness will likely backfire for those individuals with an oppressive conscience who say to themselves, after they say, "Who cares?"—"You should care because it is the right/necessary/moral thing to do, and if you don't care, things will get worse for you because other people might get hurt." For such individuals, new issues likely emerge as the result of what originally was intended to be a method to give/get relief from the old ones. Passive-aggressive individuals might instead feel troubled that others think they do not care about the important things in life.

Using Crisis Interventions

In a crisis, direct behavioral methods, such as learning ways to confront excessive anger already beginning to erupt, can be helpful for passive-aggressives. Passive-aggressives are sometimes in a crisis because they are in the midst of a divorce or have just been fired from their jobs; if they need immediate help, anger management and crisis intervention might be chosen as being better therapeutic approaches. Crisis intervention methods include:

Stop thought therapy. Here individuals tell themselves in a loud inner voice, "stop it," in the middle of temptation to brood about/discharge some annoyance or another, doing so as a way to temporize to get past an acutely difficult situation.

Relaxation. Some passive-aggressives can be helped to reduce anger and anger buildup through such direct methods as exercise and breathing control.

Directly expressing anger. Teaching the patient to modify anger's destructive, circuitous expression by instead expressing (a little) anger more directly, and in a way that is more to the point. This can result in the passive-aggressive adopting a mode of anger expression that can actually be more empathic and so less hurtful to others than is sneaky anger, where the salutary defensive benefits for the passive-aggressive individual are far greater than they are for the victim of the passive-aggressive.

Sensitivity training. Here the passive-aggressive adept at picking up negative cues is taught to as well pick up those that are (in actuality) positive.

Cognitive revision. In cognitive terms, passive-aggressives can view others in a more positive light if they try to modify what Beck calls thinking according to "exclusive causes,"[2] "dramatically broadening perspective,"[3] thus realizing that two different points of view *both* can be meaningful in the sense of being both rational and correct, perhaps with the only differences involving overall emphasis/interpretation. Positive thinking can be the favorable result of successful intervention here, so that one instead of responding negatively to a third party's lateness might think, not "she's being obstructionstic" but "she'll be here soon," temporarily assuaging one's anger until the other person arrives and mitigating the passive-aggressive response to the person when he or she actually comes into view.

CHAPTER EIGHTEEN

Anger Management

Four key methods that can help passive-aggressives deal with their anger in a healthier fashion are:

- Abreaction/talking things out
- Fight
- Flight
- Forbearance. (These methods are similar to and overlap with the ways victims of passive-aggressives can deal with the passive-aggressives in their lives, as described in Chapter 16.)

One: Abreaction/Talking Things Out

Passive-aggressives can abreact (vent) their *appropriate* anger either in or outside of the therapy hour, with different considerations applying in each case.

Abreaction of Appropriate Anger in the Therapy Hour

Therapists can encourage the abreaction of *appropriate* anger in the therapy hour (in a controlled way) by urging the patient to ventilate to a therapist serving as a sympathetic, nonjudgmental, nonpunitive listener. As Rank suggests, speaking of abreacting death wishes in depression, "In the treatment of many 'depressives,' the appearance of [anger] against others is . . . a sign of the inner unburdening and strengthening of the ego."[1]

Abreaction of Appropriate Anger Outside the Therapy Hour

Some therapists suggest that talking about one's *appropriate* anger outside the therapy hour can, even for passive-aggressives, be a good way to reduce anger and its buildup. They often suggest that one or both partners, or an entire family, call for and have a conference. They recommend that these discussions take place in a nonconfrontational, uncritical atmosphere, with the goal of modifying the anger affect in the direction of softening it and so reducing its impact on others (otherwise known as giving "an anger report"). They suggest that information, not body blows, be exchanged, and that the discussions that take place focus not on being angry itself but on resolving what is causing the anger. To avoid catching others off guard, they suggest giving ample warnings before unloading an affect-laden problem in an affect-laden way on somebody psychologically unprepared to hear this. Name calling and swearing are to be avoided.

Two recommendations stand out:

- Take responsibility for yourself to the extent that that is warranted.
- Make your points in a nonthreatening manner by expressing complaints as concerns and annoyances as discomforts. For example, a victim can say not, "I just hate you for always being late," but "Please be on time; I know it's partly me, but I really dislike waiting—don't we all?"—thus employing an element of self-blame to "detoxify" what could otherwise come across as raw, hurtful criticism. In one case, instead of confronting and criticizing his wife for making him jealous, a man said, "I am particularly sensitive that way, and I know it, so it would help me if you didn't do anything to aggravate my paranoia." In effect, he was apologetically admitting, "I only complain about your behavior because I fear it," and so instead of demanding change he was asking for increased empathy in the form of reassurances.

However, passive-aggressives should be cautious about expressing much in the way of anger outside the therapy hour. Some therapists endorse frank discussions of anger as a kind of mantra. Wetzler feels "that anger is an acceptable emotion because it is an inherent component of all human relationships, especially romantic ones" and says that "the question is not whether to express it, but what is the best way to clear the air."[2] Others disagree. According to Keating, for example, "It is not always helpful to express our feelings."[3] Especially, expressing feelings of anger can have negative consequences—on oneself, the targets of one's anger, and on one's social standing. For example, anger avoiders can get depressed when, encouraged to express their anger, they "get it out," only to suddenly and unexpectedly recognize, with chagrin, how angry they really are, and how hurtful they can be, and perhaps have really become. The targets of their anger can also get depressed—especially when their tolerance for anger is low because of something in their makeup. For example, paranoid targets, even those who in reality actually provoked the anger in the first place, are less likely to well tolerate expressions of anger than are targets who condemn and so bury anger with all other examples of overdone emotionality.

Overall, what might in other circumstances be a good idea might fail when the target, the person doing the provoking, is passive-aggressive him- or herself. Passive-aggressive partners tend to (angrily) view calls to "sit down and talk about it" as a rejection of them, an attempt to control them, or a ploy to humble them—and as such are efforts to be resisted in all the usual passive-aggressive ways, and at all costs.

Few people, passive-aggressive or not, welcome hearing what angry people have to say, and also fewer hear it as being purely informational, and potentially helpful. They hear only "what I did wrong" and become in turn angry themselves. For example, a man's wife accepted an assignment at the last minute, one that was going to make them both late for an important professional party both were planning to attend. The husband, getting angry, reminded his wife that his own professional commitments were as important as hers. The man asked for and expected his simple request to be honored and his wife give him respect and consideration, but he forgot that passive-aggressives do not usually grant requests, but instead use them to start/continue a struggle. So after he got the almost predictable negative response from his wife, the husband decided that since the provocation was mild it was better to maintain the relationship whole, as well as to spare himself further attack, by keeping quiet.

Two: Fight

Passive-aggressives often feel less angry after establishing ground rules—involving setting limits on what they are willing to tolerate from others. Formulations that are the equivalent of saying that, "Good fences make for good neighbors" constitute poetic statements of the psychology of fight (as well as a comment on the calming nature of flight, as well as a description of what can be a passive-aggressive behavior in its own right!)

Three: Flight

As previously mentioned in the discussion of victims and flight/removal in Chapters 9 and 10, passive-aggressive patients can deal with their anger by distancing themselves from its source. Many cultures have built-in mechanisms of physical removal or "shunning" that amount to socially sanctioned ways to avoid enmeshments with provocative, disappointing, or otherwise difficult people. Alternatively, when actually shunning the person is not practical or even possible, as it might be in a closed space, appropriate anger can still be dealt with—by shunning that person within one's mind.

Keating suggests that distraction is one, and a good, form of internal flight: to get "hostile feelings to dissipate . . . quickly."[4] Another good way of shunning the anger within is to try to see the person who is the trigger of one's anger in a new light. This method is primarily directed to diminishing the significance of what that person says or does. One partner in a relationship can choose to ignore, overlook, or even laugh at a meaningful relational provocation. For example, a psychologist's husband, a man without special training, routinely himself answered the questions others put to the psychologist even when those were about highly technical clinical matters. The psychologist stifled her urge to get very angry, her way to survive the onslaught. She understood that her husband had status problems of his own. Also, she loved him so much that she wanted him to feel like an equal—which, indeed, considering his native ability to make sensible psychological formulations (almost as good as hers) he essentially approximated being. Empathy, leading to an awareness of what her husband was thinking and feeling, helped her view her husband's annoying response as being of minor significance, and to treat is as no significant threat to anyone's overall well-being or to the well-being of their relationship. Instead of overreacting, she taught herself to be less angry in those situations where very little was at stake.

As mentioned above, relaxation techniques can in selected cases help passive-aggressive people shun the anger within. For Potter-Efron and Potter-Efron, calmness is the order of the day. They suggest that their patients train themselves to relax. They feel relaxation can be achieved by following a "set of simple and clear actions": "sit down . . . speak quietly. . . . breathe fully and evenly [and] don't jump: to conclusions."[5]

The extent to which tranquilizers both calm and influence personality favorably is controversial. Kramer in *Listening to Prozac* suggests the possibility that Prozac can change character in a positive way.[6] Theoretically, at least, antidepressants and tranquilizers can diminish anger enough to dim passive-aggressive thought and behavior.

However, the effect that medication has on anger is not always positive. There may be a negative effect as exemplified by a common response to alcohol. Alcohol can soothe—up to the point that it removes inhibitions, when what anger remains can emerge explosively, undoing all the (questionable) benefits of being self-sedated. Nicotine can have a para-doxically dangerously sedative effect as well.

Some observers agree with Malinow, who recommends "a minor tran-quilizer . . . to help deal with anxiety" and antidepressants for coexisting or supervening depression. Malinow also recommends exercising caution about the amount of medication given in one prescription to passive-aggressives[7]—an important consideration for patients who may express their hostility to their therapists by taking an overdose.

Four: Forbearance

Methods of forbearance involve exercising patience and restraint with others, and giving oneself some adjustment room. Many passive-aggressives have found that respecting others' limitations is a productive alternative response in those professional situations, e.g., in bureaucracies and espe-cially in the military, where externals are unlikely to change.

As mentioned throughout, it is often easier to exercise patience and restraint after developing personal empathy and altruism that can, as Beck puts it, "buffer antagonism toward other peoples."[8] Along similar lines, Keating suggests "understanding some of the syndromes of diffi-cult people"[9] as a way to avoid being and getting angry with them. (This principle seriously applies to understanding others' passive-aggression.) Many people, as Perry and Flannery observe, make an "existential choice" to stay in a difficult relationship. For example, they might decide to keep a "burdensome or cantankerous" aging parent at home "rather than plac-ing [the] parent in a nursing home," just accepting the relationship largely as it is.[10]

Existential forbearance choices are often a key factor in ensuring the success of a marriage. Wetzler, giving advice to victims of passive-aggressives equally applicable to the passive-aggressives themselves, sug-gests that it can be helpful to "learn to let some things roll off your back."[11] Wetzler also says, "There's an unspoken rule in many marriages: you have to know when to overlook certain of your spouse's neurotic tics . . . and say nothing, to keep the peace . . . Perfection is not part of the human condition."[12]

Passive-aggressives often become better socialized when they stop strug-gling with other people and just *compromise*. Some therapists promote forbearance by presenting *themselves* as a compromiser and use the thera-pist as an example of someone to identify with as that ideal person admi-rably slow to anger, e.g., "the exact same thing happened to me but when it did I didn't much care."

Being Assertive But Not Aggressive

Anger management is often well served by helping passive-aggressives learn to be assertive as distinct from aggressive. A therapist might suggest that a patient say some angry things that are on his or her mind, but only those things carefully selected to help, not harm, the cause. Some situations work when patients say "Yes and no clearly"; "tell people when [they] feel pushed around and where"; and "make [their] own choices."[13]

Taubman, in language common for the day, helped her people become assertive women without being "a Pushy Broad, Castrating Bitch or Aggressive Dame."[14] Her method dealt directly with the problems of self-expression and self-assertion found in many passive-aggressives. For example, she called her people's attention to "flashing red lights" like, "This may seem silly (unimportant), but. . . ."—and similar statements that "qualify . . . you, your ideas, your opinions, your feelings." Her goal was to help change entrenched patterns of self-effacement and develop and reinforce new patterns, with success in one area ultimately catalyzing a successful freeing of the person in a general way, and more specifically relieving hostility buildup that could potentially spill over into passive-aggressive seething, bitterness, and spitefulness. Extra benefits of such an approach are that it builds the self-respect that comes from healthy self-expression and diminishes resentment over not having expressed oneself directly, appropriately, and effectively.

While some therapists advocate expressing anger directly instead of indirectly and passive-aggressively—doing so not only to clear the air but also to help make anger an acceptable emotion rather than one that is just part of a maladaptive interpersonal game plan—the more cautious therapists considering the dynamics of human relationships always remember that no one likes to be the target of anger, and that, as any true passive-aggressive knows, even a little anger when covertly expressed, and however abstractly, can do a lot of damage to a relationship. This principle especially holds true when one contemplates defriending someone on Facebook.

Some therapists actually advocate expressing anger indirectly, that is, passive-aggressively, but this time by design. They feel that sometimes anger avoidance is not passive-aggression but part of a different/bigger, and more serious problem. They then suggest that anger avoiders recognize the huge overall cost of anger avoidance to their personal well-being. Anger avoiders can lose sleep, become depressed due to suppressing rage and retroflexing it on themselves, and develop physical problems like headaches or asthma. They can also come to be mistreated by those who feel that people who never get openly angry are people who are both asking for abuse and are safe to abuse. With anger avoiders, even passive-aggressive expressions of anger can be a step in the right direction. Expressing anger indirectly, that is, passive-aggressively, can be helpful in those situations in which there is no better alternative. Here passive-aggression becomes less of an emotional problem than an existential solution, a way to express one's anger in a somewhat safe, socially acceptable, personally creative fashion, at least to the extent that a given situation will safely allow this.

However, passive-aggressives can going overboard this way experience an escalating defensive breakdown as they lose control of their anger. Those with the potential to escalate to break down are well advised to focus on the issue, not the emotions behind it. They also might be advised to soften the blow of their anger on their victims by keeping alert to what they are saying while they are saying it, thus helping themselves as passive-aggressives unable to fully control their temper at least to minimize its effects on their victims, and thus its consequences to themselves.

Apologizing?

A useful anger management technique for helping the passive-aggressive individual improve his or her relationship with him or herself and others involves reassuring the other person that "all my anger ultimately has no significant implication," as in, "Just because I get angry with you doesn't mean I am going to ask you for a divorce." Patients who simultaneously get angry and say they are sorry, however passive-aggressive that technique is itself, have at least found a way to mollify the effects of anger on their victims. And this method can go far in helping them prevent the hurt, retaliation, and subsequent sadomasochistic escalation that so often follow upon a little to a big blowup.

Apologizing for one's not fully controllable anger can be particularly helpful for passive-aggressives who have aimed their dilute vitriol on those targets who are paranoid. Being passive-aggressive is generally somewhat safer than being overtly violent. But it is still potentially dangerous with targets who are unstable due to being paranoid/suspicious types. Some particularly damaging instances of spousal abuse have occurred when a partner of a paranoid individual has miscalculated and unapologetically provoked or threatened his or her paranoid partner, causing him or her to in turn experience a big loss of self-control. For example, a woman miscalculated when she flirted with another man in her husband's presence. She had intended only to make her husband a *little* jealous, but, failing to fully understand the true extent of her husband's capacity for jealousy, she unwittingly made him very angry indeed. Then her husband accused her of wanting to sleep around, whereupon instead of apologizing for seemingly having been cruising about, she made light of it and blamed her husband for being extremely suspicious. And that is when her husband hit her.

Passive-aggressives should always keep their goals firmly in mind in the midst of their (modified) blowups. If they are planning a divorce, they can allow more hurtful things to come through than if they are planning to have the relationship last. Here they might confine themselves to mentioning only trivial issues—perhaps after displacing their anger from something important, like, "You make plans without asking me," to something unimportant, like, "You never turn out the light and close the closet doors after you are through using the closet."

Anger-prone individuals can deal with their anger by diverting the topic to something less hot—one good way to cool tempers and avoid a fight. Developing this ability is a central aspect of what the passive-aggressive individual needs to learn how to do.

Notes

Introduction

1. American Psychiatric Association. (2013). *Diagnostic and Statistical Manual of Mental Disorders,* (5th ed.). Arlington, VA: American Psychiatric Association, 645–646.

2. Wetzler, S., and Jose, A. (2012). Passive-Aggressive Personality Disorder: The Demise of a Syndrome. In *The Oxford Handbook of Personality Disorders.* Thomas A. Widiger (Ed.). Oxford Handbooks Online, 29–30.

3. American Psychiatric Association. (2013). *Diagnostic and Statistical Manual of Mental Disorders,* (5th ed.). Arlington, VA: American Psychiatric Association, 645–646.

4. Ibid., 645–646.

5. Murphy, T., and Oberlin, L. (2016). *Overcoming Passive-Aggression: How to Stop Hidden Anger from Spoiling Your Relationships, Career, and Happiness.* Philadelphia, PA: Perseus, 4.

6. Wetzler, S., and Jose, A. (2012). Passive-Aggressive Personality Disorder: The Demise of a Syndrome. In *The Oxford Handbook of Personality Disorders.* Thomas A. Widiger (Ed.). Oxford Handbooks Online.

7. Ibid., 23.

8. Ibid., 15.

9. Ibid., 14.

10. Ibid., 15.

11. Ibid., 18.

12. Hopwood, C. J., et al. (2009). The Construct Validity of Passive-Aggressive Personality Disorder. *Psychiatry,* 72(3), 256–267. Retrieved from www.ncbi.nlm.hih.gov/pmc/articles/PMC2862968/

13. Fine, M. A., Overholser, J. C., and Berkoff, K. (1992). Diagnostic Validity of the Passive-Aggressive Personality Disorder: Suggestions for Reform. *American Journal of Psychotherapy*, 46, 472.

14. Stricker, G. (1983). Passive-Aggressiveness: A Condition Especially Suited to the Psychodynamic Approach. In *Passive-Aggressiveness: Theory and Practice.* New York: Brunner/Mazel, 5.

15. Wetzler, S., and Jose, A. (2012). Passive-Aggressive Personality Disorder: The Demise of a Syndrome. In *The Oxford Handbook of Personality Disorders.* Thomas A. Widiger (Ed.). Oxford Handbooks Online, 18.

16. Potter-Efron, R., and Potter-Efron, P. (1995). *Letting Go of Anger.* Oakland, CA: New Harbinger, 19.

17. Ibid. (paraphrase).

18. Hafter-Gray, S. Personal Communication, 1/3/2017.

19. Reich, W. (1949). *Character Analysis.* New York: Orgone Institute Press, 227 a paraphrase.

20. Benjamin, L. S. (1996). *Interpersonal Diagnosis and Treatment of Personality Disorders.* New York: Guilford Press, 297.

21. Bowles, P. (2006). *Without Stopping.* New York: HarperColllins, 28.

Chapter 1

1. Berne, E. (1964). *Games People Play.* New York: Grove Press, 93.

2. Fine, M. A., Overholser, J. C., and Berkoff, K. (1992). Diagnostic Validity of the Passive-Aggressive Personality Disorder: Suggestions for Reform. *American Journal of Psychotherapy*, 46, 471.

3. Gunderson, John G. (1997). Personality Disorders: Passive-Aggressive (Negativistic) Personality. Psychiatry in Medicine. *The Merck Manual of Medical Information: Home Edition.* Whitehouse Station, NJ: Merck Research Laboratories, 1553.

4. Hopwood, C. J., et al. (2009). The Construct Validity of Passive-Aggressive Personality Disorder. *Psychiatry* 72(3), 256–267. Retrieved from www.ncbi.nlm .hih.gov/pmc/articles/PMC2862968/

5. Fine, M. A., Overholser, J. C., and Berkoff, K. (1992). Diagnostic Validity of the Passive-Aggressive Personality Disorder: Suggestions for Reform. *American Journal of Psychotherapy,* 46, 471.

6. Wetzler, S. (1993). *Living with the Passive-Aggressive Man. Coping with Hidden Aggression—From the Bedroom to the Boardroom.* New York: Simon & Schuster, 191.

7. Millon, T. (1981). *Disorders of Personality: DSM-III: Axis II.* New York: John Wiley & Sons, 246.

8. Reich, W. (1949). *Character Analysis.* New York: Orgone Institute Press, 218, 227.

9. Millon, T. (1981). *Disorders of Personality: DSM-III: Axis II.* New York: John Wiley & Sons, 61.

10. Wilde, O. (1985). Lady Windermere's Fan. *Plays: Oscar Wilde.* New York: Viking Penguin, 54.

11. Potter-Efron, R., and Potter-Efron, P. (1995). *Letting Go of Anger.* Oakland, CA: New Harbinger, 41.

12. Wetzler, S. (1993). *Living with the Passive-Aggressive Man. Coping with Hidden Aggression—From the Bedroom to the Boardroom.* New York: Simon & Schuster, 145.

13. Prout, M. F., and Platt, J. (1983). The Development and Maintenance of Passive-Aggressiveness: The Behavioral Approach. In *Passive-Aggressiveness: Theory and Practice*. New York: Brunner/Mazel, 27.

14. Millon, T. (1981). *Disorders of Personality: DSM-III: Axis II*. New York: John Wiley & Sons, 10.

Chapter 2

1. Sprock, J., and Hunsucker, L. (1998). Symptoms of Prototypic Patients with Passive-Aggressive Personality Disorder: DSM-IIIR Versus DSM-IV Negativistic. *Comprehensive Psychiatry*, 39, 287.

2. Millon, T. (1981). *Disorders of Personality: DSM-III: Axis II*. New York: John Wiley & Sons, 313.

3. Ibid.

4. Beck, A. T. (1999). *Prisoners of Hate*. New York: HarperCollins, 59.

5. Benjamin, L. S. (1996). *Interpersonal Diagnosis and Treatment of Personality Disorders*. New York: Guilford Press, 297.

6. Ibid.

7. Ibid.

8. Sullivan, H. S. (1953). *The Interpersonal Theory of Psychiatry*. New York: W. W. Norton, 345.

9. Ibid., 57.

10. Yeomans, F., and Caligor, E. Narcissistic Personality Disorder. Challenge of Understanding and Diagnosis. *Psychiatric News*, April 1, 2016, 1, 27.

11. Fonagy, P., and Campbell, C. Update on Diagnostic issues for Borderline Personality Disorder. *Psychiatric Times*, June 2016, 1, 52.

12. Reich, W. (1949). *Character Analysis*. New York: Orgone Institute Press, 219.

Chapter 3

1. Reich, W. (1949). *Character Analysis*. New York: Orgone Institute Press, 218.

2. Ibid., 4.

3. Freud, S. (1957). The Economic Problem in Masochism 1924/1958. In J. D. Sutherland (Ed.) and J. Riviere (Trans), *Collected Papers* 2, 76–99.

4. Quality Assurance Project, The. (1991). Treatment Outlines for Avoidant, Dependent and Passive-Aggressive Personality Disorders. *Australian and New Zealand Journal of Psychiatry*, 404–411.

5. American Psychiatric Association. (1994). *Diagnostic and Statistical Manual of Mental Disorders* (4th ed.). Washington, DC: American Psychiatric Association, 735.

6. Ibid., 634.

7. Berne, E. (1964). *Games People Play*. New York: Grove Press, 93.

8. Beck, A. T. (1999). *Prisoners of Hate*. New York: HarperCollins, 41.

9. Ibid., 26.

Chapter 4

1. Benjamin, L. S. (1996). *Interpersonal Diagnosis and Treatment of Personality Disorders*. New York: Guilford Press, 268.

2. Millon, T. (1981). *Disorders of Personality: DSM-III: Axis II*. New York: John Wiley & Sons, 268.

3. Fine, M. A., Overholser, J. C., and Berkoff, K. (1992). Diagnostic Validity of the Passive-Aggressive Personality Disorder: Suggestions for Reform. *American Journal of Psychotherapy*, 46, 472.

4. Wetzler, S. (1993). *Living with the Passive-Aggressive Man. Coping with Hidden Aggression—From the Bedroom to the Boardroom*. New York: Simon & Schuster.

5. Malinow, K. L. (1986). Passive-Aggressive Personality. In *Personality Disorders: Diagnosis and Management*. Malabar, FL: Robert E. Krieger, 127.

6. Freud, S. (1922). *Group Psychology and the Analysis of the Ego* (James Strachey, Trans.). New York: Boni and Liveright. Chapter VI, Note 1.

7. American Psychiatric Association. (1994). *Diagnostic and Statistical Manual of Mental Disorders* (4th ed.). Washington, DC: American Psychiatric Association.

8. Fine, M. A., Overholser, J. C., and Berkoff, K. (1992). Diagnostic Validity of the Passive-Aggressive Personality Disorder: Suggestions for Reform. *American Journal of Psychotherapy*, 46, 471.

9. Wetzler, *Living with the Passive-Aggressive Man*, 37.

10. Ibid., 93.

11. Oldham, J. M., and Morris, L. B. (1995). The New Personality Self-Portrait. New York: Bantam Books, 223.

12. Wetzler, *Living with the Passive-Aggressive Man*, 93.

13. Ibid., 92.

14. Benjamin, L. S. (1996). *Interpersonal Diagnosis and Treatment of Personality Disorders*. New York: Guilford Press, 268.

15. Wetzler, S., and Jose, A. (2012). Passive-Aggressive Personality Disorder: The Demise of a Syndrome. In *The Oxford Handbook of Personality Disorders*. Thomas A. Widiger (Ed.). Oxford Handbooks Online, 29–30.

16. Ibid., 22.

17. Wetzler and Jose, Passive-Aggressive Personality Disorder: The Demise of a Syndrome. In *The Oxford Handbook of Personality Disorders*. Thomas A. Widiger (Ed.). Oxford Handbooks Online, 21.

18. Ibid., 22.

19. Horner, A. personal communication, 1973.

20. Fine, M. A., Overholser, J. C., and Berkoff, K. (1992). Diagnostic Validity of the Passive-Aggressive Personality Disorder: Suggestions for Reform. *American Journal of Psychotherapy*, 46, 471.

21. American Psychiatric Association. (1994). *Diagnostic and Statistical Manual of Mental Disorders*, (4th ed.). Washington, DC: American Psychiatric Association, 735.

22. Millon, T. (1981). *Disorders of Personality: DSM-III: Axis II*. New York: John Wiley & Sons, 255.

23. Wetzler, S. (1992). *Living with the Passive-Aggressive Man. Coping with Hidden Aggression—From the Bedroom to the Boardroom.* New York: Simon & Schuster, 85.

24. Rosenthal, E. (1992, August 18). Troubled marriage? Sibling relations may be at fault. *The New York Times,* C1, C9.

25. Millon, T., and Davis, R. D. (1996). *Disorders of Personality: DSM-IV and Beyond.* New York: John Wiley & Sons, 568.

26. Burns, D. D., and Epstein, N. (1983). Passive-Aggressiveness: A Cognitive-Behavioral Approach. In *Passive-Aggressiveness: Theory and Practice.* New York: Brunner/Mazel, 75.

27. Beck, A. T. (1999). *Prisoners of Hate.* New York: HarperCollins, 72.

28. Potter-Efron, R., and Potter-Efron, P. (1995). *Letting Go of Anger.* Oakland, CA: New Harbinger, 10.

29. Ibid., 11.

30. Ibid., 10.

31. Ibid., 10.

32. Berne, E. (1964). *Games People Play.* New York: Grove Press, 173.

33. Ibid., 173.

34. Ibid., 174.

35. Ibid., 112.

36. Ibid., 113.

37. Ibid., 113.

38. Perry, J. C. (1989). Passive-Aggressive Personality Disorder. *Treatments of Psychiatric Disorders.* Washington, DC: American Psychiatric Association, 165.

39. Meissner, William W. (1985). Theories of Personality and Psychopathology: Classical Psychoanalysis. In *Comprehensive Textbook of Psychiatry/IV.* Harold I. Kaplan and Benjamin, J. Sadock (Eds.). Baltimore, MA: Williams and Wilkins, 396.

40. Millon, T., and Davis, R. D. (1996). *Disorders of Personality: DSM-IV and Beyond.* New York: John Wiley & Sons, 550.

41. Ibid., 550.

42. Millon, T. (1981). *Disorders of Personality: DSM-III: Axis II.* New York: John Wiley & Sons, 264.

43. Ibid., 265.

44. Ibid., 265.

Chapter 5

1. Small, I. F., Small, J. O., Alig, Vincent B., and Moore, Donald F. (1970). Passive-Aggressive Personality Disorder: A Search for a Syndrome. *American Journal of Psychiatry,* 126, 7.

2. Reich, W. (1949). *Character Analysis.* New York: Orgone Institute Press, 227.

3. Wetzler, S. (1992). *Living with the Passive-Aggressive Man. Coping with Hidden Aggression—From the Bedroom to the Boardroom.* New York: Simon & Schuster, 111.

4. Millon, T. (1981). *Disorders of Personality: DSM-III: Axis II*. New York: John Wiley & Sons, 33.

5. Stricker, G. (1983). Passive-Aggressiveness: A Condition Especially Suited to the Psychodynamic Approach. In *Passive-Aggressiveness: Theory and Practice*. New York: Brunner/Mazel, 11.

6. Benjamin, L. S. (1996). *Interpersonal Diagnosis and Treatment of Personality Disorders*. New York: Guilford Press, 267.

7. Ibid., 293.

8. Stricker, Passive-Aggressiveness: A Condition Especially Suited to the Psychodynamic Approach, 12.

9. Wicks, R. (1983). Passive-Aggressiveness Within the Religious Setting. In *Passive-Aggressiveness: Theory and Practice*. New York: Brunner/Mazel, 214.

10. Wetzler, *Living with the Passive-Aggressive Man*, 62.

11. Keating, C. J. (1984). *Dealing with Difficult People*. Ramsey, NJ: Paulist Press, 150.

12. Mahrer, A. R. (1983). An Existential-Experiential View and Operational Perspective on Passive-Aggressiveness. In *Passive-Aggressiveness: Theory and Practice*. New York: Brunner/Mazel, 100.

13. Ibid.

14. PDM Task Force. (2006). *Psychodynamic Diagnostic Manual*. Silver Spring, MD: Alliance of Psychoanalytic Organizations, 58.

15. Perry, J. C., and Flannery, R. B. (1989). Passive-Aggressive Personality Disorder. In *Treatments of Psychiatric Disorders*. Washington, DC: American Psychiatric Association, 166.

16. Perry and Flannery, Passive-Aggressive Personality Disorder, 166.

17. Ibid., 166.

18. Brody, Sylvia. (1982). Psychoanalytic Theories of Infantile Development. *Psychoanalytic Quarterly*, 51, 526–595.

Chapter 6

1. Potter-Efron, R., and Potter-Efron, P. (1995). *Letting Go of Anger*. Oakland, CA: New Harbinger, 33.

2. Wetzler, S. (1992). *Living with the Passive-Aggressive Man. Coping with Hidden Aggression—From the Bedroom to the Boardroom*. New York: Simon & Schuster, 106.

3. Potter-Efron and Potter-Efron, *Letting Go of Anger*, 19.

4. Berne, E. (1964). *Games People Play*. New York: Grove Press, 113.

5. Bonds-White, F. (1983). A Transactional Analysis Perspective on Passive-Aggressiveness. In *Passive-Aggressiveness: Theory and Practice*. New York: Brunner/Mazel, 54.

6. Berne, *Games People Play*, 180.

7. Bonds-White, F. (1983). A Transactional Analysis Perspective on Passive-Aggressiveness. In *Passive-Aggressiveness: Theory and Practice*. New York: Brunner/Mazel, 54.

8. Berne, *Games People Play*, 116–122.

9. Ibid., 179.

10. Sprock, J., and Hunsucker, L. (1998). Symptoms of Prototypic Patients with Passive-Aggressive Personality Disorder: DSM-IIIR Versus DSM-IV Negativistic. *Comprehensive Psychiatry, 39*, 287–295.

11. Millon, T., and Davis, R. D. (1996). *Disorders of Personality: DSM-IV and Beyond*. New York: John Wiley & Sons, 561.

12. Malinow, Kenneth L. (1986). Passive-Aggressive Personality. In *Personality Disorders: Diagnosis and Management*. Malabar, FL: Robert E. Krieger, 125.

13. Millon, T., and Davis, R. D. (1996). *Disorders of Personality: DSM-IV and Beyond*. New York: John Wiley & Sons, 261.

14. Steckel, W. (1965). *Sadism and Masochism*. New York: Grove Press.

15. Reich, W. (1949). *Character Analysis*. New York: Orgone Institute Press.

16. Millon, T. (1981). *Disorders of Personality: DSM-III: Axis II*. New York: John Wiley & Sons, 245.

17. American Psychiatric Association. (1994). *Diagnostic and Statistical Manual of Mental Disorders* (4th ed.). Washington, DC: American Psychiatric Association, 735.

18. Fenichel, O. (1945). *The Psychoanalytic Theory of Neurosis*. New York: W. W. Norton, 144.

19. Wetzler, *Living with the Passive-Aggressive Man,* 182.

20. Berne, *Games People Play*, 114–116.

21. American Psychiatric Association. (1994). *Diagnostic and Statistical Manual of Mental Disorders*, (4th ed.). Washington, DC: American Psychiatric Association, 735.

22. Murphy, T., and Oberlin, L. (2016). *Overcoming Passive-Aggression: How to Stop Hidden Anger from Spoiling Your Relationships, Career, and Happiness*. Philadelphia, PA: Perseus, 164.

23. Millon, T. (1981). *Disorders of Personality: DSM-III: Axis II*. New York: John Wiley & Sons, 246.

24. Fine, M. A., Overholser, J. C., and Berkoff, K. (1992). Diagnostic Validity of the Passive-Aggressive Personality Disorder: Suggestions for Reform. *American Journal of Psychotherapy, 46*, 480.

25. Mahrer, A. R. (1983). An Existential-Experiential View and Operational Perspective on Passive-Aggressiveness. In *Passive-Aggressiveness: Theory and Practice*. New York: Brunner/Mazel, 100.

26. Millon, T., and Davis, R. D. (1996). *Disorders of Personality: DSM-IV and Beyond*. New York: John Wiley & Sons, 568.

27. Berne, *Games People Play*, 114–116.

28. Fenichel, *The Psychoanalytic Theory of Neurosis*, 163.

29. Wetzler, *Living with the Passive-Aggressive Man*, 138.

30. American Psychiatric Association. (1994). *Diagnostic and Statistical Manual of Mental Disorders* (4th ed.). Washington, DC: American Psychiatric Association, 735.

31. Berne, *Games People Play*, 112–113.

Chapter 7

1. Murphy, T., and Oberlin, L. (2016). *Overcoming Passive-Aggression: How to Stop Hidden Anger from Spoiling Your Relationships, Career, and Happiness.* Philadelphia, PA: Perseus, 152–166.

2. Bateson, G. "The Double Bind," personal communication, 1961.

3. Wetzler, S. (1992). *Living with the Passive-Aggressive Man. Coping with Hidden Aggression—From the Bedroom to the Boardroom.* New York: Simon & Schuster, 175.

4. Gunderson, J. G. (1997). Personality Disorders. In *The Merck Manual of Medical Information: Home Edition.* Whitehouse Station, NJ: Merck Research Laboratories, 427.

5. Kernberg, Otto F. (1994). Leadership Styles and Organizational Paranoiagenesis. In *Paranoia: New Psychoanalytic Perspectives.* Madison, CT: International Universities Press, 66–71.

6. Paris, J. (1999). A Diathesis-Stress Model of Personality Disorders. *Psychiatric Annals,* 29, 693–697.

7. Millon, T., and Davis, R. D. (1996). *Disorders of Personality: DSM-IV and Beyond.* New York: John Wiley & Sons, 264.

Chapter 9

1. Burns, D. D., and Epstein, N. (1983). Passive-Aggressiveness: A Cognitive-Behavioral Approach. In *Passive-Aggressiveness: Theory and Practice.* New York: Brunner/Mazel, 77.

Chapter 10

1. Mahrer, A. R. (1983). An Existential-Experiential View and Operational Perspective on Passive-Aggressiveness. In *Passive-Aggressiveness: Theory and Practice.* New York: Brunner/Mazel, 117.

2. Kernberg, Otto F. (1994). Leadership Styles and Organizational Paranoiagenesis. *Paranoia: New Psychoanalytic Perspectives.* Madison, CT: International Universities Press, 61–79.

3. Bateson, G. (1961), personal communication, 1961.

4. Kernberg, O. F. (1994). Leadership Styles and Organizational Paranoiagenesis. In *Paranoia: New Psychoanalytic Perspectives.* Madison, CT: International Universities Press, 61–69.

5. Berne, E. (1964). *Games People Play.* New York: Grove Press, 95.

6. Taubman, B. (1976). *How to Become an Assertive Woman.* New York: Pocket Books, 129.

Chapter 11

1. Steckel, W. (1965). *Sadism and Masochism.* New York: Grove Press, 33.

2. Stricker, G. (1983). Passive-Aggressiveness: A Condition Especially Suited to the Psychodynamic Approach. In *Passive-Aggressiveness: Theory and Practice.* New York: Brunner/Mazel, 8.

3. Kaslow, F. W. (1983). Passive-Aggressiveness: An Intrapsychic, Interpersonal, and Transactional Dynamic in the Family System. In *Passive-Aggressiveness: Theory and Practice.* New York: Brunner/Mazel, 149.

4. Reich, W. (1949). *Character Analysis.* New York: Orgone Institute Press, 219.

5. Rank, O. (1959). *Life Fear and Death Fear. In The Myth of the Birth of the Hero.* New York, Vintage Books, 277.

6. Steckel, *Sadism and Masochism,* 28.

7. Beck, A T. (1999). *Prisoners of Hate.* New York: HarperCollins, 85.

8. Ibid., 83.

9. Rank, *Life Fear and Death Fear,* 277.

10. Millon, T. (1981). *Disorders of Personality: DSM-III: Axis II.* New York: John Wiley & Sons, 250.

11. Reich, *Character Analysis,* 219 or 223.

12. Ibid., 223.

13. Deutsch, H. (1944). *The Psychology of Women.* New York: Grune and Stratton, 281–288.

14. American Psychiatric Association. (1994). *Diagnostic and Statistical Manual of Mental Disorders* (4th ed.). Washington, DC: American Psychiatric Association, 733.

15. Schumann, R.

16. Chadwick, G. E. Album cover, *Fourth String Quartet.*

17. Anthiel, *Bad Boy of Music.* Garden City, NY: Doubleday, 1945.

18. Rachmaninoff, S. *Prelude in C-Sharp Minor.*

19. Freud, S. (1957). The Psychogenesis of a Case of Homosexuality in a Woman. Freud, S. The Economic Problem in Masochism 1924/1958. In J. D. Sutherland (Ed.) and J. Riviere (Trans), *Collected Papers,* 2, 76–99.

20. Boito, A.

21. Shostakovich, D.

22. Wagner, R.

23. Bartok, B.

Chapter 12

1. Berne, E. (1964). *Games People Play.* New York: Grove Press, 176.

2. Pinsker, H. (1998). The Supportive Component of Psychotherapy. *Psychiatric Times,* 15, 2.

3. Oldham, J. M., and Morris, L. B. (1995). *The New Personality Self-Portrait.* New York: Bantam Books, 405.

4. Benjamin, L. S. (1996). *Interpersonal Diagnosis and Treatment of Personality Disorders.* New York: Guilford Press, 110.

5. Ibid., 282.

6. Murphy, T., and Oberlin, L. (2016). *Overcoming Passive-Aggression: How to Stop Hidden Anger from Spoiling Your Relationships, Career, and Happiness.* Philadelphia, PA: Perseus, 1–178.

7. Brandt, A. (2013). *Keys to Eliminating Passive-Aggressiveness.* New York: Norton, 9.

8. Pinsker, H. (1998). The Supportive Component of Psychotherapy. *Psychiatric Times* 15, 60–61.

9. Oldham, J. M., and Morris, L. B. (1995). *The New Personality Self-Portrait.* New York: Bantam Books, 404.

10. Quality Assurance Project, The. (1991). Treatment Outlines for Avoidant, Dependent and Passive-Aggressive Personality Disorders. *Australian and New Zealand Journal of Psychiatry*, 405.

11. Oldham and Morris, *The New Personality Self-Portrait*, 225.

12. Millon, T. (1981). *Disorders of Personality: DSM-III: Axis II.* New York: John Wiley & Sons, 272.

13. Quality Assurance Project, The. (1991). Treatment Outlines for Avoidant, Dependent and Passive-Aggressive Personality Disorders. *Australian and New Zealand Journal of Psychiatry*, 404.

14. Wetzler, S. (1992). *Living with the Passive-Aggressive Man. Coping with Hidden Aggression—From the Bedroom to the Boardroom.* New York: Simon & Schuster, 93.

15. Beck, A T. (1999). *Prisoners of Hate.* New York: HarperCollins, 231.

16. Fenichel, O. (1945). *The Psychoanalytic Theory of Neurosis.* New York: W. W. Norton, 476.

17. Oldham and Morris, *The New Personality Self-Portrait*, 225.

Chapter 13

1. Oldham, J. M., and Morris, L. B. (1995). *The New Personality Self-Portrait.* New York: Bantam Books, 407.

2. Beck, A. T. (1999). *Prisoners of Hate.* New York: HarperCollins, 249–251.

3. Burns, D. D., and Epstein, N. (1983). Passive-Aggressiveness: A Cognitive-Behavioral Approach. In *Passive-Aggressiveness: Theory and Practice.* New York: Brunner/Mazel, 75.

4. Beck, *Prisoners of Hate*, 232.

5. Ibid., 252–254.

6. Burns and Epstein, Passive-Aggressiveness: A Cognitive-Behavioral Approach, 73.

7. Ibid., 232 or 253.

8. Millon, T. (1981). *Disorders of Personality: DSM-III: Axis II.* New York: John Wiley & Sons, 272.

9. Burns and Epstein, Passive-Aggressiveness: A Cognitive-Behavioral Approach, 75.

10. Ibid., 73.

11. Benjamin, L. S. (1996). *Interpersonal Diagnosis and Treatment of Personality Disorders.* New York: Guilford Press, 260.

12. Brandt, A. (2013). *Keys to Eliminating Passive-Aggressiveness.* New York: Norton, 34–35.

Chapter 14

1. Oldham, J. M., and Morris, L. B. (1995). *The New Personality Self-Portrait.* New York: Bantam Books, 407.

2. Ibid., 407.

3. Wetzler, S., and Jose, A. (2012). Passive-Aggressive Personality Disorder: The Demise of a Syndrome. In *The Oxford Handbook of Personality Disorders.* Thomas A. Widiger (Ed.). Oxford Handbooks Online, 29–30.

4. Oldham, J. M., and Morris, L. B. (1995). *The New Personality Self-Portrait.* New York: Bantam Books, 407.

5. Berzon, B. (1996). *The Intimacy Dance.* New York: Plume, 182.

6. Brandt, A. (2013). *Keys to Eliminating Passive-Aggressiveness.* New York: Norton, 34–35.

7. Beck, A. T. (1999). *Prisoners of Hate.* New York: HarperCollins, 232–233.

8. Fenichel, O. (1945). *The Psychoanalytic Theory of Neurosis.* New York: W. W. Norton, p. 273.

9. Ibid., 279.

Chapter 15

1. Wetzler, S. (1992). *Living with the Passive-Aggressive Man. Coping with Hidden Aggression—From the Bedroom to the Boardroom.* New York: Simon & Schuster, 4.

2. Millon, T., and Davis, R. D. (1996). *Disorders of Personality: DSM-IV and Beyond.* New York: John Wiley & Sons, 555–556.

3. Millon, T. (1981). *Disorders of Personality: DSM-III: Axis II.* New York: John Wiley & Sons, 272.

4. Reich, W. (1949). *Character Analysis.* New York: Orgone Institute Press, 246.

Chapter 16

1. Burns, D. D., and Epstein, N. (1983). Passive-Aggressiveness: A Cognitive-Behavioral Approach. In *Passive-Aggressiveness: Theory and Practice.* New York: Brunner/Mazel, 96.

2. Beck, A. T. (1999). *Prisoners of Hate.* New York: HarperCollins, 83.

3. Prout, M. F., and Platt, J. (1983). The Development and Maintenance of Passive-Aggressiveness: The Behavioral Approach. In *Passive-Aggressiveness: Theory and Practice.* New York: Brunner/Mazel, 35.

4. Keating, C. J. (1984). *Dealing with Difficult People.* Ramsey, NJ: Paulist Press, 150.

5. Berne, E. (1964). *Games People Play.* New York: Grove Press, 154–162.

6. Millon, T. (1981). *Disorders of Personality: DSM-III: Axis II.* New York: John Wiley & Sons, 272.

7. Kaslow, F. W. (1983). Passive-Aggressiveness: An Intrapsychic, Interpersonal, and Transactional Dynamic in the Family System. In *Passive-Aggressiveness: Theory and Practice.* New York: Brunner/Mazel, 137.

8. Millon, *Disorders of Personality: DSM III: Axis II,* 250.

9. Berne, *Games People Play,* 159–162.

Chapter 17

1. The Mindfulness Workbook for OCD. (2013). *A Guide to Overcoming Obsessions and Compulsions Using Mindfulness AND Cognitive Behavioral Therapy.* Oakland, CA: New Harbinger Publications, Inc.

2. Beck, A. T. (1999). *Prisoners of Hate.* New York: HarperCollins, 85.

3. Ibid., 83.

Chapter 18

1. Rank, O. (1959). *Life Fear and Death Fear. In The Myth of the Birth of the Hero.* New York, Vintage Books, 277.

2. Wetzler, S. (1992). *Living with the Passive-Aggressive Man. Coping with Hidden Aggression—From the Bedroom to the Boardroom.* New York: Simon & Schuster, 115.

3. Keating, C. J. (1984). *Dealing with Difficult People.* Ramsey, NJ: Paulist Press, 150.

4. Ibid.

5. Potter-Efron, R., and Potter-Efron, P. (1995). *Letting Go of Anger.* Oakland, CA: New Harbinger, 71–73.

6. Kramer, P. (1993). *Listening to Prozac.* New York: Penguin.

7. Malinow, Kenneth L. (1986). Passive-Aggressive Personality. *Personality Disorders: Diagnosis and Management.* Malabar, FL: Robert E. Krieger, 130.

8. Beck, A. T. (1999). *Prisoners of Hate.* New York: HarperCollins, 229.

9. Keating, C. J. (1984). *Dealing with Difficult People.* Ramsey, NJ: Paulist Press, 150.

10. Perry, J. C., and Flannery, R. B. (1982). Passive-Aggressive Personality Disorder. *Journal of Nervous and Mental Disease,* 170, 164–173.

11. Wetzler, *Living with the Passive-Aggressive Man,* 115.

12. Ibid., 155.

13. Potter-Efron and Potter-Efron, *Letting Go of Anger,* 40–44.

14. Taubman, B. (1976). *How to Become an Assertive Woman.* New York: Pocket Books, 1.

Index

About the Author

Martin Kantor, MD, is a Harvard-trained psychiatrist who has been in full private practice in Boston and New York City, and active in residency training programs at hospitals including Massachusetts General in Boston, MA, and Beth Israel in New York, NY. He also served as assistant clinical professor of psychiatry at Mount Sinai Medical School and clinical assistant professor of psychiatry at the University of Medicine and Dentistry of New Jersey–New Jersey Medical School. Kantor is a full-time author whose published works include more than 25 other books, including Praeger's *Obsessive-Compulsive Personality Disorder: Understanding the Overly Rigid, Controlling Person; Now That He's Out: The Challenges and Joys of Having a Gay Son; Now That You're Out: The Challenges and Joys of Living as a Gay Man; Homophobia: The State of Sexual Bigotry Today;* and *Essential Guide to Overcoming Avoidant Personality Disorder.*